Praise for *Collaboration and Co-Teaching: Strategies for English Learners*

"This easy-to-read book empowers educators to work collaboratively in planning and teaching to meet the needs of English language learners in co-taught classrooms. This book makes a contribution toward successfully educating students in diverse classrooms."
Richard Andrew Villa, President, Bayridge Consortium, Inc.

"Honigsfeld and Dove have written a comprehensive book on collaboration between mainstream and ESL teachers. This is an essential read for teachers and administrators who wish to effectively implement collaborative strategies that benefit ELLs in their schools."
Judie Haynes, Professional Development Provider, EverythingESL.net

"This book is a road map for collaborative practice with a focus on English language learners. The vignettes offer a window into the complex and diverse challenges of teaching in linguistically and culturally diverse contexts. The what, when, where, how, and why of collaborative practice are discussed, and the book provides valuable online resources and helpful references for further research and exploration."
Dorit Kaufman, Professor of Linguistics, Director of Professional Educational Program, Stony Brook University, NY

"This text is a guide to successful practice, from laying the initial groundwork, to classroom and curriculum planning, to administrative and school design, to evaluation design, with examples and forms that can be utilized by the reader throughout. The authors present a realistic look, with optimism for this exciting venture of collaboration and co-teaching in the context of ELLs, as well as challenges and pitfalls, but always with helpful solutions."
Jana Noel, Professor and Community Engagement Faculty Scholar, California State University, Sacramento

"This groundbreaking book provides a strong foundation for both teachers and administrators who want to establish more supportive, inclusive learning environments for their English language learners. This research-based work explores the many facets of collaboration and provides the reader with the tools to begin co-teaching. Its practical ideas and questions help teachers move collaboration and co-teaching to the next level."
Heidi Bernal, Director, English Language Learner Department, Saint Paul Public Schools, MN

"Through intriguing questions and illustrative vignettes, Honigsfeld and Dove masterfully guide us in understanding the essentials of collaboration when planning, implementing, and assessing instruction for students who are acquiring English as an additional language. A must-read for educators wishing to create a professional leaning community where insights about ESL instruction can be shared."
Diane Lapp, Distinguished Professor of Education, San Diego State University, CA

"This important book fills a critical need for current information about the collaborative process and should be in every educator's professional library."
Scott W. C. Lawrence, Director of Curriculum, East Granby Public Schools, CT

We dedicate this book to all educators who are committed to working with English language learners. We also dedicate this book to our respective families who are our daily inspirations, Howie, Benjamin, and Jake; Tim, Dave, Jason, Christine, Sara, and Meadow Rose.

Collaboration and Co-Teaching

Collaboration *and* Co-Teaching

STRATEGIES FOR ENGLISH LEARNERS

ANDREA HONIGSFELD
MARIA G. DOVE

Foreword by **Margo DelliCarpini**

CORWIN
A SAGE Company

For information:

Corwin
A SAGE Company
2455 Teller Road
Thousand Oaks, California 91320
(800) 233-9936
Fax: (800) 417-2466
www.corwin.com

SAGE Ltd.
1 Oliver's Yard
55 City Road
London EC1Y 1SP
United Kingdom

SAGE India Pvt. Ltd.
B 1/I 1 Mohan Cooperative
   Industrial Area
Mathura Road, New Delhi 110 044
India

SAGE Asia-Pacific Pte. Ltd.
33 Pekin Street #02-01
Far East Square
Singapore 048763

Printed in the United States of America.

Library of Congress Cataloging-in-Publication Data

Honigsfeld, Andrea, date
Collaboration and co-teaching : strategies for English learners / Andrea Honigsfeld and Maria G. Dove.
    p. cm.
Includes bibliographical references and index.
ISBN 978-1-4129-7650-3 (pbk. : alk. paper)
   1. English language—Study and teaching—Foreign speakers. 2. Language arts—Ability testing.
3. Curriculum planning. 4. Literacy—Evaluation. I. Dove, Maria G. II. Title.

LB1576.H635 2010
428.2′4—dc22   2010008587

This book is printed on acid-free paper.

10 11 12 13 14 10 9 8 7 6 5 4 3 2 1

Acquisitions Editor:	Dan Alpert
Associate Editor:	Megan Bedell
Editorial Assistant:	Sarah Bartlett
Production Editor:	Cassandra Margaret Seibel
Copy Editor:	Mark Bast
Typesetter:	C&M Digitals (P) Ltd.
Proofreader:	Theresa Kay
Cover Designer:	Michael Dubowe

Contents

Foreword

If you are reading this book, there is a good chance that you are a teacher, teacher educator, or administrator who has asked a question: How can we better serve the English language learners in our PreK–12 grade settings? While this is a complex and multifaceted issue, Andrea Honigsfeld and Maria Dove take a brilliant step toward providing an answer that makes sense and can be implemented in a number of different contexts.

It is well documented that U.S. schools are experiencing rapid growth in terms of the number of students whose native language is not English. In fact, the data show that enrollment in public schools in the United States for ESL students between the years 1991 and 2000 grew by 105 percent, compared to a 12 percent overall growth rate among the general school population (Kindler, 2002). Combined with this is the fact that many general-education teachers, who are specialists in their specific disciplines, are often underprepared to work with ELLs in the general-education classroom, and ESL teachers, while specialists in TESOL (Teaching English to Speakers of Other Languages) pedagogy and theory, often are not aware of the actual curricular demands placed on ELLs in general education. In fact, research has found that only 26 percent of teachers reported taking part in professional development that addresses issues of ELLs (NCES, 2001). In addition, only 27 percent of teachers report being *very well prepared* to work with ELLs in the general-education classroom (U.S. Department of Education, NCES, 2001). There is usually some requirement in teacher education programs that involves understanding the needs of ELLs, but research tells us that only 20 percent of programs offer a specific course on this topic (U.S. Government Accountability Office, 2009). Finally, the acquisition of the academic language needed, Cognitive Academic Language Proficiency, as Cummins (1979) names it, takes years to acquire. Students entering school and simultaneously acquiring language and content skills, under the best of circumstances, can take seven to ten years to develop this type of language, depending on their level of academic preparation upon entering school as a second- or additional-language learner (Collier & Thomas, 1989). Combined with the aforementioned growth in the ELL population and the level of preparedness among teachers who have ELLs in their general-education classrooms, it seems that we might be reaching a tipping point in terms of providing the most effective service to students who need both to be successful in their general education, content classes and acquire English as an additional language, both for social and academic purposes. While ESL teachers are in the best position to build these language skills in a highly contextualized and sheltered setting, such as a pull-out ESL program, the content or general-education teacher is the one qualified to deliver the discipline-specific material. In a traditional pull-out program, these activities take place in isolation from each other and may not be connected to the extent that they need to be. As a teacher educator who works with both ESL and content-area teachers, I have often heard the lament from the subject area teacher: *I'm not really sure what happens in the ESL classroom . . . what the ESL teacher does with the students.* Conversely, the ESL teachers I work with tend to be unclear on the types of skills and language necessary for success in general education. An example of this can be seen in the following reflection of a TESOL teacher candidate who participated in a jointly scheduled methods class (TESOL and secondary-level English) where the aim was to build collaborative relationships across the disciplines during the teacher education experience. This candidate's writing focused on what she learned about her own practice and the actual curricular demands of the secondary-level English curriculum that her ELL students have to master as a result of working with an English education teacher candidate:

> I was teaching very different kinds of writing. We did a lot of journal entries and letters and five paragraph essays, which I thought was the kind of thing they [ESL students] needed for their classes. Then, the English teachers in my collaboration group started talking about the critical-lens essay, and I had no idea what this was. When I found out, I realized that this is a really hard kind of essay for ESL students to write since you need a lot of different things. You need background knowledge, intense information on two novels, and, hardest [*sic*] of all, the ability to interpret a quote, which can be metaphorical. I said to myself, "Wow, I've been really wasting my and their time by focusing on this five-paragraph essay!" (Roxie[1], reflective journal entry, November, 2007 [DelliCarpini, 2009])

This teacher candidate learned from her English education colleagues in the class about the actual demands that the curriculum placed on students and reflected that, while the writing activities she was working on were good ways for her learners to develop written communication skills in English, the format the writing was taking was not exactly what would be most helpful for them in this particular academic endeavor. When teachers collaborate and co-teach, the content and language become interconnected in a way that is not possible when students receive content instruction in one class and language instruction in another.

Co-teaching between ESL and general-education teachers is not without its challenges. Aside from the usual constraints of time, administrative support, and the needed skills to form effective co-teaching partnerships, the issue of positioning between the ESL and general-education teacher has emerged in the literature as one that could potentially prevent an effective partnership from ever occurring. For example, Arkoudis (2006) discusses that effective collaboration between ESL and general-education teachers assumes an equitable relationship between the two, but in fact, ESL teachers are frequently marginalized and have low status in the schools where they work. Based on this marginalization, meaningful co-teaching and collaboration can be a challenge. However, this challenge can be overcome: When teachers are provided the necessary support, underlying theory, and have the ability to practice and reflect on practices, these partnerships can be successful and benefit both teachers and students. The supported act of building collaborative relationships can ameliorate the negative effects of not understanding each other's discipline. In addition, strong collaborative partnerships can have a positive effect on the whole school community: When teachers work across disciplines, combining skills to ensure the success of ELLs, all students benefit, the community of learners becomes more inclusive, and all teachers share in the responsibility of the education and success

---

1. Pseudonym

of students who are learning English in that school community—another factor that can break down some of the barriers that may exist in terms of teacher positioning.

If we are truly committed to enhancing outcomes and developing effective educational contexts for English language learners, collaboration and co-teaching must become part of the landscape. Students do not learn in isolation; in fact, they learn best and retain the most when they are able to see the interconnectedness not only between their school subjects and their own lives, but how the different subjects they are learning connect to each other. When teachers engage in collaborative partnerships, students are receiving interconnected and relevant instruction that targets their needs and positions them as key members of the general-education learning communities to which they belong.

In *Collaboration and Co-Teaching: Strategies for English Learners,* Andrea Honigsfeld and Maria Dove have developed a theoretically grounded text that provides readers with underlying knowledge and theory regarding collaboration and co-teaching in general and specifically between ESL and general-education teachers. The text is engaging and user-friendly and offers what I consider to be a "one-stop" approach in terms of developing collaboration and co-teaching skills in both preservice and inservice teachers. Honigsfeld and Dove have addressed all of the issues that, in my experience, have critical impact on the success of these relationships and provide vignettes, examples, and opportunities for development of both knowledge and skills through activities. These features allow readers to not only understand the collaborative and co-teaching process, but to also see, through the vignettes, co-teaching, and collaboration in practice, both the successful and challenging experiences. In addition, this text also provides a section in each chapter on the role of program administrators, therefore increasing the ability for teachers engaged in collaboration and co-teaching to be supported in their efforts.

Honigsfeld and Dove open this text with an excerpt from the Rudyard Kipling poem accompanying "The Elephant's Child," inviting you to take a journey with them to explore ESL and general-education teacher collaboration and co-teaching. The journey takes readers through the *what, when, where, how,* and *why* of collaborative practices and deconstructs the process in a way that can be implemented across contexts, whether in a teacher education program, professional-development venue, or the PreK–12 grade setting. As I read this text, I saw a wonderful world of possibilities opening up before me in terms of building collaborative relationships in the preservice and inservice teachers with whom I work, and I believe that this book will become a road map for your own journey into ESL and general-education teacher collaboration and co-teaching.

Margo DelliCarpini
Editor, *TESOL Journal*
TESOL Program Coordinator
Department of Middle & High School Education, Lehman College
The City University of New York

Preface

I keep six honest serving-men
(They taught me all I knew)
Their names are What and Why and When
And How and Where and Who.

Rudyard Kipling

Rudyard Kipling took his readers on many journeys, from England to India, from Africa to Australia, through novels, short stories, and poems. His famous quote above (from the poem accompanying "The Elephant's Child") inspired us to take you, our reader, on a journey from teacher collaboration to co-teaching. It is a journey unlike any of Kipling's, yet it is always challenging, exciting, and out of the ordinary! We each started our own journeys of collaboration at the onset of our teaching careers 20–25 years ago. We have been exploring the *Whos, Whats, Whens, Wheres, Whys,* and *Hows* of teacher collaboration and co-teaching for the sake of our English language learners ever since. The more questions we asked, the better we understood our own experiences—why some things worked and others did not. The more questions we asked, the more valuable insight we received from our colleagues and friends who also engage in collaboration—about working with English language learners in a wide range of settings from preschool to college. The more questions we asked, the more we discovered that while there is an expanding body of literature on the topic of teacher collaboration and co-teaching, most of it is not concerned with the needs of English language learners (ELLs).

In recent professional-development sessions, we asked several groups of general-education teachers, English-as-a-second-language (ESL) specialists, and district and school administrators what questions come to their minds when they hear the topic of the workshop they will be attending is teacher collaboration and co-teaching for the sake of ELLs. Here are some of the questions that we captured during our warm-up activity:

- Who should collaborate in a school building?
- How often should collaborative teaching teams meet?
- How could the administration best support teacher collaboration?
- Does co-teaching mean both teachers teach at the same time?
- Who would set up teacher collaboration and co-teaching in a building?
- Who would be included in a collaborative teacher team?
- What is the role of the guidance department in teacher collaboration?
- How can teacher collaboration help beginner ELLs?
- Why should I collaborate? Are there incentives? What are the benefits?

The abundance of questions ranged from novice-level, sincere inquires, such as, *Who should collaborate?* to more complex, buildingwide concerns such as, *How would administrators support teacher collaboration more effectively?* We found similar patterns of questions each time we worked with teachers on collaborative strategies and co-teaching.

Thanks to our day-to-day practice, answers first grew out of teaching our English-as-a-foreign-language and English-as-a-second-language classes collaboratively. Later on, we found more answers while preparing teacher candidates for the field of ESL through a graduate teacher education program, while working as instructional coaches and mentors assisting new teachers both in the general-education and ESL setting or while offering professional-development workshops to experienced teachers. The more questions we answered, the more questions were raised. Each person we encountered had a unique perspective on what educators could and should do to help ELLs. Kipling got it right for us again:

But different folk have different views,

I know a person small—

She keeps ten million serving-men,

Who get no rest at all!

She sends 'em abroad on her own affairs,

From the second she opens her eyes—

One million Hows, two million Wheres,

And seven million Whys!

Are there one million unanswered *Hows,* two million *Wheres,* and seven million *Whys* of teacher collaboration? Probably not! Do you have a few questions? If you are reading these pages, you probably do, and this book is written for you! The concepts of teacher collaboration, collaborative schools, and co-teaching are not new; however, our invitation to all teachers (general-education, content area, and ESL specialists alike) to set out on a journey from collaboration to co-teaching may be new in many schools. Enjoy your trip through the following nine chapters, each centered on an essential question.

Chapter 1 establishes the framework for the rest of the book ("What Is This Book About?"). Chapter 2 explores the importance of teacher collaboration, offers a rationale for collaborative practices and co-teaching, and synthesizes relevant research in 10 key areas ("Why Is Collaboration Needed?"). Chapter 3 identifies all stakeholders in a multilingual educational community and describes their unique roles and responsibilities in developing a school culture that fosters teacher collaboration and co-teaching for the benefit of English language learners ("Who Does Teacher Collaboration and ESL Co-Teaching Concern?"). Chapter 4 highlights the collaborative practices that ESL and general-education teachers may choose to participate in ("What Are the Essential Components of an Integrated, Collaborative ESL Program?"). Chapter 5 identifies the nuts and bolts of collaborative and co-teaching practices ("How Do Teachers Plan, Instruct, and Assess ELLs Collaboratively?"). Chapter 6 explores the time frames available for collaborations ("When Do Teachers and ESL Specialists Collaborate and Co-Teach?"). Chapter 7 describes the different physical and virtual environments that teachers use in order to enhance their collaborative processes ("Where Do Teachers and ESL Specialists Collaborate and Co-Teach?"). Chapter 8 promotes reflective practices and presents informal assessment and evaluation techniques ("What Next? Reviewing and Evaluating Integrated, Collaborative ESL Programs). Finally, Chapter 9 introduces six exemplary ESL teachers and their collaborative partners and presents their experiences working in collaboration in a case study format ("Portraits of Collaboration").

We hope you enjoy your journey exploring the possibilities that teacher collaboration holds for ESL programs and the education of English language learners. In addition, it is our wish that the information and personal stories we have shared regarding co-teaching and inclusive programs to benefit ELLs may inspire you to devise, experiment with, and evaluate innovative programs for this special student population.

Acknowledgments

We extend a special thank you to all the teachers and administrators who—directly or indirectly—supported the development or inclusion of the case studies, classroom examples, and authentic snapshots presented in this book: Yanick Chery-Frederic, Maria Ciarametaro, Dr. Thomas P. Dolan, Susan Dorkings, Susan Elliott, Lisa Fuentes, Aminda Gentile, Lisa Greiner, Dr. Evelyn Holman, Angela Hudson, Lynne Manouvrier, John O'Mard, Sandy Pensak, Lucia Posillico, Nathaniel Raynor, Ronald Ross, Linda Scalice, and Michael Singleton.

We appreciate the willingness of all the teachers featured in Chapter 9—who also served as coauthors of their case studies—to share their collaborative experiences: Barbara Suter and Vera Zinnel, Caryn Bachar, Nancy Berg and Matt Fliegel, Linda Rauch, Susan Dorkings, Christine Rowland, and Seth Mactas.

Our most sincere appreciation goes to Kelley Cordeiro, the coauthor of Chapter 9, for her many contributions to the manuscript; Joshua L. Garfinkel and Nathaniel Raynor for being our critical friends; and Erin Gilmartin for technical assistance with library research.

We would also like to acknowledge that this text has been significantly improved by the constructive feedback offered by our reviewers: Heidi Bernal, Director of ELL, Saint Paul Public Schools, MN; Margo DelliCarpini, Editor, *TESOL Journal*, TESOL Program Coordinator, Department of Middle & High School Education, Lehman College, The City University of New York, Bronx, NY; Karen Duke, Jackson Preparatory Magnet, Saint Paul, MN; Scott W. C. Lawrence, Director of Curriculum, East Granby Public Schools, CT; Helaine W. Marshall, Director, Language Programs, Long Island University, Brookville, NY; Joann Miles, ESL Teacher, Manorhaven and Salem Elementary Schools, Port Washington, NY; Karen Owen, Staff Development Director, Escambia School District, FL; Ellie Paiewonsky, Supervisor II, Nassau BOCES BETAC, Duffy Center, Hicksville, NY; Nathan Raynor, ESL Teacher, Grades K–5, Manorville, NY; Franklin (Bud) Read, Supervisor of Academics, Colonial School District, New Castle, DE; Kusum Sinha, Assistant Superintendent, Croton-Harmon School District, NY; Anne M. Wilding, TESOL Field Placement Supervisor, Stony Brook University, Department of Linguistics, NY.

We thank Dan Alpert for being the most insightful and encouraging editor we could have asked for. We would like to express our gratitude to Dan publicly for believing in this project from the beginning and for supporting it ever since. Our sincere appreciation goes to the entire Corwin team, especially to Megan Bedell, Sarah Bartlett, and Cassandra Seibel for their work on the manuscript preparation and production process.

We would like to thank all the teachers with whom we co-taught and who helped us develop our own collaborative practices, in particular Dolly Ging, Eileen Haydock, Joanne Lufrano, Alison Roberts, Sandy Rubin, Sandy Schlaff, and Joyce Smithok.

The richness of the content and variety of ideas could not have been possible without the generous input and feedback of those who have attended professional-development trainings with us or participated in our research projects. We also wish to acknowledge individuals who have encouraged us to pursue this project, including Maureen Walsh, EdD, and Bernadette Donovan, OP, PhD; Audrey Cohan, EdD; and all our colleagues at Molloy College, Rockville Centre, New York.

Last but not least, without the ongoing support of our immediate and extended families and friends this book could not have happened. You know who you are and we love you!

About the Authors

Andrea Honigsfeld is Associate Dean in the Division of Education at Molloy College, Rockville Centre, New York. She teaches graduate education courses related to cultural and linguistic diversity, linguistics, ESL methodology, and action research. Before entering the field of teacher education, she was an English-as-a-foreign-language teacher in Hungary (Grades 5–8 and adult), an English-as-a-second-language teacher in New York City (Grades K–3 and adult), and taught Hungarian at New York University.

She was the recipient of a doctoral fellowship at St. John's University, where she conducted research on individualized instruction and learning styles. She has published extensively on working with English language learners and providing individualized instruction based on learning style preferences. She received a Fulbright Award to lecture in Iceland in the fall of 2002. In the past eight years, she has been presenting at conferences across the United States, Great Britain, Denmark, Sweden, the Philippines, and the United Arab Emirates. She frequently offers staff development primarily focusing on effective differentiated strategies and collaborative practices for English-as-a-second-language and general-education teachers. Her coauthored book *Differentiated Instruction for At-Risk Students* (2009) and coedited book *Breaking the Mold of School Instruction and Organization* (2010) are published by Rowman and Littlefield.

Maria G. Dove is Assistant Professor in the Division of Education at Molloy College, Rockville Centre, New York, where she teaches courses to preservice and inservice teachers in the graduate education TESOL program. Having worked as an English-as-a-second-language teacher for over 30 years, she has provided instruction to English language learners in public-school settings (Grades K–12) and in adult English language programs in Nassau County, New York.

During her years as an ESL specialist, she established co-teaching partnerships, planned instruction through collaborative practices, and conducted ESL co-taught lessons in general-education classrooms with her fellow K–6 teachers. She has served as a mentor for new ESL teachers and coaches both ESL and general-education teachers on co-teaching strategies. She has published several articles and book chapters on her experiences with co-teaching, differentiated instruction, and the education of English language learners. She regularly offers professional-development workshops regarding the instruction of English language learners to local school districts as well as at state and national conferences.

What Is This Book About?

That is what learning is. You suddenly understand something you've understood all your life, but in a new way.

Doris Lessing

OVERVIEW

The goals of this chapter are to offer a rationale for this book and to provide insight into its purpose and organization. We offer important background information on demographic trends for English language learners (ELLs) and compare various program models serving ELLs across the United States. We examine how to benefit ELLs through a framework of collaborative teaching practices and define key concepts related to teacher collaboration and co-teaching for the benefit of English language learners. After we describe various current program models to support ELLs and present a historical perspective on teacher collaboration, we make a claim for teacher collaboration for the sake of ELLs in today's schools.

Voices From the Field

Kaman and her younger sister Feng arrived with their family from Shanghai just two weeks before the school year began. They hardly had settled into their American home when, filled with a strange mix of concern and excitement, they entered their new school. Kaman, a sixth grader, and Feng, a second-grade student, spoke little English, although Kaman had some facility with understanding and reading the language.

(Continued)

(Continued)

When Feng reached her classroom, her eyes opened wide and a huge smile appeared across her petite face. She was amazed to see youngsters who looked just like her, as there were many Asian families in the neighborhood. When the teacher led her by the hand to her seat, she seemed undisturbed by the unfamiliar words she heard everyone speaking. Feng was undaunted by her lack of English language skills. She clearly made her thoughts known to her classmates and her teacher by using simple gestures and pointing to the things she needed. Several of her classmates taught her some new words such as "water," "lunch," and "bathroom," which she had trouble pronouncing, but she felt wholly satisfied with her newfound understanding and word approximations. And when it came time for math, Feng not only was able to understand the lesson, she provided one of her new friends the answers to some of the number problems. Feng was having a great first day at her new American school.

In contrast, Kaman's day was filled with intermittent waves of anxiety and fear. When she entered her new classroom, the teacher was busy, organizing science textbooks that had just arrived, and her new classmates basically ignored her. Kaman stood for some time in the back of the room waiting for all the desks to fill before she chose one for herself. She was disturbed and distracted by all the foreign sights, sounds, and smells around her. Kaman tried to learn what was expected of her by observing her fellow students, but she felt as if she was always one step behind the others. She copied everything the teacher wrote on the board, although the teacher said so many things he did not write, and Kaman was unable to understand him. She also did not understand all of the abbreviations the teacher used when writing the homework assignments. Surprisingly, no one seemed to be aware of Kaman's limited English skills on her first day in her new school, but as the day ended, Kaman dreaded the thought of what might happen when she was found out.

Vignette Reflection

Although Kaman and Feng come from the same household, their psychological and emotional needs differ greatly. On occasion, older siblings, in spite of their better facility with the English language, have more difficulty adjusting than their younger brothers and sisters.

When teachers and administrators meet to plan educational programs and curriculum, Heidi Hayes Jacobs (2004) asks them to consider the "empty chair" in the room that represents the school's students. Jacobs contends that the best interest of these youngsters should be reflected in all that educators do. In order to explore the diverse needs of English language learners, teachers and administrators must be mindful of the distinct challenges of these students along with their various individual needs. In their best interest, educators must develop strategies to share pertinent information about these youngsters to better prepare them for classroom instruction.

WHAT GUIDED US WHEN WE WROTE THIS BOOK?

We invite our readers to explore the many possibilities of teacher collaboration for the benefit of ELLs. Whether you have earned an ESL teaching license, an endorsement from your state, work with ELLs in a sheltered-content class, or are a general-education teacher perhaps without formal ELL training, there are shared goals in common. It is our hope that all service providers strive to deliver the best possible instruction to ELLs collaboratively.

We designed this book to be a valuable resource that assists both novice and experienced teachers in their endeavors to provide effective *integrated, collaborative* instruction for ELLs. Why is this type of instruction necessary?

Much has been written about the cognitive, academic, and linguistic needs of ELLs (Cummins, 2001; Irujo, 1998; Nieto, 2002). Many guidebooks and professional-development materials have been produced on teacher collaboration and co-teaching for inclusive classrooms (Conderman, Bresnahan, & Pedersen, 2009; Villa, Thousand, & Nevin, 2008). Much has been published about effective strategies general-education teachers can use to offer more culturally and linguistically responsive instruction for ELLs (Calderón, 2007; Carrasquillo & Rodriguez, 1996; Gibbons, 2002; Haver, 2003; Hill & Flynn, 2006). However, very few resources are available to help general-education teachers and ESL specialists collaborate effectively on all grade levels. Our goal is to fill that gap by offering a user-friendly and comprehensive guide that considers all types and levels of collaboration.

We recognize that a variety of ESL program models, diverse local needs, and considerable regional differences in ESL services exist. We also acknowledge that each ELL is unique, as is every educator reading this book. We respond to this diversity by addressing the spectrum of current, collaborative practices. These range from informal and occasional exchanges of teaching ideas, to systemic and formal initiatives such as curriculum alignment and parallel teaching, to the most complex form of collaboration, which is co-teaching embedded in the context of a vibrant professional learning community (PLC) (DuFour & Eaker, 1998).

With increasing numbers of ELLs in the general-education classrooms, there are a number of program models available to ESL service providers. Schools need to examine all available program models and instructional delivery systems to be able to provide the best services for a growing population of ELLs. There is a documented need for teachers to work together formally and informally, inside and outside the classroom, and during academic learning time (ALT) or instructional time and professional-development time. Our book offers a vehicle to explore the world of collaboration by answering essential questions that we used as chapter titles. Additionally, we define the role school administrators play in collaboration, offer comprehensive guidelines on conducting collaborative program evaluations, and outline how the book can be used as a professional-development tool to help build professional learning communities that focus on ELLs' needs.

THE PURPOSE

The purpose of this book is manifold and as follows:

1. To define teacher collaboration, collaborative team teaching, and co-teaching in the context of ESL

2. To explore how teacher collaboration and co-teaching can provide an effective framework for integrated ESL practices to accommodate the academic, sociocultural, and linguistic needs of diverse English language learners

3. To establish a vehicle for professional development toward creative collaboration between ESL and general-education teachers

4. To offer a framework for implementing an effective co-teaching model to differentiate instruction for ELLs

5. To recount real-life vignettes that depict challenges and successes teachers experienced in collaborative partnerships

6. To share extensive case studies of ESL teachers' collaborative experiences at the elementary, middle, and high school levels

7. To offer guidelines to school district administrators on how to create a collaborative instructional model to support ELLs

8. To provide insight into areas of best practice where further research is needed

STRUCTURE AND ORGANIZATION OF THE BOOK

Our title reflects a broad perspective: *Collaboration and Co-Teaching: Strategies for English Learners.* We invite you to take your own journey and encourage you to choose your own collaborative paths, using this book as a roadmap. Each chapter examines both formal and informal teacher collaboration practices as well as co-teaching with the ESL specialist. The chapters are structured in a similar fashion for consistency. Recurring features are intended to provide easy access to the content of the book.

Overview: We offer a descriptive preview of the entire chapter by highlighting the key ideas that are included.

Voices From the Field: We present a short, authentic vignette about a different teacher at the elementary, middle, or high school level in each chapter. Their personal and professional experiences are directly connected to the content of the chapter. We periodically revisit the story as it relates to our discussion of the dilemmas, challenges, and successes presented following the vignette.

Following the above introductory features, the main body of each chapter addresses both general collaborative practices and specific co-teaching experiences with ESL specialists. Each chapter ends with the following recurring features:

Administrators' Roles: We recognize that teacher collaboration and co-teaching practices may develop as grassroots initiatives. We have both been involved in such pioneering experiences. We also recognize that collaboration goes beyond what individual teachers do; it involves school and district level administrators, support staff, the entire school faculty, and the larger educational community. Building a professional learning community—in which a culture of collaboration is the norm and co-teaching is instructionally and logistically supported—needs building administrators' full support. In each chapter, we address the role of school leadership and offer key points to be considered when creating an integrated, collaborative model of ESL services.

Summary: At the conclusion of each chapter, we briefly synthesize the main ideas and their implications for teachers working in diverse contexts.

Discussion Questions: We anticipate that our book will be useful in both preservice teacher education courses and inservice professional-development situations. We invite you to continue exploring the topics presented in each chapter. The end-of-chapter questions are designed to prompt further reflections for the individual reader and to initiate group discussions and collaborative inquiry for teacher groups.

Key Resources: We offer a list of online resources at the end of each chapter that allows you to search for more information on the topic.

In addition, each chapter includes interactive discussion points and graphic representations of the content.

Chapter 9 stands apart from the first eight chapters. Instead of following the previously established template, it exhibits six case studies to demonstrate the variety of collaborative experiences in an elementary, middle, and high school. This final chapter is designed to aid in the synthesis of the ideas in the book in a cohesive and authentic way.

We wish to emphasize that teacher collaboration is a vehicle for ongoing, site-based professional development through mentoring (for novice teachers), peer coaching (for midcareer teachers), and establishing teacher leadership roles (for more experienced teachers). Thus, our book is designed to further ideas on how to engage in a collaborative inquiry process, a collegial circle, or a teacher study circle (TSC).

THE ELL POPULATION

Recent demographic changes among school students in the United States are well documented. Projections for the next 10, 15, and even 50 years abound. Data sources and statistical approaches vary from source to source, as does terminology. Most federal and state agencies use the term *Limited English Proficient* (LEP) when referring to children who do not communicate well in English, if it is not their first language. On the other hand, schools, teacher educators, and advocacy groups tend to employ the title *English Language Learners* (ELL) or *English Learners* (EL) to focus on the child and not the deficiency. In a 2008 NCELA publication, Ballantyne, Sanderman, and Levy make yet another type of distinction:

> The term *English language learners (ELLs)* . . . refers to those students who are not yet proficient in English and who require instructional support in order to fully access academic content in their classes. ELLs may or may not have passed English language proficiency (ELP) assessments. The subset of ELLs who have not yet achieved ELP as measured by the particular assessment procedures of their state are often referred to as Limited English Proficient (LEP) students. (p. 2)

In this book, we use the acronym *ELL* to show an appreciation for the student and to avoid placing undue emphasis on his or her limitations. Among many others, Payán and Nettles (2008) report that there are over 5.1 million ELLs in U.S. schools representing roughly 10 percent of total public school enrollment and speaking over 450 languages or dialects. The number of ELLs has risen by close to 60 percent in the past 10 years. Nearly 60 percent of ELLs qualify for a reduced-price or free lunch. These demographic trends are anticipated to continue in the next decade, so reexamining what schools do to respond to them is of utmost importance.

COLLABORATION

The concepts of teacher collaboration and collaborative schools are not new; however, our invitation to all teachers (general-education, content area, and ESL specialists alike) to set out on a journey beginning with collaboration and moving toward co-teaching *for the sake of English language learners* may be new in many schools.

The word *collaboration* comes from "co-labor," or "work together." According to *Merriam-Webster's Collegiate Dictionary,* to *collaborate* means "to work jointly with others or together especially in an intellectual endeavor."

In the *Merriam-Webster Thesaurus* (online), *collaboration* is defined both as

1. the state of having shared interests or efforts (association)
2. the work and activity of a number of persons who individually contribute toward the efficiency of the whole (teamwork)

Several educational researchers and practitioners have offered their definitions and descriptions of collaboration. Many others emphasize the importance of collaboration as an essential skill for bringing about much-needed educational and social change.

- As early as 1990, Smith and Scott claimed that "collaboration depends inherently on the voluntary effort of professional educators to improve their schools and their own teaching through teamwork" (p. 2). They confirmed Lieberman and Miller's (1984) position that the norm continues to be "self-imposed, professionally sanctioned teacher isolation" (p. 11).
- Collaboration is a style of interaction between at least two co-equal parties voluntarily engaged in shared decision making as they work toward a common goal (Cook & Friend, 1995).
- According to Reich, new skills needed by twenty-first-century workers are abstraction, system thinking, experimentation, and collaboration (as cited in Thornburg, 2002). "Collaboration is important for two crucial reasons. First, many of the challenges facing us today cut across a wide range of disciplines, which can often only be bridged through teamwork. Second, by interacting with others, we can often discover new approaches to problems" (p. 34).
- One of the most compelling reasons for collaboration, Risko and Bromley (2001) suggest, is that it "moves professionals and families from the deficit model to one that affirms and is responsive to students' strengths, backgrounds, beliefs, and values" (p. 11). They also posit that collaboration "reduces role differentiation among teachers and specialists, resulting in shared expertise for problem solving that yields multiple solutions to dilemmas about literacy and learning" (p. 12).

These definitions yield common themes, including an emphasis on being engaged in collaboration *voluntarily*, having a common goal (e.g., enhancing instruction for students, school improvement), participating in interdisciplinary endeavors, and finding multiple creative solutions.

Co-Teaching as a Unique Form of Teacher Collaboration

Co-teaching is traditionally defined as the collaboration between general and special education (SPED) teachers on all of the teaching responsibilities for all of the students assigned to a classroom (Gately & Gately, 2001). This definition has frequently been expanded to allow the collaborative partnership between a general-education teacher and a service provider or specialist other than a SPED teacher, such as a remedial math teacher, a reading specialist, a teacher of the gifted and talented, a speech-language pathologist, and, more recently, the English-as-a-second-language (ESL) teacher.

Villa et al. (2008) suggest that "co-teaching involves the distribution of responsibility among people for planning, instruction, and evaluation for a classroom of students" (p. 50). It is a unique professional relationship in which "partners must establish trust, develop and work on communication, share chores, celebrate, work together creatively to overcome the inevitable challenges and problems, and anticipate conflict and handle it in a constructive way" (p. 5).

To date, limited resources are available on co-teaching practices shared by ESL and general-education educators. Emerging research has documented the challenges of developing effective collaborative relationships and co-teaching practices (Davison, 2006; DelliCarpini, 2008, 2009; Hurst & Davison, 2005). Documentary accounts of successful collaborative and co-teaching practices have also surfaced (Kaufman & Crandall, 2005). Often times, educators working with special needs children, youths who are at risk, ELLs, or gifted students look to borrow, adapt, and synthesize information and ideas from a related field. Thus, resources such as DuFour and Eaker's (1998) work on professional learning communities, Richard Villa and colleagues' (2008) contributions, and Margaret Friend's (2005, 2008) publications on co-teaching in the inclusive setting have been influential among ESL specialists.

Collaboration and the
Twenty-First-Century Educational Community

Several professional organizations also place a special emphasis on collaboration, which is one of the twenty-first-century competencies our K–12 students need to be prepared for today's world. The Partnership for 21st Century Skills (2007) outlined contemporary professional development as that which promotes professional learning communities for teachers and emphasizes classroom learning that advances modern skills for students. Professional development "encourages knowledge sharing among communities of practitioners, using face-to-face, virtual and blended communications" (par. 5).

In 2001, the National Staff Development Council (NSDC) also added collaboration to its process standards. "Staff development that improves the learning of all students provides educators with the knowledge and skills to collaborate" (NSDC Standards for Staff Development, 2001, para. 2). As early as 1992, the Interstate New Teacher Assessment and Support Consortium (INTASC) established a set of model standards to support states in their teacher education program design. One of the 10 standards (no. 10) was devoted to collaboration, ethics, and relationships. It stated that "the teacher fosters relationships with school colleagues, parents, and agencies in the larger community to support students' learning and well-being" (INTASC, 1992, p. 33). Similarly, in 2008, Standard 6 of nine teacher education standards developed by the Association of Teacher Educators (ATE) focuses on collaboration. It suggests that teacher educators

> collaborate regularly and in significant ways with relevant stakeholders to improve teaching, research, and student learning. Accomplished teacher educators adopt a collaborative approach to teacher education that involves a variety of stakeholders (e.g., universities, schools, families, communities, foundations, businesses, and museums) in teaching and learning. Collaboration to design and implement teacher education promotes the collective practice that increases efficacy and knowledge of teacher education. (pp. 6–7)

In a 2008 Edutopia article, Will Richardson claims that the *Information Age* is now being replaced by the *Collaboration Age*. We believe that collaboration has been fostered and made more accessible due to the advances in information technology. Perhaps the Information Age is not being replaced by the Collaboration Age as much as it is being incorporated into this new paradigm.

In response to an April 2009 report from the National Commission on Teaching and America's Future (NCTAF) on teacher retention, the NEA responded by affirming that collaboration is key to keeping teachers. As NEA President Dennis Van Roekel states, "Quality teaching is engendered when teachers work together to analyze student progress, plan curriculum and instructional strategies and involve parents in their children's schooling" (NEA, 2009, par. 3).

Effective Teacher Collaboration

Our belief that effective collaboration benefits students (and teachers alike) is affirmed by the well-deserved attention it receives in the educational community. We build on several available collaborative frameworks by synthesizing their essential dimensions and adapting them to the context of a culturally and linguistically diverse school. We take a broad look at what exemplifies effective teacher collaboration, what essential frameworks need to be established in order for ESL and general-education teachers to work together effectively, and how integrated approaches to ESL services benefit all stakeholders.

PROGRAM MODELS SERVING ENGLISH LANGUAGE LEARNERS

Have you wondered what types of program models are available across the United States to respond to the growing needs of English language learners (ELLs) or how they compare? Let's take a quick bird's-eye look at the ESL landscape.

After students are classified as English language learners, several program models are available in some schools, while in others only one type of support program is available. Depending on what source you consult, program models are categorized in numerous ways ranging from three main models (Rossell, 2003) to as many as six or even more (Genesee, 1999). To help navigate the maze of programs, let's focus on the following four most common program models:

1. Structured English Immersion

2. English as a Second Language Programs

3. Bilingual Education (Transitional or Maintenance)

4. Dual Language or Two-Way Enrichment Bilingual Programs

Structured English Immersion

In 1998, Proposition 227 was passed in California, enforcing that "all children in California public schools shall be taught English as rapidly and effectively as possible" (*Proposition 227*, par. 7). In 2000, Proposition 203, a similar decision, was publicly voted on in Arizona, requiring

> pupils who are "English learners" to be taught in English immersion classes during a temporary transition period not normally intended to exceed 1 year. Once pupils have acquired a good working knowledge of English and are able to do regular schoolwork in English, they are required to be transferred to classrooms where students either are native English language speakers or already have

acquired reasonable fluency in English ("English language general education classrooms"). (*Ballot Proposition #203, p. 1*)

Both states, along with several others such as Massachusetts, increased their English immersion programs. According to guidelines for the implementation of *Structured English Immersion programs,* ELLs are placed in self-contained classes where they receive English and content instruction all day. Some argue that Structured English Immersion (SEI) may resemble a *sink or swim* approach of much earlier times, according to which English language learners were placed in general-education classrooms and were expected to master general-education curriculum with or without support from the classroom teacher. However, advocates of Structured Immersion suggest that

> SEI offers LEP children an ideal format. The goal is for these children to gain fluency in English as quickly as possible in a nonthreatening setting and to move gradually into the general education, the place where the challenging classes abound and they can learn alongside the other children. (Haver, 2003, p. xv)

Clark (2009) notes that most state student performance assessments are conducted in English, thus districts face an added challenge to enhance ELLs' proficiency in an expedited time frame; otherwise the districts are subject to increased scrutiny and possible sanctions. Yet, when Thompson (2009) gave students a voice, they claimed that despite their documented academic gains in isolated, self-contained fast-track English classes, their social isolation added to racism and segregation in the school:

> "I am thankful to my teachers because the little bit of English I am able to speak, I speak because of them," Amalia Raymundo, from Guatemala, said during a break between classes. But, she added, "I feel they hold me back by isolating me."
>
> Her best friend, Jhosselin Guevara, also from Guatemala, joined in. "Maybe the teachers are trying to protect us," she said. "There are people who do not want us here at all." (Thompson, 2009, par. 5–6)

Academic gains were reported at the expense of social integration!

English as a Second Language (ESL) Programs

In an ESL program, students who are identified as English language learners (ELL) receive specially designed language and academic instruction for the entire school day, or some part of it, offered by an English-as-a-second-language specialist. The more proficient students are, the fewer hours they tend to spend with the ESL teacher. In some states, education departments developed closely monitored guidelines for the number of periods each ELL is entitled to receive ESL services. For example, in New York State,

> freestanding ESL programs must be implemented in school districts which have fewer than 20 LEP students at the same grade level in the same building who speak the same native language other than English. The freestanding ESL program includes two components: a language arts instructional component and a content area instructional component. The language arts instructional component is delivered through instruction in English language arts and English as a second

language. The content area instructional component is delivered through instruction in English and ESL methodologies. (NYSED, 2009, p. 3)

The Commissioner's Regulation also outlines the amount and type of English language instruction or Native Language Arts (NLA) required at three language proficiency levels. Table 1.1 outlines the required units of study for K–8 and 9–12 students. (A unit of study is equivalent to 180 minutes per week.)

In Tennessee, state guidelines specify that

at the elementary level, an endorsed ESL teacher must provide direct services one to two hours per day for prefunctional, beginning and intermediate English Language Learners. Students at the advanced level may have programs more tailored to their needs including, but not limited to, visits in classroom without or with limited numbers of ELLs for subjects for which they are most proficient. They should receive up to one hour of direct service each day until these transitions begin to take place. (Tennessee State Board of Education ESL Program Policy, 2007, p. 3)

Similarly, advanced ELLs and students at the secondary level must receive services based on Tennessee state policy. Most other state education departments post their own guidelines on their Web sites to offer a framework for required services.

Types of ESL Programs

ESL programs take several alternative forms. The most prevalent are the pull-out and push-in (or plug-in) models. As indicated by their names, the ESL specialist either (a) provides ESL services in a designated area outside the classroom (usually in a specially equipped ESL classroom)—thus the name *pull-out,* or (b) he or she offers language support in the general-education classroom, also referred to as *inclusion* or *plug-in* ESL.

Table 1.1   Required Units of Study

English Language Requirements						
English Proficiency Level	Grades K–8			Grades 9–12		
	Number of Units			Number of Units		
	ESL	NLA*	ELA	ESL	NLA*	ELA
Beginning	2	1	-	3	1	-
Intermediate	2	1	-	2	1	-
Advanced	1	1	1	1	1	1

* If in bilingual program

Pull-Out Programs

Pull-out programs may also be referred to as self-standing ESL instruction. The ESL specialist either follows a specially designed ESL curriculum that is based on the participating students' individual language and academic needs, or he or she might develop a curriculum closely aligned with the general-education curriculum. Within the pull-out setting, ELLs benefit from small-group instruction and the unique adaptations to the general-education curriculum that the ESL specialist is able to offer.

Push-In, Plug-In, or Inclusive ESL Programs

If the ESL specialist provides instruction in the general-education classroom, there are a few additional options to consider:

1. Will the ESL teacher pull ELLs aside to a learning center or a designated area in the classroom and teach a stand-alone ESL curriculum?

2. Will the ESL teacher pull ELLs aside to a learning center or a designated area in the classroom and support the general-education curriculum by following the lesson conducted by the classroom teacher?

3. Will the ESL teacher and ELLs be integrated into the general-education teacher's lesson through differentiated instructional strategies?

4. Will the ESL teacher and the general-education teacher collaboratively plan and carry out the instruction following one of several possible co-teaching models? (For implementation of teacher collaborations, see Honigsfeld & Dove, 2008; Vaughn, Schumm, & Arguelles, 1997; or Wertheimer & Honigsfeld, 2000.)

Self-Contained ESL Classes

When the ELL population is large enough, self-contained ESL classes may be serviced by teachers certified both in ESL and a content specialty. Newcomer schools or classes may be established in school communities with large recent immigrant groups. Boyson and Short (2003) report on 115 newcomer programs at the middle and high school level located in 30 states at 196 school sites. More than half of the newcomer programs Boyson and Short have reviewed were found in California, New Jersey, New York, and Texas. Such programs recognize that

> recent immigrants may face even more challenges than other English language learners as they attempt to adjust to a new country and culture. One approach to easing that adjustment is the newcomer school . . . like New York City's award-winning International High School, a stand-alone school enrolling only recent immigrants. These schools provide immigrant students with intensive English-language instruction, content-area support in their native languages, and culturally responsive student and social services. (Rance-Roney, 2009, p. 35)

Vignette Revisited

Which ESL program might be best for Feng or Kaman? Are some programs better for beginning-level ESL students? Should the age of the youngster be considered or does the child's prior schooling matter? Each program designed for ELLs provides valuable assistance and essential instruction to ensure academic growth and language development, and schools often have more than one model of instruction to meet students' individual needs. Feng may thrive in an integrated, push-in ESL program due to her young age and relaxed disposition in the general-education classroom. However, Kaman may not wish to stand out in her class, afraid of being embarrassed, and her psychological needs might best be served initially in a pull-out program model.

Administrative Decision Making About ESL Program Models

How do administrators make these classroom-level organizational decisions? The following factors each contribute to the decision-making process:

1. Number of ELLs on each grade level (Should ELLs be clustered or distributed evenly across the classes?)

2. Availability of ESL support personnel (Are there highly qualified and certified ESL teachers or ESL teaching assistants?)

3. Classroom space (Is there a separate ESL classroom for pull-out services or is there a shortage of classroom space such as in some large urban schools?)

4. The instructional philosophy of the district or school (Are general-education teachers and ESL specialists encouraged to collaborate, are they given common preparation periods to plan together?)

ESL programs across the United States tend to follow the national TESOL *PK–12 English Language Proficiency Standards* (2006) and state or local standards. Most standards-related documents we reviewed share several essential elements. The ESL standards are organized by grade level or grade cluster, recognizing age-appropriate goals in language acquisition. They typically address the four language domains: listening, speaking, reading, and writing. There is some variation in whether standards address the four main content areas—ELA (English Language Arts), social studies, math, and science—or merely focus on social and instructional language and literacy skills.

Bilingual Education (Transitional or Developmental)

Bilingual Education has been at the center of political and educational debates for decades (Krashen, 1999). There are just as many proponents as opponents of bilingual education; however, carefully designed, longitudinal research studies showing the effectiveness of these program models cannot, and should not, be ignored (Collier & Thomas, 2002, 2007). The two main subtypes of bilingual education focus on the ultimate outcome of the program:

1. Is it to help students exit the bilingual classroom and enter the general-education, "English only" setting as soon as possible? or

2. Is it to maintain and further enhance students' native language and literacy skills while simultaneously helping them develop English language proficiency and literacy?

The first is often referred to as Transitional Bilingual Education, whereas the second is labeled as Maintenance, Developmental, or Late-Exit Bilingual Education and may also be considered for use as an enrichment program.

Within each program model, there are several other factors to consider. The most prevalent feature is the amount of time spent on each of the target languages. When

Thomas and Collier (2002) examine various bilingual-education programs, they describe one-way bilingual programs (both the transitional and developmental) as either following a 90/10 or a 50/50 model. In the 90/10 model, students initially receive 90 percent of instruction in their native language, which is then gradually reduced to about 50 percent by the fifth grade. In the 50/50 model, one or two teachers use both the native language and English for an approximately equal amount of time for instructional purposes throughout the implementation process.

Dual Language or Two-Way Immersion Programs

Dual-language models are among emerging program initiatives focusing on enrichment for both native and nonnative speakers of English. "In many states—especially in Texas, New Mexico, New York, California, Washington, Illinois, and the Washington, D.C. metropolitan area—dual language is expanding to many new schools" (Thomas & Collier, 2002, p. 17). Dual-language programs used in the United States tend to fall into one of the following two categories:

1. Minority-language-dominant programs. These programs follow an instructional pattern of using the minority language either for 90 percent or 80 percent of the time.

2. Balanced programs. These are programs in which the instructional time is equally divided between the minority language and English (Howard & Sugarman, 2001). It has been recommended that these programs systematically separate the two languages by day or other time schedule, subject matter, teacher, or a possible combination of these factors (Calderón & Minaya-Rowe, 2003; Cloud, Genesee, & Hamayan, 2000).

What Works Best?

You might be wondering which of the above is the best possible program model for English language learners. If we believe and agree that one size does *not* fit all, there cannot be *one* right answer to this question. Each model has its merits; each model has numerous documented success stories and its own share of challenges, the discussion of which goes beyond the scope of this book.

What Zigler and Weiss noted in 1985 still holds true: Research on program effectiveness must "go beyond the question of whether or not a program 'works' to ask *what works, for whom, how, when, and why*" (p. 199, emphasis added). Their message is still valid, though the educational context has changed considerably since the 1980s. We live in an age of increased accountability and standardized assessments. We witness or participate in continued debates on the impact of No Child Left Behind, including its impact on English language learners.

We also concur with Crawford (2008), who states that "decisions on how to teach English learners are being made not in the classroom, but in legislative chambers and voting booths; not on the basis of educational research data, but on the basis of public opinion, often passionate but rarely informed" (p. 59). Our commitment is to take on a pronounced role of advocacy to help schools and communities learn about the needs of ELLs and the organizational, curricular, and instructional options we can offer them. All stakeholders engaged in a local decision-making process collaboratively may be able to come to a resolution on what program models to use for which students, how to initially pilot new programs, when to maintain existing programs, and why and how to revise them.

WHAT CAN WE LEARN FROM THE HISTORY AND RESEARCH ON COLLABORATIVE PRACTICES?

In 1965, in a landmark publication entitled *The Sociology of Teaching,* Waller was among the first to explore the dynamics of teaching and identified four wishes that many share in a school:

1. Response: We wish to seek out as well as offer appreciation to each other.

2. Recognition: We wish to acknowledge and be acknowledged as individuals in a group.

3. New Experience: We wish to break away from routines and monotony.

4. Security: Yet, at the same time, we wish to protect existing structures.

Waller (1965) also cited Faris, who called attention to another wish of a social nature: the desire for participation. How many of these wishes are still at work 45 years later?

It was Dan Lortie's *Schoolteacher: A Sociological Study,* published in 1975, that first called attention to teacher isolation as a major obstacle to improvement in American schools. As Lortie describes the day-to-day lives of teachers, he frequently points out the lack of extensive opportunities or well-defined structures for collaboration among teachers. He observes that "mutual isolation during most of the day is the rule in many schools" (p. xi), which undoubtedly results in the loss of valuable knowledge. He also notes that "those in professional development help when they bring teachers together, and principals are also in a position to increase opportunities for teachers to work together and to share know-how" (p. xi).

Close to three decades ago, Judith Warren Little (1982) examined the differences between more and less effective schools and found that the more effective ones had a greater degree of collegiality. She discusses unique characteristics of collegiality (or collaboration) in schools where teachers participate in the following activities:

1. Teachers engage in frequent, continuous, and increasingly concrete and precise talk about teaching practice.

2. Teachers are frequently observed and provided with useful critiques of their teaching.

3. Teachers plan, design, evaluate, and prepare teaching materials together.

4. Teachers teach each other the practice of teaching. (pp. 331–332)

We translated Little's (1982) frequently quoted four key ideas into a framework of four Cs, in which *collaborative* serves as a defining adjective, followed by a key dimension of behavior that teachers engage in collaboratively:

1. Collaborative Conversations: Enhanced communication among all teachers

2. Collaborative Coaching: A climate that allows for critical feedback

3. Collaborative Curriculum: Curriculum and materials alignment

4. Collaborative Craftsmanship: Continuous improvement of the craft of teaching, while coordinating time, resources, and support for each other

Table 1.2 reveals how we co-constructed meaning from Little's (1982) original findings and transferred the concept of collegiality to the linguistically and culturally diverse school context that we see in the twenty-first century.

Table 1.2 The Four Cs of Collaboration

Collaborative Conversations	Collaborative Coaching
Talk about	*Engage in peer coaching to improve*
• Students' needs • Students' lives • Students' work • Curriculum • Instruction • Teachers' own struggles • Teachers' own successes • What matters to you, the teacher	• Lesson planning • Lesson delivery • Unit design • Use of supplementary materials • Adapted content • Modified instruction • Assessment
Collaborative Curriculum	Collaborative Craftsmanship
Align	*Explore*
• Lesson objectives (language objectives and content objectives) • Unit goals • Curriculum maps • Supplementary materials • Resources • Adapted texts and materials	• ELLs' background knowledge • ELLs' prior learning • Peer coaching • Planning instruction collaboratively or in the context of co-teaching • Effective methods for aligning curriculum and objectives • Using time more effectively • Making the most of collaborative efforts

TEACHER COLLABORATION IN TODAY'S SCHOOLS

Collaboration may start out as a small, grassroots effort, involving only two or three teachers who share the responsibility for some of the same ELLs and are concerned about their students' progress.

It may involve an entire grade level. Some examples include grade clusters working together to develop or enhance curricula in elementary schools; an interdisciplinary team of math, science, social studies, English, and ESL teachers (sharing responsibility for a cluster of classes in middle schools); or a discipline-specific department (focusing on preparing all students to meet graduation requirements of high schools).

Many argue that teacher autonomy and teacher isolation continue to trouble our profession. Many more—including DuFour and Eaker (1998), Fichtman Dana and Yendol-Hoppey (2008), and Schmoker (2006)—claim that professional learning communities will bring "results now!" When we asked teachers if they collaborate, we received reassuring responses:

"My school is 95 percent ESL, we must collaborate."

"Collaboration is teachers working together, filling in where one leaves off."

"I wish I could do more of it!"

"Of course, we work well with each other."

When we further probe what they do when they "collaborate," the answers range from talking to each other in the teachers' lounge about students to co-teaching on a daily basis, with a wide variety of activities in between. Some teachers serve on CSTs (Child Study Teams), others supervise students during arrival and dismissal; some co-plan lessons, some make joint decisions about new textbooks or other instructional materials. Many schools invite tenured teachers to participate in APPR (Annual Professional Performance Review) or R&D (Research and Development) Teams or to conduct collaborative lesson studies in place of formal observations.

Collaboration efforts are further refined when teachers enter into a co-teaching arrangement. Co-teaching for English language learners is a means of reducing teacher isolation without eliminating teacher autonomy. When co-teaching teams plan lessons for ELLs, they have team-teaching autonomy, the ability and freedom to guide instruction together to meet the needs of a particular group of learners. With the development of trust over time, co-teaching team members have the power to influence how curriculum is presented to all students and to create opportunities for new ideas and strategies that can be undertaken with ELLs in mind.

We are at an interesting turning point in education. The old mores and the physical realities of schools built in the mid- to late twentieth century still continue to reinforce teacher autonomy and isolation. At the same time, there is a growing trend of and need for collaboration in both instructional and noninstructional activities and through a variety of professional-development models. To best respond to the demands of today's schools, we propose a collaborative, integrated approach to ESL services, which is outlined in the following chapters.

SUMMARY

Teacher collaboration must have intrigued educators ever since the Little Red School House expanded to include more than one teacher. Most schools still follow the early twentieth-century model of "Cells and Bells" (Nair & Fielding, 2005), with many teachers working in isolation in their own classrooms. We believe that for the sake of ELLs, there is a place and time for creative collaboration among all teachers in every school that serves ELLs. This book was born out of our strong conviction regarding the benefits of, and even stronger commitment to helping everyone find, a shared learning and teaching experience. No doubt, our ELLs need us to work together.

DISCUSSION QUESTIONS

1. Examine how teacher collaboration might impact instruction for ELLs in your school.

2. What factors determine the ESL delivery service models in your district?

3. In 1975, Lortie stated,

   Official curricula are accepted as blueprints for instruction, but when teachers seek advice, they are considerably more likely to turn to each other than to administrators; at the same time . . . in considering whether to adopt new ways of teaching they frame any such decision in terms of its match with their own personalities. (pp. xiv–xv)

   Would Dan Lortie observe the same today? What would a sociologist say about our professional lives? How far have we come? What should we still be working on?

4. Engage your colleagues in a shared-reflection session using the conclusions of Little's (1982) study. Is there still a lesson to be learned from her work? What do the findings mean for today's ESL and general-education teachers in your school? What ideas would you add to Table 1.2?

KEY ONLINE RESOURCES

NCELA
   www.ncela.gwu.edu

The Partnership for 21st Century Skills
   www.21stcenturyskills.org

Professional Learning Communities
   www.ncrel.org/sdrs/areas/issues/content/currclum/cu3lk22.htm
   http://pdonline.ascd.org/pd_online/secondary_reading/el200405_dufour.html
   www.nsdc.org/standards/learningcommunities.cfm

WIDA
   www.wida.us

2

Why Is Collaboration Needed?

If you're walking down the right path and you're willing to keep walking, eventually you'll make progress.

Barack Obama

OVERVIEW

This chapter underscores the benefits of collaboration, which supports all regular classroom responsibilities, as well as various school activities such as curriculum committees, faculty conferences, and parent-teacher meetings. Each undertaking has a definite focus and meaningful purpose to which teachers subscribe. This chapter will guide educators to embrace the importance of teacher collaboration and understand the reasons why it must be an integral part in planning and delivering instruction for ELLs. We will systematically review the challenges ELLs, their teachers, and school administrators face and why collaboration may be an answer to the demands placed on them. We will emphasize that the research base for collaborative teacher learning, teacher collaboration and co-teaching, is well established, and we will present arguments for developing a site-based professional learning community for the benefit of ELLs.

Voices From the Field

It was a warm, late-spring afternoon when the faculty at Meadow Elementary School filed into the air-conditioned auditorium for their monthly meeting. The teachers who entered segregated themselves according to their grade level or specialty area in the self-folding rows of seats toward the back of the large room. The principal stood in the middle of one row, leaned against the back of one of the seats, and faced her staff.

She opened the meeting by running through a litany of reminders regarding housekeeping issues: report card comments, state assessment schedules, PTA flower sale, Math and Pasta Night, etc. Most of the teachers remained polite and attentive while a few quietly attended to housekeeping issues of their own: grading papers, amending lesson plans, and texting a spouse about the evening's dinner plans.

After the principal mentioned preparation for student placement in the coming school year, one of the ESL teachers began to whisper to her nearby colleagues. She asked for advice on whether she should share what was discussed at the recent ESL meeting regarding ELL grade-level placement. After a brief conversation, the ESL teacher tentatively raised her hand to speak. After she was recognized by the principal, she quietly stood and offered the faculty the following information:

"The ESL teachers met last Tuesday and discussed the adoption of the SIOP Model in combination with a co-teaching approach to deliver instruction for our ELLs. In order to put this plan into place, it is necessary to cluster our ELL students in the fewest classes possible per grade level. When placing students for the coming school year, we need to keep these issues in mind."

The school auditorium began to buzz with low yet audible whispers, grunts, and whines. One first-grade teacher quickly raised her hand and stood up to speak. She was quite agitated by the news, and she asked a very serious question: "Where's the research on co-teaching for ELLs?" Before anyone else could speak, the principal interjected that the clustering of ELLs was also discussed at the last administrator's meeting, and placement of these students would be revisited before new classes were formed. She remarked that the meeting's agenda still needed to be addressed and continued with the next item on her list.

Vignette Reflection

Our vignette highlights the ongoing apprehension and frustration teachers face when they need to disclose serious issues about their particular disciplines to their colleagues. On the one hand, the ESL teacher was apprehensive to alert the other faculty members about the clustering of ESL students in fewer classes, and the classroom teacher reacted to yet another program or policy change whose tenets and rationale were not presented to the entire faculty before its proposed implementation.

Monthly full-faculty meetings allow for housekeeping issues to be addressed, but they rarely are adequate forums to discuss content curriculum or innovative instructional practices for ELLs. Whereas additional weekly faculty meetings might be devoted to staff development, grade-level and content-specialty conferences, or teacher-union meetings on a rotating basis, the lack of time scheduled for teachers to collaborate regarding the education of ELLs furthers the practice of teachers working in isolation. If all teachers could pool their resources and talents—content knowledge, cultural insights, adapted materials, management techniques, technological savvy, and understanding of second language acquisition information—it would help to ensure academic success for ELLs.

CHALLENGES ENGLISH LANGUAGE LEARNERS FACE

Whether newly arrived or U.S. born, English language learners must leap over the many hurdles they encounter along the road to becoming English proficient, socially accepted, and academically successful. Take into account, for example, that some of our youngest learners and those with interrupted formal schooling also must negotiate acquiring literacy skills along with a new language and academic content. In addition, ELLs are also faced with having to make progress on high-stakes annual assessments, some of which newly arrived students are compelled to take even though they are minimally prepared. The challenge for many of these students is great and for some, the time they have to acquire needed skills is short. Thus, the development of a shared understanding of the complex sociocultural, socioeconomic, affective, linguistic, and academic challenges that ELLs face is key to their success.

Sociocultural Factors

Culture is the combined characteristics of a group of people. It encompasses the behaviors and beliefs that distinguish or are common to a particular community. All people who are a part of the same community have their own unique culture, and it is our own culture that drives our perceptions of the world. Each cultural community has its own language, and in many ways, learning a new language is equivalent to learning a new culture (Brown, 2006).

There are various sociocultural factors that ELLs must negotiate while they acquire English. Consider the following:

Culture Shock: This term refers to the period of time when newly arrived ELLs are exposed to American culture for the first time (see Table 2.1).

Cultural Isolationism: The practice of newly arrived immigrants to live in neighborhoods where their native language is spoken. This convention facilitates day-to-day living yet keeps non-English-speaking families isolated from the general-education culture.

School Norms: Issues involving cultural differences in school settings include ideas regarding teacher respect, the questioning of teachers' subject knowledge, learning from fellow students, and what constitutes plagiarism.

Bias or Prejudice: Assumptions made by teachers and fellow students with respect to the ability of immigrant children who speak little or no English.

Table 2.1 Culture Shock: The Four Phases of Adjustment

Honeymoon	Everything about the new culture appears to be wonderful.
Shock	ELLs are overwhelmed by their new surroundings and may suffer from insomnia, eating disorders, anxiety, and depression.
Integration	Some elements of the new culture are accepted and integrated with the beliefs of the native culture.
Acculturation	The new culture is embraced even though parts of the native culture are maintained.

Vignette Reflection

This case illustrates how some teachers may harbor certain beliefs regarding the abilities and talents of English language learners. Although ELLs initially lack skills in English and may perform poorly on standardized tests, their early academic performance in American schools is not a predictor of their future achievement.

School Acculturation

Olsen (2006) notes that the structure of American schools can also be a problem for some English language learners, particularly for students who enter the system in their teen years. According to Olsen, these students may need more "time to master English, time to overcome academic gaps, time to master the curriculum" (p. 6).

Students who are not fluent in English very often are not familiar with American culture in general and, more specifically, the public school system. They may not know what is expected of them and from time to time feel detached from and lost in their new surroundings. These students may exhibit disruptive behaviors in unfamiliar situations or appear uncooperative in their new school environment; yet, their teachers may interpret their conduct differently. English language learners may appear to be inattentive, lazy, or even defiant; however, they simply might not know what the common expectations are for their participation or, more seriously, be suffering from the effects of depression due to the trauma of leaving their native homes.

Teachers need to be aware of the common adverse reactions that students and their families face when entering a new country. There are a host of new situations new arrivals must negotiate, and dealing with an unfamiliar school system is just one of them. It is prudent to withhold judgments concerning these youngsters' ability to fully participate in the school community.

Emotional and cultural concerns are just some of the many difficulties these students must handle. Some ELLs are U.S. born and have had varying degrees of exposure to American mores. Others may be foreign born, yet they have received an outstanding education in their native country, arrive with high achievement in their native language, and are equipped with the necessary academic skills to be successful. Yet still others may arrive the victims of political strife or poverty in their native lands and have had little or no formal schooling.

Why Collaboration Is Key to Addressing Sociocultural Factors

In their teacher preparation programs as well as through ongoing professional development, ESL specialists often receive more extensive training in responding to the needs of culturally and linguistically diverse students. Whether or not they are bilingual or bicultural themselves, ESL teachers are frequently called upon to serve as cultural interpreters, cultural mediators, or cultural brokers in their schools. They are asked to help immigrant families and the students in their schools to better understand American cultural norms, most specifically, to help families navigate the cultural maze of the American school system. Oftentimes, when teachers collaborate they better understand that ELLs are not only challenged by difficult content and language barriers but also have to adjust to the cultural norms of a new teaching paradigm in the United States. From the frequent use of group work, differentiated instruction, project- or inquiry-based learning, to the types of questions teachers typically ask, ELLs often experience a paradigm shift and have to redefine what a "good student" is, what he or she does to do well in school.

Socioeconomic Factors

A common issue that impacts academic advancement for English language learners is the large number of students who come from economically disadvantaged homes. These youngsters additionally are confronted by neighborhoods that contain high crime and gang activity (Lachat, 2004). Some students' illegal status may cause them additional anxiety, whereas others lack access to proper health care, experience frequent change in neighborhoods and schools, or need to work after school to contribute financially to their households.

Evans (2004) describes poor-quality housing, lack of educational resources in the home, greater incidence of family disruption, and greater mobility as some of the disadvantages that affect children from some homes challenged by poverty. Yet, classroom teachers must address daily students who are distracted often by fear, instability, and uncertainty. Some of these students need to acquire English language skills as well. Since socioeconomic factors may impede the progress of some ELLs, special attention must be paid to students and their families who struggle to make ends meet.

Why Collaboration Is Key to Addressing Socioeconomic Factors

Collaborating teachers may share and combine their instructional resources to provide students with supplies and other assistance. When both general-education teachers and ESL specialists collaborate not only with each other but all other school personnel (social workers, guidance counselors, Parent-Teacher Association members, parent-school liaisons), as well as members of community organizations, a concerted effort is made to inform families in need about available support services and community-based resources.

Affective Factors

Many of us who have studied a second language have met with varying degrees of success. Much of our personal achievement with learning a new language may have to do with a range of personality factors. Consider these questions when identifying the traits of successful second language learners:

1. What are the reasons for learning a second language?

2. What can be gained from knowing a new language?

3. Is there a willingness to learn?

4. Is there a strong belief that learning a second language can be accomplished?

5. Does the learner believe it is worth the time and attention?

6. Can fear and apprehension about learning a new language be overcome?

Many aspects of our emotions affect how we learn. Here is a list of variables that can assist or hinder your students' progress toward acquiring a second language:

- Ability to take risks
- Amount of confidence
- Sense of self-esteem
- Degree of shyness
- Level of anxiety
- Problems with learned helplessness
- Types of motivation
- Value placed on second language learning

Since one of Krashen's (1981) five well-known second language acquisition theories focuses on the affective filter, we also recognize the importance of motivation, self-confidence, and anxiety as factors influencing second language acquisition.

Why Collaboration Is Key to Addressing Affective Factors

According to a recent report on the impact social-emotional learning has on K–8 students, Payton et al. (2008) note that

> students who appraise themselves and their abilities realistically (self-awareness), regulate their feelings and behaviors appropriately (self-management), interpret social cues accurately (social awareness), resolve interpersonal conflicts effectively (relationship skills), and make good decisions about daily challenges (responsible decision making) are headed on a pathway toward success in school and later life. (p. 5)

When teachers, administrators, and all members of a school community agree on the importance of developing the "whole" child, focusing on each student's social-emotional learning, a commitment to address the social-emotional needs of ELLs becomes a shared concern.

Linguistic Factors

Consider the task of learning a new language. Think about the complexities it entails. You need not only know the proper words to use; you also must have a sense of how the words can be stringed together into a complete thought. Beyond those simple basics, there is a whole host of information you must master in order to become fluent in the target language:

- Clear pronunciation
- Correct word order usage
- Distinction between formal and informal language
- Use of idiomatic expressions and colloquialisms
- Knowledge of social and academic language
- Facility with the conventions of writing

Why Collaboration Is Key to Addressing Linguistic Factors

ESL teachers use language learning techniques to assist ELLs in developing the necessary skills to become fluent in English. Ongoing collaborative practices between ESL and general-education teachers provide a clear path for sharing strategies to support new-language acquisition in the general-education classroom. Table 2.2 outlines some of the approaches ESL teachers apply when developing language competence with ELLs.

Table 2.2 Instructional Strategies to Develop Language Competencies

What ELLs Need for Language Competencies	What Teachers Need to Do to Develop Language Competencies
Vocabulary	• Preteach essential vocabulary • Use explicit instruction • Provide opportunities to use new words in speaking, reading, and writing
Grammar	• Teach grammar skills in context • Use students' actual speaking and writing to provide mini-lessons • Provide lessons that include both inductive and explicit grammar teaching • Include one aspect of grammar as a part of students' writing assignments
Literacy Skills	• Read aloud to students • Access prior knowledge • Explicitly teach phonological awareness of problematic sounds • Promote writing to increase reading skills • Integrate the teaching of vocabulary • Have ELLs reread familiar texts to increase fluency
Pragmatics	• Explicitly teach cross-cultural differences in social settings • Create role-playing activities for students to practice compliments, greetings, refusals, etc. • Share stories that identify American cultural norms and expectations

Background Knowledge

When someone tells us a story, we tend to form pictures in our minds about what is happening in the story. As the storyteller reveals further details, we change our minds' visual patterns to try to match what is being said. In essence, we use our own experiences regarding what we have already seen and heard to visualize and make sense of what we are being told. However, if the storyteller introduces something that is unfamiliar to us in the storyline, we may have no point of reference to understand what is being said. If sufficient explanation and details are not provided, we can no longer comprehend what is being spoken.

Students who have had limited experiences in a global sense or who come from areas of the world that are underdeveloped technologically have a difficult time connecting with some of the academic content they need to learn. ELLs may have school experiences that differ greatly from those in American schools. However, these students also have a vast amount of knowledge that can be tapped into to enhance their academic understanding.

Why Collaboration Is Key to Addressing Background Knowledge

When ESL and general-education teachers collaborate, they exchange techniques and strategies to capitalize on students' prior learning and build their background knowledge. They agree that all students have prior knowledge and unique personal experiences they can use when learning new content and skills. All teachers must investigate the authentic cultural backgrounds of their ELLs. Teachers must use their students' cultural backgrounds to help them make connections. All students can build upon their existing knowledge to connect what they already know with new information.

Academic Factors

From California to New York State, numerous students across the United States come from non-English-speaking backgrounds. These students often face challenges that their English-speaking peers do not. Many need to acquire a new language while learning academic content through English-only instruction. Their lack of English language skills frequently makes the school curriculum less accessible to them, and many end up dropping out of school due to their poor achievement.

How to best meet the needs of English language learners is just one of the many demands classroom teachers face. In light of No Child Left Behind reforms in which all students are expected to achieve, teachers must design and implement content-area instruction with ELLs in mind as well as maintain high expectations for the success of this special population of students. With classrooms becoming more linguistically and culturally diverse, teachers with support from school administrators need to focus on making curriculum accessible to all learners.

Best practices regarding academic development for ELLs point to specific strategies general-education teachers can adopt for regular use in their classrooms to support the language and content acquisition of language minority students. These strategies include providing academic work for ELLs that is culturally meaningful and that builds on the students' own background knowledge, allowing opportunities for students to work in pairs or small groups so that native-language skills can support learning, and engaging students in complex, critical-thinking activities that are appropriate for particular ELLs' English language proficiency. How do general-education teachers begin to develop assignments that are culturally meaningful? Why should content-area specialists permit ELLs to use their native language, and when is it appropriate? What does an ELL's English language proficiency have to do with designing tasks that include critical thinking? How can complex thought be attained through the use of simplified language?

Prior Schooling

Investigating a student's educational background can provide teachers with the needed insight and guidance to begin planning a program for a newly enrolled ELL. Some questions that might be addressed are the following:

- When did the student first begin school?
- Did the child attend preschool?
- Does the student have literacy skills in his or her native language?
- Was schooling interrupted for any reason in the native country?
- Has the child's family moved back and forth between their native country and the United States for prolonged periods of time?
- Has the student received bilingual, ESL, or other support services in the previous school?
- Did the child study English in his or her native country?

Having information regarding a student's former school experience is key to any planning process. However, O'Day and Bitter (2003) found that the planning process by itself did not impact how students met with academic success. Planning is merely a first step in the overall process. Teachers need to incorporate specific strategies on an ongoing basis in order for academic growth to occur. Furthermore, building teacher capacity through collaboration and the development of professional learning communities is another essential ingredient for effective instruction.

Curricular Variations

Students may come from backgrounds that have provided them with excellent literacy and mathematics skills in their native language. They may also be well versed in the areas of music, art, global studies, and science. Yet when they arrive in the United States, apart from having to learn a new language, these students may not be well prepared for the curriculum taught in American schools nor the assessments they have to take in order to meet state and local achievement standards.

Eva's story. When she first arrived from Egypt eight months ago, Eva entered the eighth grade at a suburban middle school. Although Eva did not speak a word of English, she quickly developed her social communications skills. Her clear pronunciation of English and her outgoing nature made it seem as if her English language skills were much more advanced.

In her native country, Eva excelled in mathematics and science. She loved working with technology, and at her home in the United States, she had all the latest gadgets and technical devices: a digital video camera that doubled as a still camera, a hydrogen-powered model rocket, and a voice-activated robot, among others. Eva was capable of searching for information on the Internet with ease, and she assisted the other children in her ESL group with their class projects.

As the school year began to close, Eva had the daunting task of studying for the upcoming state social studies assessment in American history. Although Eva studied about some aspects of American life in her native country, she certainly did not study the subject to the extent that her American peers had. Additionally, her lack of academic language in English made studying for the state assessment a tremendous undertaking.

Other circumstances as well can contribute to ELLs' lack of facility with local curricula. Some students frequently move from place to place, and this in turn creates a lack of continuity in the information they acquire in the schools they attend.

Zhi's story. A bright and energetic boy, Zhi was eight years old when his family moved to the United States from Shanghai five years ago. They first lived in Los Angeles, where Zhi's father took a job in the restaurant industry, and Zhi attended his first American school. Although he had no knowledge of English, Zhi entered second grade at an urban elementary school, where he made good progress developing his speaking, reading, and writing skills in English.

After two and a half years, Zhi's father had a better job opportunity, and his family moved once again to a small suburb just outside of New York City. By this time, Zhi was in the middle of fifth grade. His new class was engaged in studying the history of New York State, but Zhi had no background knowledge on the subject. Furthermore, his new school used a mathematics curriculum that was different from the way he was taught in Los Angeles. Zhi began to struggle a bit more academically, and he lost some of his confidence in his ability as well.

When his father's brother arrived a year and a half later, Zhi was happy to be reunited with his cousins. However, both families decided to pool their resources, and Zhi's family moved once again, this time to Cary, North Carolina, where his father and uncle opened their own restaurant. Now, Zhi is attending a middle school where he must again adjust to a new school environment. Zhi not only needed to deal with changing school expectations and curricula, his frequent moves from place to place interrupted his schooling and confounded his ability to meet with academic success.

In spite of Zhi's many academic talents and the quality of teaching and learning available, family circumstances have placed Zhi and the teachers in charge of his instruction in a challenging situation. Teachers often struggle to engage ELLs in the process of acquiring the necessary academics to meet the goals set by state standards when there are family and social issues, among others, that are beyond the scope of the classroom and beyond the control of the individual teacher.

High-Stakes Testing

Much time, effort, and nervous energy is consumed by American schools due to the requirements for ELLs to participate in standardized assessments. Classroom teachers spend an inordinate amount of time in some districts preparing all students to take these tests through drills, practice, and review with sample assessments. Test preparation in turn leaves less room for instruction that requires students to use critical thinking and higher-order reasoning skills and strategies. In essence, the practice of test preparation waters down the curriculum to a common denominator: students' enhanced use of test-taking skills and strategies. What does this practice mean for English language learners? What is being eliminated from their curriculum in order to develop their test-taking ability?

It has already been established that most ELLs have assistance from an ESL teacher or other support professionals from one to two class periods. The rest of their day is spent in general-education classes. During the time when test preparation is being conducted, general-education teachers most likely would not be supporting the language development of ELLs in their classes. These teachers would be engaged in instructing all students on test-taking strategies. Furthermore, some districts require ESL teachers to use a portion of their instructional time to prepare ELLs for standardized tests.

It is questionable what these assessments actually reveal about the abilities of English language learners. Do the mathematics assessments provide an accurate picture of an ELL's mathematical or reading ability? Can we conclude that an ELL's lack of achievement on an American history assessment means he has little facility with social studies? What are the emotional implications and long-term effects for requiring English language learners to participate in assessments for which they are clearly not ready?

Why Collaboration Is Key to Addressing Academic Factors

In the course of a typical student schedule, ESL or bilingual education services only are furnished one to two periods of study per day. English language learners typically spend the majority of the school day in general-education classes that offer no learning support other than what the general-education teacher can provide, along with whatever technology is available in the classroom. Formal training for regular classroom teachers to meet the needs of these diverse learners is crucial yet woefully inadequate.

When ESL and general-education teachers have sufficient time to collaborate, they can begin the process to change how curriculum and assessment is planned for ELLs. They can share their personal knowledge that can facilitate learning for these youngsters, and they can devise alternative assessment procedures for ELLs to accurately demonstrate what they have learned. Through collaborative practices, ESL teachers have the opportunity to share their extensive knowledge base with their general-education counterparts. Such a knowledge base includes

1. the distinction between academic and social language; more specifically understanding the differences among conversational fluency, discrete language skills, and academic-language proficiency (Cummins, 2001);

2. the impact age, motivation, attitude, confidence, classroom climate, and learning style have on second language acquisition;

3. issues related to acquiring the new school culture such as understanding academic expectations, discipline, formality, and social adjustment; and

4. national and state learning standards for ELLs.

There is no formula for determining the special needs of English language learners; each ELL is unique in his or her own way. In addition, these students bring their own set of challenges to school with them when they enroll. That is why we are such strong advocates for teacher collaboration. So very often, ongoing professional conversations between ESL teachers, general-education teachers, and other school personnel can help all educators to better understand the unique behaviors of ELLs.

CHALLENGES TEACHERS FACE

It is our fervent contention that collaborative practices among teachers and school cultures that promote professional learning communities are the best means for finding solutions to the growing demands of English language learners. In much of this book, we detail the challenges all teachers encounter in their attempts to plan and deliver instruction for ELLs. Yet, in this chapter, we feel compelled to present the five most important reasons teachers need to collaborate.

Curriculum Continuity and Accessibility

No longer can ESL teachers sit back and deliver isolated skill lessons to their ELLs in vocabulary, grammar, reading, and writing. Programs developed for English language learners must be comprehensive and long-term to accomplish language and content-area objectives. Frequently, ESL teachers modify existing curriculum intermittently for students in their programs. This modified curriculum is rarely shared with classroom or other ESL teachers. If a comprehensive program that examines all levels of language proficiency and content instruction were carefully devised over time, it would have long-term benefits for the instruction of ELLs as well as assist teachers in economizing their planning and preparing of revised materials and resources.

Curriculum mapping that identifies the goals and learning objectives in the core subject areas can help assure curriculum continuity for ELLs. It is a method for documenting the content material, related skills and strategies, and the assessment procedures for each core subject taught. A comprehensive grade-level curriculum map can be an important resource for ESL teachers to have in order to plan instruction for ELLs that is congruent with their general-education classrooms.

Materials for English language learners often need to be adapted according to students' levels of proficiency to make the curriculum more accessible. In order for this to be accomplished, teachers need adequate professional development to understand how to accommodate the learning needs of ELLs. Ongoing teacher collaboration between ESL and general-education teachers can help meet this demand.

Differentiating Instruction

In order to meet the needs of every child, conscientious educators often attempt to modify the content, materials, activities, or the instructional delivery of their lessons. Teachers generally determine the strategies they use based on the abilities and particular learning styles of their students. However, why should one teacher plan for so many different students? Why *do* teachers differentiate instruction to ensure that all students can learn?

Tomlinson (1999) suggests that using differentiated approaches based on learners' readiness levels, interests, and learning profiles (which include cultural and linguistic differences, gender, age, learning styles, prior experiences, etc.) assures meaningful engagement in all learning activities. Differentiated instruction takes time to develop, so incremental implementation is recommended. The challenge of adapting new strategies could also be supported by professional-development activities that foster reflective practices and encourage conversations and collaboration with colleagues who have experience using differentiated instructional techniques.

Accountability

Test-driven curriculum beleaguers teachers who are charged with being responsive to students' individual needs yet must be concerned with their youngsters achieving high scores on state standardized tests. Pressure is often brought to bear on teachers who oppose *teaching to the test,* and many succumb to its constraints. All too often, practitioners find it necessary to eliminate enrichment activities due to a lack of class time, which is taken up by teaching test-taking skills. These omitted learning activities often are the hands-on experiences that are so beneficial to English language learners.

Teachers should be accountable for the instruction they provide to their students. Unfortunately, a teacher's worth is all too often judged by the results students obtain on high-stakes testing. As a result, focusing on standardized-test preparation causes teachers to lose sight of the necessary learning objectives for their students. This emphasis on test preparation in general-education classrooms is a particular frustration for teachers and a misuse of class time for English language learners.

Engaging the Families of ELLs

Communication with students' homes is an important practice for teachers in order to keep parents informed of their child's progress. Yet, it is most challenging to connect with the families of English language learners. The language barrier between the school and immigrant families can make communication difficult. Often, a third party must be relied upon to convey information to the family.

Parents who do not speak English may not be aware of the school's expectations for students to arrive at school on time, to complete their homework, and to attend school regularly. These parents may not be aware of state and local learning standards or the importance of their children's performance on standardized tests. Teachers need to acquire the necessary strategies to include these families in the education of their children.

Time Constraints

Teachers most often are dissatisfied with the available time they have to meet the demands of their responsibilities and participate in professional development to improve their facility with classroom instruction. Most teachers are willing to collaborate with their peers; yet, most do not have sufficient time in their schedules to engage in collaborative conversations on a regular basis.

CHALLENGES SCHOOL ADMINISTRATORS FACE

Program Compliance and Accountability

According to NCLB (No Child Left Behind), ELLs "will meet the same challenging state academic content and student academic achievement standards as all children are expected to meet" (NCLB, 2001, §3102(2)). As stated by more recent guidelines of the U.S. Department of Education, Office of Elementary and Secondary Education (2007),

> Under Title I of the ESEA, States must include LEP students in their assessments of academic achievement in reading/language arts and mathematics, and must provide LEP students with appropriate accommodations including, to the extent practicable, assessments in the language and form most likely to yield accurate data on what LEP students know and can do in the academic content areas until they have achieved English language proficiency. States must also annually assess LEP students for their English language proficiency. Additionally, beginning with

the 2007–2008 school year, States must administer science assessments and include LEP students in those assessments. (p. 3)

Ever since 2001, when NCLB was written into law, school and district administrators have become more compelled than ever to focus their attention on student performance as defined by high-stakes standardized assessments. As Glatthorn and Jailall (2008) point out, "one consequence of NCLB is that it has placed the curriculum at center stage by requiring schools to align curriculum, instruction, and assessment as a basis for better student achievement results" (p. ix). In order to achieve those desired outcomes, they recommend a comprehensive alignment of all seven types of curricula, such as the recommended, written, taught, supported, learned, assessed, and hidden curriculum, preferably executed at the school level. Under these demands, most educational leaders, particularly principals, have experienced a marked shift in their roles from being managers of their buildings to being instructional and curriculum leaders, who have a solid understanding of all content and specialty areas' curricula and instructional strategies. As such, they are now expected to offer clear guidance regarding teaching and learning and are under constant scrutiny to demonstrate continued school improvement. Since NCLB requires disaggregating subgroup data, ELLs' test scores and performance on standardized tests constitute an additional, growing challenge for school leaders.

A Safe, Secure, and Culturally Responsive Learning Environment

School safety is a shared concern by most educators across the United States. According to a 2006 NCES report, 96 percent of high schools, 94 percent of middle schools, and 74 percent of primary schools that responded to the survey reported incidents of crime. Regarding illegal drugs, 44 percent of high schools, 27 percent of middle schools, and 1 percent of primary schools reported that students were found to be distributing them while at school. With a 42 percent rate, middle schools stood out as the most likely place where bullying may occur at least once a week, as opposed to 21 percent of high schools and 24 percent of primary schools.

In response to such alarming statistics, the American Association of School Administrators (AASA) recommends that school leaders create safe and nurturing places for all students by following the "ABC's of School Safety": Awareness, Balance, and Control. The three steps school leaders are suggested to take include (a) raising awareness about safety, (b) taking a balanced approach to it, and (c) implementing several school safety controls that result in a secure learning environment.

Safe and secure will not be enough, though! Yet another challenge school leaders encounter is what Ladson-Billings (1994) refers to as creating a culturally responsive learning environment and culturally congruent, meaningful learning opportunities. With increasing cultural and linguistic diversity among the school-age population, all school personnel must recognize the importance of including students' cultural framework as reference in all aspects of learning.

Supervision, Evaluation, and Professional Development

Supervising and evaluating all teaching and non-teaching staff as well as providing opportunities for ongoing professional development for the faculty are demands school leaders need to balance with all other aspects of their jobs. In *Bringing Out the Best in*

Teachers: What Effective Principals Do, Blase and Kirby (2009) summarize several critical actions and behaviors they observed among the most effective principals. We adapted their findings and created the following list of reflective questions for school leaders:

- How do I praise teachers for their professional accomplishments associated with school goals?
- How do I communicate and model high expectations for student achievement?
- How do I support teacher involvement in significant schoolwide decisions?
- How much professional autonomy do I grant teachers regarding curriculum and instruction when they exhibit professional readiness?
- How do I support teachers with material resources, protection of instructional time, professional development, and assistance with student discipline and parental concerns?
- How do I encourage individual growth through advice, feedback, and professional development?
- How do I exercise my authority?
- How do I consistently model effective practices congruent with principals' ethical code?

When school goals embrace diverse student needs and teachers' collaborative practices support all learners' social, emotional, academic, and linguistic development, all students are better able to achieve. School cultures should provide a secure, supportive environment for teachers as well as encourage risk taking and experimentation with innovative practices. If teachers are better able to hone their instructional skills, it will directly affect the achievement of ELLs together with all learners.

Considering, Responding to, and Balancing the Needs of All Stakeholders

In an educational institution, well-known stakeholders who stand to gain from its success can be identified as students, faculty, and administrators as well as parents and community members (Godwin & Gross, 2005). The challenge all school leaders face, regardless of geographic location, is that they must understand, value, and respect all stakeholders' perspectives and needs as they make important decisions about local policy and practice. (See a detailed discussion of all stakeholders in a school community in Chapter 3.)

Building Partnerships

The practice of teachers working in collaborative teams is consequential to the development of school-learning communities, which can be effective catalysts for instructional change. These collaborative partnerships comprised of general-education teachers and subject-area specialists in conjunction with school administrators are a tremendous source of teacher empowerment. Sharing their expertise and providing feedback in collaborative settings are activities that enable teachers to be a part of the decision-making process in their school. It is particularly important for all teachers with special knowledge of English language learners to have a venue to act as advocates for these diverse learners.

A current trend is for school district administrators to promote teacher collaboration and the formation of professional learning communities as opportunities for staff development. Some of these in-service programs have included grade-level or subject-level teacher teams who work together for specific purposes. Team-learning objectives often consist of lesson planning, curriculum mapping, and best-practice sharing. In addition to grade- and subject-level meetings, the following fall under the learning-community umbrella: coaching, mentoring, reciprocal classroom observations, shared leadership, and study groups (Roberts & Pruitt, 2009). All of these collaborative practices require time and careful structure to make them effective.

When teachers are able to consistently work together as teams, ELLs' class participation and academic performance are often much improved. In spite of its many positive aspects and benefits, some teachers are frustrated by collaborative-team efforts. They may not know what is expected of them or may harbor certain assumptions about the team's purpose that are not readily shared by others in the group. Some practitioners, by their participation in collaborative teams, believe they may be relinquishing control over what is being taught in their own classrooms. Others do not understand the collective purpose of team effort and think they would be much more productive on their own.

Thus, shared professional collaboration continues to be a challenge for some school districts. This is partially due to the lack of a proper collaborative framework, set expectations for its purpose, and sufficient time scheduled for meetings to regularly occur. As part of any overall collaborative plan, activities and associated expectations should be identified to make professional learning communities as productive as possible.

Creating a Positive School Culture

Based on the demands placed upon students, teachers, and school administrators, we concur with Deal and Peterson (1999) regarding their research and analysis of a positive school climate. They found that schools with a strong, positive school culture were not only safe and secure places for all to learn but shared a common set of norms and values and demonstrated success in the following areas:

- Fostering effort and productivity
- Improving collegial and collaborative activities that in turn promote better communication and problem solving
- Supporting successful change and improvement efforts
- Building commitment and helping students and teachers identify with the school
- Amplifying energy and motivation of staff members and students
- Focusing attention and daily behavior on what is important and valued (pp. 7–8)

Prominent among Deal and Peterson's (1999) findings are the benefits of collaborative practices, a shared commitment to school improvement efforts, and a special focus on the diverse school population. Similarly, based on an extensive meta-analysis of studies on successful school leadership, Marzano, Waters, and McNulty (2005) establish that a school leader has at least 21 responsibilities.

In order to create a purposeful community from which a strong leadership team can be created, Marzano et al. (2005) narrow the list to nine items as being the most essential. The short list includes being the optimizer, offering affirmation, sharing ideals and beliefs, demonstrating situational awareness, having visibility, building relationships, enhancing communication, building culture, and offering input. Aligned to Deal and Peterson's (1999) work, of these nine, we conclude that building a culture, meaningfully creating shared values, norms, and beliefs that "positively influences teachers, who, in turn, positively influence students" (Marzano et al., p. 47), is most likely one of the most fundamental challenges and responsibilities school leaders face.

WHY COLLABORATION IS THE ANSWER TO THE DEMANDS TEACHERS AND ADMINISTRATORS FACE

Since the first Little Red School House opened up, an age-old problem has perpetuated: Most teachers often work in isolation from each other. Elmore (2000) emphasizes the isolation of teaching as a vocation (p. 30). He further suggests that "individual teachers invent their own practice in isolated classrooms, small knots of like-minded practitioners operate in isolation from their colleagues within a given school, or schools operate as exclusive enclaves of practice in isolation from other schools" (p. 21). On the other hand, collaboration allows teachers and administrators to build a learning community, as shown in the following examples:

- When teachers move from isolation to collaboration, collaboration breaks the isolation cycle and allows for "respecting, acknowledging, and capitalizing on differences in expertise" (Elmore, 2000, p. 25). Teachers with general-education, content-specific expertise offer their knowledge of the subject matter content, general-education curricula, and local, state, and national content-related standards and assessments to all other teachers on staff. At the same time, ESL specialists have the opportunity to share their expertise in second language acquisition, cross-cultural understanding, bilingualism and biculturalism, and literacy development. As a result, *students benefit.*

- When the school leadership is collaborative, both the responsibilities and the decision-making power are shared in a more democratic fashion. Such collaborative leadership is often referred to as distributed leadership (Spillane & Diamond, 2007), which suggests mutual interdependence among multiple members of the school: "Leadership for instruction typically involves principals, assistant principals, teacher leaders, and classroom teachers who work independently as well as collaboratively to influence instruction" (p. 8). What collaborative leadership means for ELLs is that multiple school community members' knowledge and expertise in curriculum, instruction, and leadership capacities are used to make the school a more effective and nurturing place to be. As a result, *students benefit.*

- When the entire school community shares a collaborative culture, members of that community work together effectively guided by shared norms, values, and principles. Diverse experiences, ideas, and points of view are respected rather than negated, marginalized, or trivialized. Thus even if people disagree, their shared purpose helps them move forward. As Glickman (1998) and many others after his seminal work *Renewing American Schools* report, in successful schools teachers are always questioning their current practices to be able to improve them. Teachers work collaboratively as they offer feedback to each other and plan instruction in coordination. Members of such successful schools "exercise collective autonomy . . . in making professional decisions about matters of schoolwide teaching and learning" (p. 28) and participate in collegial discussions about how to continuously improve instruction and enhance the learning environment for all students. Finally, the norm is both to be critical consumers of educational information as well as to produce data and information "by seriously studying their students and programs and by considering outside information before making schoolwide decisions" (p. 28). As a result, *students benefit.*

WHY CO-TEACHING IS A POSSIBLE ANSWER TO CHALLENGES TEACHERS AND ADMINISTRATORS FACE

Teacher collaboration and a team approach to the teaching profession may become all-important notions for a number of critical reasons. As early as 1992, Fradd discussed the promising positive outcomes of teacher collaboration implemented to serve all kids with special needs, including ELLs. The most important question on teachers' and administrators' minds might be, "Does it yield increased student achievement?" An emerging line of research is documenting the impact of teacher collaboration and co-teaching on ELL student learning. Pardini (2006) describes the results of an ongoing, multiyear initiative in the St. Paul Public Schools in Minnesota, where traditional ESL programs are completely replaced by a collaborative program model. ESL and general-education teachers at all grade levels team teach. Pardini notes that

> between 2003 and 2005, the gap in reading achievement between the district's ELL and non-ELL students fell from 13 to 6 percentage points, as measured by the percent of students showing proficiency on the Minnesota Comprehensive Assessment. In math, the gap fell from 6.7 to 2.7 percentage points. The district's ELL students also did well when compared with their peers statewide, outscoring them in each of the last three years in reading and math as measured by the Test of Emerging Academic English. (p. 21)

In fact, ELLs in Saint Paul Public Schools have made steady gains on all standardized tests administered in the state in closing the achievement gap between ELL and non-ELL students.

As a final note, in a most recent report, the National Commission on Teaching and America's Future (NCTAF) (April 2009) called attention to alarming demographic trends among teachers and administrators. Since more than half of educators working in the K–12 setting are Baby Boomers, many of them may retire within the next five years. In the 2010–2011 school year alone, more than 100,000 experienced teachers are expected to leave full-time positions, whereas in the next decade more than 50 percent of currently practicing veteran teachers could retire.

A possible solution suggested by the NCTAF is forming teacher teams, which would allow veteran teachers to stay on in part-time or consulting/mentoring roles as they team taught with novice teachers. The consequences of such a shift may be far reaching: "This could be the decade in which we move beyond the notion that the stand alone teacher can do everything and instead reinvent American education to give us a global competitive edge for years to come" (p. 4).

RESEARCH SUPPORT FOR ENHANCED ESL SERVICE DELIVERY

Ten broad topics of research and/or related areas of best practice promoted by leading educational organizations will serve to offer support and to establish a strong case for collaborative practices designed to serve ELLs. Our goal is to outline a broad, foundational framework for a collaborative model of ESL services. We believe that a *shared knowledge and understanding* of both seminal research and emerging empirical findings will help all educators in a school community to build a stronger academic program for ELLs. We also trust that ongoing, *collaborative explorations* of best practices engage educators in meaningful professional learning and result in positive change. The outcome? Enhanced teaching and learning for ELLs and all other students and continued, powerful, job-embedded professional development for all teachers. Seminal research in the following 10 essential areas of educational knowledge is summarized in the Research Appendix.

1. Second language acquisition/English language development

2. Acculturation and culturally responsive teaching

3. Bilingualism and native language use

4. ELLs' literacy development

5. Developing ELLs' academic language proficiency

6. Effective instructional strategies

7. Curriculum alignment and curriculum mapping

8. Teacher teaming and co-teaching

9. Teacher learning

10. Professional development and learning communities

Vignette Revisited

In our opening vignette, a concerned first-grade teacher asked an insightful question: "Where's the research on collaboration or co-teaching for ELLs?" Like many general-education teachers, ESL practitioners try innovative ideas with their students often without the benefit of critically evaluating available research. Information we present in Appendix A regarding related research and best practices might help both our first-grade and ESL teachers to better understand the need for collaboration when working with ELLs.

ADMINISTRATORS' ROLE: CREATING A SCHOOL COMMUNITY TO SUPPORT EFFECTIVE INSTRUCTION FOR ELLS

Based on the demands on students, teachers, and administrators outlined earlier in this chapter, and the research base that supports teacher collaboration, shared knowledge base, and collaborative inquiry, we suggest that school leaders do the following:

1. Create an inclusive, welcoming school learning community with a shared vision of respect and acceptance of everyone's cultural heritage and background

2. Build a professional learning community that continually engages in collaborative inquiry on all students' needs, including ELLs' linguistic, academic, and cultural challenges

3. Establish "flexible teaming" that allows for both horizontal (on grade level) and vertical (across grade level) teacher teams, as well as cross-disciplinary teamwork to support ELLs' curricular, instructional, and extracurricular needs

SUMMARY

The need for collaboration in pursuit of the academic success of English language learners has been identified through the challenges of students, teachers, and administrators. Each of these stakeholders has particular demands they must confront and an important investment in the success of collaborative practice.

DISCUSSION QUESTIONS

1. Reflect on your own teaching experiences and generate a list of challenges you face. Are they similar to or different from the demands on teachers discussed in this chapter? Compare your list with the one presented in this chapter and highlight the differences. Explore possible explanations for the differences.

2. In collaboration with your colleagues, develop a proposal for your school and district administrators to implement a collaborative ESL service delivery model, with the possibility of including co-teaching.

3. In 2008, The Council of Chief State School Officers published the revised *Educational Leadership Policy Standards.* Review the standards below and identify aspects of the standards that are intended to support a collaborative school culture, teacher collaboration, co-teaching, and building a professional learning community. Generate a list of recommendations for your principal to put these standards into operation and apply them to your own school context.

Standard 1

An education leader promotes the success of every student by facilitating the development, articulation, implementation, and stewardship of a vision of learning that is shared and supported by all stakeholders.

Functions:

A. Collaboratively develop and implement a shared vision and mission

B. Collect and use data to identify goals, assess organizational effectiveness, and promote organizational learning

C. Create and implement plans to achieve goals

D. Promote continuous and sustainable improvement

E. Monitor and evaluate progress and revise plans

Standard 2

An education leader promotes the success of every student by advocating, nurturing, and sustaining a school culture and instructional program conducive to student learning and staff professional growth.

(Continued)

(Continued)

Functions:

A. Nurture and sustain a culture of collaboration, trust, learning, and high expectations
B. Create a comprehensive, rigorous, and coherent curricular program
C. Create a personalized and motivating learning environment for students
D. Supervise instruction
E. Develop assessment and accountability systems to monitor student progress
F. Develop the instructional and leadership capacity of staff
G. Maximize time spent on quality instruction
H. Promote the use of the most effective and appropriate technologies to support teaching and learning
I. Monitor and evaluate the impact of the instructional program

Standard 3

An education leader promotes the success of every student by ensuring management of the organization, operation, and resources for a safe, efficient, and effective learning environment.

Functions:

A. Monitor and evaluate the management and operational systems
B. Obtain, allocate, align, and efficiently utilize human, fiscal, and technological resources
C. Promote and protect the welfare and safety of students and staff
D. Develop the capacity for distributed leadership
E. Ensure teacher and organizational time is focused to support quality instruction and student learning

Standard 4

An education leader promotes the success of every student by collaborating with faculty and community members, responding to diverse community interests and needs, and mobilizing community resources.

Functions:

A. Collect and analyze data and information pertinent to the educational environment
B. Promote understanding, appreciation, and use of the community's diverse cultural, social, and intellectual resources
C. Build and sustain positive relationships with families and caregivers
D. Build and sustain productive relationships with community partners

Standard 5

An education leader promotes the success of every student by acting with integrity, fairness, and in an ethical manner.

Functions:

A. Ensure a system of accountability for every student's academic and social success
B. Model principles of self-awareness, reflective practice, transparency, and ethical behavior
C. Safeguard the values of democracy, equity, and diversity
D. Consider and evaluate the potential moral and legal consequences of decision-making
E. Promote social justice and ensure that individual student needs inform all aspects of schooling

Standard 6

An education leader promotes the success of every student by understanding, responding to, and influencing the political, social, economic, legal, and cultural context.

Functions:

A. Advocate for children, families, and caregivers
B. Act to influence local, district, state, and national decisions affecting student learning
C. Assess, analyze, and anticipate emerging trends and initiatives in order to adapt leadership strategies

KEY ONLINE RESOURCES

Professional Organizations

American Association for Applied Linguistics (AAAL)
www.aaal.org

American Association of School Administrators (AASA)
www.aasa.org

American Educational Research Association (AERA)
www.aera.net

American Federation of Teachers (AFT)
www.aft.org

Association for Supervision and Curriculum Development (ASCD)
www.ascd.org

Council of Chief State School Officers
www.ccsso.org

International Reading Association (IRA)
www.reading.org

National Association for Bilingual Education (NABE)
www.nabe.org

National Association for Multicultural Education (NAME)
www.nameorg.org

National Council of Teachers of English (NCTE)
www.ncte.org

National Education Association (NEA)
www.nea.org

National Staff Development Council (NSDC)
www.nsdc.org

Teachers of English to Speakers of Other Languages (TESOL)
www.tesol.org

Research Centers

Center for Advanced Research on Language Acquisition (CARLA)
http://carla.acad.umn.edu

Center for Applied Linguistics (CAL)
www.cal.org

Center for Language Minority Education and Research
www.clmer.csulb.edu

Center for Research on Education, Diversity & Excellence (CREDE)
http://crede.berkeley.edu

Collaborative for Academic, Social, and Emotional Learning (CASEL)
www.casel.org

Mid-Continent Regional Educational Laboratory
www.mcrel.org

National Center for Research on Evaluation, Standards, and Student Testing at UCLA
www.cse.ucla.edu

Northwest Regional Educational Laboratory
www.nwrel.org

WestEd: A Research, Development, and Service Agency
www.wested.org

Other Related Resources

Education Week on the Web
www.edweek.org

Edutopia on the Collaboration Age
www.edutopia.org/collaboration-age-technology-networking

Kansas University
www.specialconnections.ku.edu

Marilyn Friend's Corner
http://forumoneducation.org/marilynfriend/marilynfriend.shtml

Marilyn Friend's Web Site
www.powerof2.org

Office of English Language Acquisition, Language Enhancement, and Academic Achievement for Limited English Proficient Students (OELA)
www.ed.gov/about/offices/list/oela/index.html

Richard Villa
www.ravillabayridge.com

Teaching Diverse Learners
www.alliance.brown.edu/tdl

The U.S. Department of Education's National Clearinghouse for English Language Acquisition
www.ncela.gwu.edu

3

Who Does Teacher Collaboration and ESL Co-Teaching Concern?

We are caught in an inescapable network of mutuality, tied in a single garment of destiny. Whatever affects one directly, affects all indirectly.

Martin Luther King, Jr.

OVERVIEW

The goal of this chapter is to identify all stakeholders in a multilingual educational community and to describe their unique roles and responsibilities in developing and sustaining a collaborative school culture. We will present and analyze the unique experiences (both benefits and challenges) each constituent encounters while teachers engage in collaborative practices and co-teaching for the benefit of English language learners. We will consider the roles played by those who initiate, design, implement, monitor, and evaluate collaborative practices for the sake of ELLs.

Voices From the Field

Ms. Kovacs teaches sixth-grade math in a large suburban middle school with a growing Spanish-, Portuguese-, and Urdu-speaking immigrant population. She sees a total of 127 students every day. She is mindful of the varied learning needs in her classes, but she feels pressured to cover the state-mandated curriculum to prepare her students for the annual math assessment. "I have to move through the curriculum very quickly; I can't slow down!" she notes. Many of her colleagues nod in agreement, sharing a similar concern.

(Continued)

(Continued)

Ms. Kovacs is genuinely alarmed about her ELLs. When she says, "I know they are not getting most of what I am doing," she is revealing both her sincere self-reflection and frustration.

Despite having participated in several professional-development workshops on ESL strategies and differentiated instruction, she continues to feel hesitant about modifying her math lessons for both her students with special needs and her ELLs. During her lunch break, Ms. Kovacs occasionally seeks out the ESL teacher to discuss concerns about some of their mutual students. She has had several conversations with the guidance counselor, the school social worker, her assistant principal, and one with the nurse, too. She welcomes the literacy coach into her classroom and frequently asks for resources and ideas on how to modify her math lessons, assignments, and homework. But she needs more . . .

Vignette Reflection

Our vignette is just one example of the many teacher voices we hear at staff development workshops as well as at local and national conferences on the teaching of ELLs. It expresses the strong desire teachers have to participate in ongoing, regularly scheduled dialogues with their colleagues. Yet, teacher isolation persists because it is deeply rooted in overall school practices, and desired opportunities for teachers to learn from one another are lacking within many school systems, which in turn impacts the power of instruction for ELLs.

ALL STAKEHOLDERS

Who walks though the front door of your school in the course of a day? In the course of a week? Or by the end of the year? Whose voice is heard? Who makes decisions? Who is involved in every aspect of the school life? Who is included in the school community and who is not? Who abides by those decisions and who hesitates? In order to establish a collaborative school community, we must identify the stakeholders first: What is unique about them? How do they benefit from collaborative school practices? Finally, what are their roles and responsibilities when teacher collaboration becomes enhanced and co-teaching is introduced for the sake of English language learners?

Our Students

English-Speaking General-Education Students

Simplicio (2007) described the twenty-first-century students or "millennial" students as those who go to well-equipped schools with ample resources and attend classes taught by well-qualified teachers. Overall, this might be the case. However, when describing the general U.S. student population, he acknowledges that while "millennial students are better informed, more technologically savvy, and worldlier, they are also more diverse, more demanding, needier, and harder to teach than any other students in the past" (p. 2).

Harder to teach? It depends who you ask. Needier? Many would claim so. Technologically savvy? It depends on which side of the digital divide they happen to grow up. More diverse? Definitely! Walk into any classroom in the United States, or across the globe, for that matter, and you will find that students represent diversity not only in race, gender, ethnicity, languages, and socioeconomic status; they also bring a variety of life experiences, display a range of learning styles, represent multiple intelligences, and show varied interests, talents, and readiness levels. With such apparent diversity, one teacher alone cannot respond to every student's needs. Many teachers still work in isolation.

What are the benefits for general-education students when their teachers collaborate? They receive the following:

- More differentiated instruction due to collaborative teacher planning
- More varied instructional materials and resources
- More carefully crafted lessons
- More authentic and meaningful assessments that are adapted to the needs of students who are struggling or at risk
- More appropriate instructional adaptations for students who are struggling or at risk

Furthermore, if general-education teachers engage in co-teaching and if general-education students are taught by two rather than one teacher, students will experience the following:

- Fewer interruptions due to pull-out programs at the elementary level
- More individualized or personalized attention due to reduced teacher-student ratio in all K–12 classes
- Enhanced social and emotional development due to enhanced awareness of classmates' needs
- More chances to learn about cooperation with their classmates
- More opportunities to observe cooperation, interaction, and communication by their teachers collaborating in action

A few words of caution. General-education students need to be prepared to welcome and accept all of their classmates, including ELLs. It is the teachers' responsibility to foster development of heightened sensitivity to students' needs and an understanding of the basic premise that "fair does not mean equal." When a co-taught class is set up, students need to be ready to adhere to the principles and dynamics of a collaborative classroom: Both teachers should be treated with the same respect. Each teacher will take on the role of leading a lesson or providing support to the other. Students will also need the opportunity to come to an understanding that each classmate may have different needs and that two teachers will respond to these needs through collaborative planning, co-teaching, and differentiated instruction.

LEP: Limited English Proficient (aka Language Enriched Pupils)

Who are our LEP students? From a deficit model, they are limited in their language proficiency. We much prefer to emphasize the richness of culture and language they bring to the classroom and call them, as Fradd (1998) does, *Language Enriched Pupils.*

Cultural and linguistic diversity are no longer unique to big cities or urban, inner-city schools. Many rural and suburban school districts face the same challenges of addressing the needs of a multilingual student body. According to the *Census Brief 2000: Language Use and English-Speaking Ability,* with a record 39 percent, California had the largest percentage of non-English language speakers age five or older. Next came New Mexico (37%), Texas (31%), New York (28%), Hawaii (27%), and finally Arizona and New Jersey in a tie (26%). However, the largest increases in non-English language speakers have been experienced by six other states (the percentage of increase indicated in parenthesis): Nevada (193%), Georgia (164%), North Carolina (151%), Utah (110%), Arkansas (104%), and Oregon (103%).

The diversity of languages spoken in U.S. homes has also increased manifold. According to the same *Census Brief*, the top 10 languages spoken in the United States (after English and Spanish) were Chinese, French, German, Tagalog, Vietnamese, Italian, Korean, Russian, Polish, and Arabic. The top 10 languages spoken in New York State by English language learners and their families show a slightly different picture. These languages are Spanish, Urdu, Russian, Chinese, Haitian Creole, Bengali, Korean, Arabic, Polish, and Albanian (*NYS Native Language Arts Standards*, 2006). In California, Spanish is followed by Vietnamese, Filipino, Cantonese, Korean, Mandarin, Hmong, Punjabi, Armenian, and Farsi. In Arkansas, Spanish or Spanish-Creole, German, French including Patois and Cajun, and Vietnamese top the list. The patterns of languages and ethnic groups will vary from state to state and region to region, but effective collaboration and co-teaching can equally benefit any multilingual community.

Language Proficiency Levels. There is considerable variation in how many language proficiency levels are differentiated to describe our ELLs. The number ranges from three to six language proficiency levels. In New York State, there are three: Beginning, Intermediate, and Advanced. In Texas there are four levels: Beginning, Intermediate, Advanced, and Advanced High. In California, there are five: Beginning, Early Intermediate, Intermediate, Early Advanced, and Advanced. Similarly, in Indiana, ELLs may be labeled as Beginner, Early Intermediate, Intermediate, Advanced, or Fluent English Proficient, whereas in Maryland, they are Low Beginning, High Beginning, Low Intermediate, High Intermediate, or Advanced level ELLs.

The WIDA (World-Class Instructional Design and Assessments) consortium (www.wida.us) also differentiates six levels of proficiency: Entering, Beginning, Developing, Expanding, Bridging, and Reaching. WIDA, established in 2002, had 23 member states (Alabama, Delaware, District of Columbia, Georgia, Hawaii, Illinois, Kentucky, Maine, Mississippi, Missouri, New Hampshire, New Jersey, New Mexico, North Carolina, North Dakota, Oklahoma, Pennsylvania, Rhode Island, South Dakota, Vermont, Virginia, Wisconsin, and Wyoming) at the time of this book's publication.

In 2004, WIDA co-published the *English Language Proficiency Standards for English Language Learners in Kindergarten Through Grade 12*, which also served as the foundation for the *National TESOL Standards* published two years later (Teachers of English to Speakers of Other Languages, 2006). The new TESOL standards represent a marked shift to focus on content-based ESL proficiency as well as identifying five levels of proficiency.

ELL SNAPSHOTS

ELLs are a diverse group. Yet parts of their personal histories often have a lot in common. Meet Jose, Tianika, Andy, Gerry, and Kristina. You might recognize their stories, which belong to students with different names. Or one day children like them might be in your classes, each with their own story.

Jose was born in the United States. Raised by a hardworking extended family, he never left his community, except for short trips to the Dominican Republic. Now he is five and ready for kindergarten. Jose speaks fluent Spanish but has had no play dates with English-speaking friends, no exposure to *Sesame Street* or *Dora the Explorer,* no preschool experience where English nursery rhymes and the alphabet are taught to three-year-olds. Like his siblings and cousins, he is a child of first-generation immigrants who live in a relatively secluded metropolitan community where most people speak the same language. Store signs are in two languages but mostly are frequented by shoppers who share the same native tongue. Most day-to-day business can be conducted successfully in the native tongue. Now Jose is leaving his "linguistic island" and embarking on a new experience: learning English and, to compound matters, learning *in* English.

Tianika is 15. She used to go to private school in Nigeria, speaks two dialects of Hausa, and is literate in two languages other than English (being a child of diplomats who have lived in Russia and France). Her teachers assume her silence comes from lack of ability, and they often group her with students who are struggling learners. In fact, she turns out to be a high-achieving, very focused student who is often frustrated by not being able to express herself well in English. She is self-conscious of her heavy accent and seems rather shy and reluctant to make friends with her classmates.

Andy is a serious, rather reserved 11-year-old. He barely speaks English with his classmates and hardly ever raises his hand in class. Andy is a completely different person after school: He studies diligently every day, he takes karate and music lessons, he goes to Chinese school on Saturdays and Bible school on Sundays. Much to his teachers' surprise, his writing is improving considerably faster than his speaking skills, and he is already outperforming his classmates on most of the math and science assessments.

Gerry is nine, but he has not spent more than three years in school in the Philippines. What he learned, though, as he guided tourists up a nearby mountain to view the Taal volcano every day, was many life lessons. He has learned to take care of his mule, he knows how to be the fastest to get back to the base and be in line for the next tourist, and he has earned enough money to support himself and his sister. He even picked up some English: "Balance ma'am, balance!" and "Thank you!" In his U.S. classroom, he is friendly and gets along with his classmates. Once recess is over, though, he is lost in the classroom and does not seem to be able to sit still, listen, or follow the lesson. He hardly comprehends any of the language or concepts presented in his class.

Kristina was adopted from a Russian orphanage. At eight years of age, she owns her own winter coat, books, schoolbag, and toys for the first time. In the orphanage, she was used to sharing, and even fighting for, the warmer coat or stronger pair of boots. She reads and writes in Russian but has only basic English skills. She receives occupational therapy, and a private tutor also works with her to improve her English. Despite all the effort, care, and nurturing they offer, Kristina's parents are seeing their daughter act aggressively and lethargically in turn. They fear Kristina is not adjusting well to life in the United States.

Presenting similar ELL portraits could continue. Each child entering school in the United States has a story—stories that we need to not only hear but actually listen to! Whether starting kindergarten or joining 11th grade near the end of the school year, each child will bring unique experiences and challenges to the classroom. What should teachers and administrators know about ELLs? How can we learn more about this population? Take a look at Figure 3.1 and consider the questions that will help you better understand each aspect of the student's background. Then review the textbox following the figure to see what additional information you need.

Figure 3.1   Key Questions About ELLs

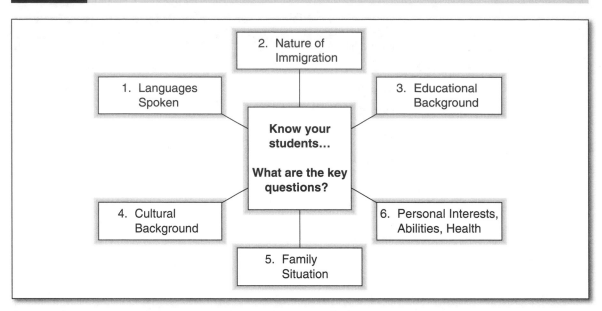

<table>
<thead>
<tr><th colspan="1">WHAT INFORMATION IS HELPFUL?</th></tr>
</thead>
</table>

1. Languages Spoken

Language(s) or dialects spoken in the home

Dominant language in the home

Receptive skills in a language or dialect other than English

Level of native-language development

Family literacy

2. Nature of Immigration

Country of origin or U.S. born

Date of arrival in United States

Unusual or traumatic experiences surrounding the immigration

3. Educational Background

Prior formal education: type of school, number of years

Additional educational opportunities provided by the family or community

4. Cultural Background

Dominant cultural background of the student and family

Basic beliefs concerning education (e.g., attendance, roles and responsibilities of teachers, students, parents)

Basic beliefs concerning family, friends, religion

Important days of celebration

5. **Family Situation**

Primary caregivers

Parents, siblings, extended family, and living situation

English-speaking relatives

Family status in the United States: permanent or temporary

Awareness of available community services and resources in their home language and culture

6. **Personal Interests, Abilities, Health**

Student's special interests, abilities, and talents

Extracurricular activities

Notable physical or health conditions that influence learning or instruction (i.e., vision, hearing, food allergies, childhood illnesses, etc.)

What are the benefits for ELLs when their teachers collaborate? ELLs receive the following:

- Greater continuity of instruction: fewer interruptions in their school day
- More carefully aligned curriculum that yields adaptations
- More differentiated instruction due to collaborative teacher planning
- Effectively coordinated interventions for students at risk through Response to Intervention (RTI) programs
- More focus on their linguistic needs: instruction at their level of language proficiency
- More focus on their academic needs: preteaching necessary skills for understanding
- Greater understanding of their school behaviors and sociocultural needs
- More empathy from all teachers

If two teachers work together to provide instruction in a co-taught setting, ELLs will experience the following:

- Greater stability at the elementary level by receiving more instruction in their regular classrooms
- More individualized attention due to reduced teacher-student ratio in all K–12 settings
- Increased exposure to their English-speaking peers
- Enhanced social and emotional development due to diverse peer interaction
- More exposure to adult linguistic models, including an additional teaching professional
- More experience with grade-appropriate content
- Greater opportunities for acculturation by staying integrated in their regular classes
- Increased confidence in their ability to learn grade-level work

A few words of caution. ELLs—especially beginners and students with interrupted formal education (SIFE)—may have significant gaps in both their academic knowledge and understanding of U.S. school norms. Due to their differing background experiences and the linguistic and academic challenges they face, they might feel more at ease in a small group, pull-out program, or in a specially designed SIFE or newcomer program to assist with their basic language development needs. Some adolescent ELLs might be struggling with accepting school procedures and adjusting to school norms and routines.

Teachers

Close to 4 million Americans spend their work days as teachers in general-education classrooms across the United States (U.S. Department of Labor, Bureau of Labor Statistics, 2010–11). Approximately 50 percent of teachers leave their assignment in the first five years (Allen, 2005); over 25 percent of new teachers leave the profession in their first three years of teaching, many more within five years (Boe, Cook, & Sunderland, 2008). According to Hull (2004), by 2013, 3.5 million new teachers will need to be hired to support increased enrollment in public schools and to replace retiring teachers. Currently, high-stakes standardized tests and ongoing test preparation, increased accountability, mandated curricula, scripted literacy programs, and lack of planning time and resources are among the top challenges classroom teachers face across the country. At the same time, more and more educators are expected to work in an inclusive setting, sometimes without collaborative support, and still must meet the needs of students with various disabilities learning alongside general-education students.

Elementary General-Education Teachers

Many elementary teachers comment that their students receive multiple support services during the day from Title I service providers, speech and language pathologists, social workers, occupational therapists, and psychologists. Academic Intervention Service (AIS) providers, reading teachers, and remedial math specialists also provide additional instruction to those who will benefit from it. Band, music, and other special practice sessions add to the time some children spend outside of the classroom. Pull-out programs abound in some schools; numerous other interruptions occur in many others.

In light of the often-fragmented nature of a school day, there is a lot to gain for elementary classroom teachers and other general-education elementary instructional staff from collaborating with ESL specialists. Their roles and responsibilities change in the process in rather complex ways.

If general-education teachers collaborate with ESL specialists, they will do the following:

- Regularly exchange ideas with colleagues trained in a different discipline
- Share their knowledge of the general-education curriculum
- Align the content curriculum mandated by state and local standards to ELLs' language proficiency levels
- Learn to adapt their curriculum to bridge the gap ELLs have in their prior knowledge
- Help ELLs socialize more successfully
- Help ELLs learn about the norms of American schools
- Modify their lessons in varied ways that may benefit other students at risk in the class
- Develop a better understanding of the unique linguistic, cultural, and academic needs of ELLs

If general-education teachers co-teach with ESL specialists, they will do the following:

- Share their classroom space, available class time and resources, and all instructional responsibilities with a colleague
- Expose ELLs to state-mandated general-education curricula along with best practices for second language learning
- Better communicate goals and objectives for limited-English-proficient students
- Enhance their academic communication skills, including interactions with ELLs, by observing an ESL specialist interact with ELLs
- More effectively facilitate small-group instruction that actively involves ELLs
- Become reflective about their shared teaching experience
- Adopt the use of strategies that are modeled by the ESL teacher

Secondary (Middle and High) School Content-Area Teachers

If content-area teachers collaborate with ESL specialists in the middle school and high school context, they will do the following:

- Enrich the curricular content mandated by state and local standards to address ELLs' unique experiences
- Actively engage ELLs in their content classes by considering their language proficiency levels
- Adapt their curriculum and instruction to bridge the gap ELLs have in their prior knowledge
- Help ELLs socialize more successfully
- Help ELLs learn about the norms of American schools
- Modify their lessons in varied ways that may benefit other students at risk in the class
- Develop a better understanding of how to address the unique linguistic, cultural, and academic needs of ELLs by watching an ESL specialist interact with ELLs

If content-area teachers co-teach with ESL specialists, they will do the following:

- Help ELLs be more engaged in each lesson that focuses on grade-appropriate content
- Reduce ELLs' tendency to become invisible or voiceless
- Focus both on content and language goals
- Better understand how able ELLs are to learn new and difficult information

Vignette Revisited

Let's see how Ms. Kovacs is faring this year. Her principal invited all teachers to participate in self-directed teacher study groups on a voluntary basis. Ms. Kovacs was among the first to sign up. Each four-to-six-member group was encouraged to explore a topic of their choice. Ms. Kovacs's team decided on effective ESL strategies, with a special emphasis on vocabulary development, scaffolding, and tiering. As a result, she no longer feels that she is without any support. She and her colleagues are working on a cohesive overall plan for their ELLs. Ms. Kovacs often returns to the teaching strategies she knows best—which meet the majority of her students' needs—but also includes strategies she has learned from her ESL colleagues. She has become mindful of her ELLs' need for adapted texts, modified assignments, and extensive work on vocabulary and content literacy skills.

A few words of caution. Both elementary and secondary general-education and content-area teachers need opportunities (a) to build a collegial relationship with ESL specialists and (b) to develop knowledge and skills related to working with ELLs. This takes needed time, administrative support and encouragement, and team-building strategies to make it successful.

ESL Specialists

ESL teachers are at the forefront of addressing the needs of ELLs. They are specially trained in second language acquisition, childhood bilingualism, culturally responsive teaching strategies, literacy development, and content-based ESL instruction. ESL teachers and the services they provide are sometimes misunderstood by the school community. During a recent professional-development session, we posed the following questions: *What is ESL?* and *What is the role of the ESL program?* Among the responses we received were the following:

- "ESL is a necessary program."
- "ESL strategies should not be considered the sole domain of the ESL teacher."
- "It is just like resource room."
- "ESL is helping kids learn English as a second language, full of growing pains. ESL could be helpful, difficult, challenging, beneficial."
- "ESL should be collaborative to be thoroughly beneficial. ESL must be done daily; it must be scaffolded and integrated."
- "ESL bridges the gap between bilingual classes and general-education instruction."
- "ESL is language acquisition. ESL should be a bridge to general-education learning."
- "ESL is extra help for English learners."
- "ESL should be an opportunity to acquire the skills necessary to succeed in an English-speaking culture."
- "ESL should coordinate with the general-education classroom. ESL should be helpful and flexible with existing instruction."
- "ESL is support and reinforcement. Individualized assessments. Gives the children a sense of accomplishment."
- "ESL should be taught collaboratively with the classroom teacher and the ESL teacher."
- "ESL should be taught using the same materials as in the regular classroom."

The comments above—collected anonymously—reveal a range of ideas, expectations, and misconceptions teachers might have about the ESL program in their respective schools. A common thread that emerges from these comments reinforces the need for enhanced communication and collaboration among all teachers who share the responsibility of teaching ELLs. General-education teachers need to know that ESL is not merely extra help or resource room; it is not a remedial program. As Nate Raynor, one ESL teacher with whom we worked, noted, "co-teaching or push-ins should *not* be merely an 'in-room pull-out,' a real-time translation service, or a kind of specialized 'super-aide.'"

What are the benefits for ESL specialists when they collaborate with classroom teachers and content-area specialists? They will be able to do the following:

- Appreciate the challenges (a) general-education elementary teachers face being in charge of classes of 20–30 students of varied needs all day long or (b) their secondary-content-area colleagues encounter as they teach up to 150 or more students per day

- Understand national, state, and local content standards better
- Enhance their knowledge of grade-appropriate content curriculum and related assessments
- Have the opportunity to offer insight into making grade-appropriate content accessible to ELLs
- Experience increased camaraderie and a stronger sense of belonging within the school

What are the benefits for ESL teachers when they co-teach? They will experience the following:

- Have the opportunity to work with an entire class of students, rather than only with small groups
- Take on the role of educating their colleagues about the needs of ELLs
- Help ensure that general-education content becomes accessible to ELLs
- Combine content and language development in a single lesson
- Develop more complex classroom management skills
- Understand the demands placed on classroom teachers and students regarding standardized test preparation

A few words of caution. ESL specialists who enter into a partnership are able to establish their roles as equals in the classroom, rather than being treated as assistants. Even though teacher assistants are also highly valuable members of such a collaborative team effort (see next section), ESL teachers should not accept the role of support personnel. To summarize what teachers who collaborate have to share, see the following textbox.

WHAT DO COLLABORATIVE TEACHERS HAVE TO OFFER EACH OTHER?

1. **Pedagogical Knowledge**
   a. Understanding child development and learning process
   b. Instructional strategies
   c. Classroom management skills
   d. Organization for differentiated instruction

2. **Content Expertise**
   a. Familiarity with the curriculum
   b. National and state content and ESL standards
   c. Strategies to best teach challenging, grade-appropriate content
   d. Anticipation of areas of difficulty for ELLs

3. **Second Language Acquisition (SLA) Processes**
   a. Basic Interpersonal Communication Skills vs. Cognitive Academic Language Proficiency (BICS vs. CALP)
   b. Stages of SLA
   c. Reasonable expectations for ELLs at each language proficiency level
   d. How to challenge but not frustrate second language learners

(Continued)

(Continued)

4. **Cross-Cultural Understanding**

   a. Twenty-first-century immigrant experience

   b. Students born in the USA

   c. Culture of schooling

   d. Fighting bias and prejudice against immigrants and language learners

   e. Acculturation vs. assimilation processes

5. **Interpersonal Skills**

   a. Communication skills (You can talk to me . . .)

   b. Relationship building (You can count on me . . .)

   c. Encouragement (I have an idea . . .)

   d. Inspiration (I can help . . .)

Teacher Assistants

In many schools, teachers are assisted by paraprofessionals, paraeducators, teacher assistants (TAs), educational assistants (EAs), teacher aids, or instructional aids. According to the U.S. Department of Labor, Bureau of Labor Statistics (2010–11), over 1.3 million teacher assistants, whose educational qualifications range from a high school diploma to some college training, are employed in the United States. Their roles also range considerably, from offering noninstructional or clerical support—such as filing paperwork, duplicating instructional materials, taking attendance, or supervising recess activities—to participating in such instructional activities as checking homework. Teacher assistants participate in other instructional activities including reinforcing what was already taught to the class, individually or in small-group settings, and helping students use print resources (dictionaries, encyclopedias, other references books) and educational devices (laboratory equipment and computers).

What are the benefits for teacher assistants when they are involved in collaborating with both classroom teachers (content-area specialists) and ESL teachers? They will be able to do the following:

- Develop or enhance their skills working with diverse student bodies
- Communicate about the needs of English language learners with more than one educator and share their insights
- Coordinate their support activities with more than one teacher
- Provide better-defined instructional support to ELLs while observing how both general-education and ESL teachers interact with this population

A few words of caution. Bilingual teacher assistants should not be required to merely offer simultaneous translations of a teacher's direct instruction. The SIOP model (Echevarria, Vogt, & Short, 2008) suggests native-language use to clarify key concepts. Misusing or overusing native-language support may merely reinforce ELLs native-language skills but will not allow language skills and content knowledge to form in the student's new language. TAs need to be positioned to receive the same respect that teachers do. They should be invited to participate in all staff meetings and professional-development opportunities that teachers are.

Other Teaching and Nonteaching School Staff

In addition to administrators, teachers, and teacher assistants, many other instructional and noninstructional school staff members interact with ELLs and their families on a regular basis, including special-subject teachers (art, physical education, music, band), librarians, remedial math and reading teachers, guidance counselors, school psychologists, social workers, and nurses. How can they be included in a collaborative approach to ESL services? *Inform and be informed* is the motto of one principal we have worked with. When the entire school staff is informed about ELLs' needs and appropriate strategies to be used with this population, everyone's professional practice is enhanced. When all staff and faculty members are invited to contribute and be informed, all students benefit.

Administrators

School administrators manage the day-to-day operation of a school and offer instructional leadership to their faculty. Principals' and assistant principals' responsibilities range from hiring faculty to creating a master schedule for all teachers, from managing student discipline to supervising and evaluating teachers and staff. At a recent administrators' retreat, we asked a large group of K–12 principals and assistant principals to share the biggest challenges they face as school leaders of culturally and linguistically diverse students. The responses included mostly questions, asking for guidance in the following areas:

- "How do you help the entire community accept the growing influx of immigrant families?"
- "How do you sensitize your teachers to the fact that cultural and linguistic differences should not be perceived as deficiencies?"
- "How do you communicate with and involve parents who do not speak English?"
- "What do you do about the self-segregation that occurs during recess and lunch among students?"
- "How do you help ELLs prepare for the standardized tests they are required to take after being in this country for merely one year?"
- "What are the best practices to accelerate ELLs' linguistic and academic development?"
- "How do you persuade your entire faculty to differentiate instruction for the benefit of ELLs and other struggling students?"

Administrators, both new and experienced, grapple with similar challenges. Quick fixes are in demand but are in short supply. Raising faculty-wide awareness about ELLs' needs, solving problems collaboratively, sharing in the decision-making process, and setting realistic common goals that are attainable for all parties are all steps in the right direction. If teachers and administrators take joint ownership of the issues surrounding ELLs and are engaged in dialogue to discuss instructional concerns and challenges, students will benefit from their collaborative efforts. These viable leadership practices, which result in student success, generate support for the decisions that are reached and policies that are enacted. What are the actions of administrators when they work to establish a collaborative school culture? They accomplish the following:

- Set common goals for the school
- Establish a common focus for the entire school regarding serving ELLs
- Build a common language about and for the sake of ELLs
- Support collaboration with effective resource management (human, time, budget, equipment, materials)
- Acknowledge and embrace teacher leadership for those who engage in regular collaborative practices
- Provide effective and appropriate professional-development opportunities to faculty at various stages of their involvement in collaboration and co-teaching
- Reach out to the community at large to expand the collaborative school culture beyond school walls

A few words of caution. Teacher collaboration and co-teaching cannot be owned or successfully championed by an administrator alone. Being sensitive to other leaders in a building, such as teachers who have earned the respect of others, may be critical to developing and fostering collaboration. Administrators may recognize that some teachers are more willing than others to collaborate. In this case, allow a small group of teachers to spearhead collaborative or co-teaching initiatives while offering incentives to those who volunteer to participate.

Parents and Community Members as Collaborative Partners

Parental Involvement

Parents and caregivers play an important part in their children's education and schooling experience. "Parents as collaborative partners" may be defined differently in different communities. However, the National PTA established these six standards for effective parental involvement in their *National Standards for Parent/Family Involvement Programs* (1997):

I. Communicating—Communication between home and school is regular, two-way, and meaningful.

II. Parenting—Parenting skills are promoted and supported.

III. Student learning—Parents play an integral role in assisting student learning.

IV. Volunteering—Parents are welcome in the school, and their support and assistance are sought.

V. School decision making and advocacy—Parents are full partners in the decisions that affect children and families.

VI. Collaborating with community—Community resources are used to strengthen schools, families, and student learning (par. 3).

Maintaining these standards is expected to result in home and school environments that equally support children's academic, social, and emotional development. If parents and teachers communicate high yet reasonable expectations for their children and provide opportunities for successful academic development, then the chances of success in school significantly increase.

What are the benefits for parents when their children receive instruction in a collaborative school culture that may also include co-teaching? Based on Epstein and colleagues' (2002) six-part model, parents benefit from the following:

- There are opportunities to help teachers more fully understand students' backgrounds and cultures, thus developing shared goals for the students. At the same time, they may receive support and assistance with understanding child and adolescent development and creating home conditions that support learning at each age, grade, and language proficiency level. (*Parenting*)
- More effective communication with all school professionals involved in their children's academic, cultural, and linguistic development is realized. (*Communicating*)
- Invitations to assist as volunteers in class-based or schoolwide events and as audiences at a range of school activities are offered. (*Volunteering*)
- Involvement with their children in academic and language learning activities at home, including helping with homework and other curriculum-related activities, increases. (*Learning at Home*)
- There is inclusion in school decisions, governance, and advocacy activities through school councils or improvement teams, committees, and parent organizations. (*Decision Making*)
- Information, resources, and services from local community groups, including businesses, agencies, cultural and civic organizations, and colleges or universities, are available. (*Collaborating With the Community*)

A few words of caution. Parents of English language learners are sometimes among the hardest-to-reach members of a school community. Often both parents work (they may even hold multiple jobs), thus they might not be available during regular school or even after school hours. Many might not have phones or might not be able to answer the phone in English. Concerted efforts and creative ways of reaching all parents are needed to be successful and will vary from school to school. This may involve recruiting bilingual community members to act as liaisons between the school and students' homes or scheduling meetings when parents are most available, such as evenings and weekends.

Community Involvement

In 2007, the Association for Supervision and Curriculum Development (ASCD) published a booklet entitled *The Learning Compact Redefined: A Call to Action*, in which the ASCD Commission on the Whole Child redefined school reform and identified communities' roles as follows:

"Communities provide

- family support and involvement;
- government, civic, and business support and resources;
- volunteers and advocates; and
- support for their districts' coordinated school health councils or other collaborative structures." (p. 3)

School districts and local communities vary from each other tremendously in size, location, demographics, and resources. However, Hugh Price (2008) suggests that all schools mobilize the communities of which they are members by achieving the following:

- Providing volunteers with clear objectives, strategies, tools, and resources to accomplish set goals
- Brainstorming long-term activities that will foster children's linguistic and academic development
- Employing media strategies to send the message of community involvement (cable newscasts, church bulletins, the Internet, shoppers' newspapers)
- Establishing a steering committee to define tasks and divide the workload among participating groups
- Remembering to keep the focus on the children and not letting adult needs and issues drive the community mobilization
- Setting up a clear and comprehensible vision that all collaborators are onboard with
- Organizing opportunities for consultation among partners to keep the interest alive and updates vocalized

What are the benefits for all community members when students receive instruction in a collaborative school culture that may also foster co-teaching? They have the opportunity to do the following:

- Volunteer in the classroom and school
- Contribute their time, talents, and resources
- Include intermediaries such as local institutions of higher education or businesses in community activities
- Witness the impact the entire community has on the school and its ELLs
- Make greater use of district resources
- Increase their interaction with graduating students and job candidates
- Experience an inclusive school culture reaching beyond the school grounds

ADMINISTRATORS' ROLE: DEVELOPING AND SUSTAINING A COLLABORATIVE SCHOOL CULTURE

Who really decides what happens in the classroom, in a school, in a district? Reeves (2006) notes that decision making may be best perceived on three levels within a school. Let's examine how such a model sheds light on supporting ELLs through the development of a collaborative school culture.

On Level 1, teachers make decisions individually and behind closed classroom doors. As such, teacher autonomy is reinforced. It is teachers' own discretion whether or not they will engage in collaborative practices. Each teacher may decide what type of collaboration and co-teaching practices he or she favors. Even when a co-teaching framework is in place, there are numerous choices to explore (for example, we offer seven possible co-teaching models in Chapter 4).

On Level 2, decisions are made collaboratively. Teachers and administrators identify and solve problems as a team. They agree on the type of collaborative model to employ (including the possibility of co-teaching) within the various ESL instructional delivery systems used in the building.

On Level 3, school administrators make sovereign decisions about issues that do not require collaborative decision making and fall outside the realm of teacher collaboration and co-teaching. Decisions regarding school safety and security fall into this level.

What defines a collaborative school culture for ELLs? We believe it is a culture in which a collective vision is developed, philosophical beliefs and values are shared, and a common purpose is articulated. In collaborative schools and districts, curricula are consistently aligned to national, state, and local content and ESL standards. Teachers implement research-based instructional practices consistently across content areas and grade levels by sharing in the three phases of instruction: planning, teaching, and assessing. Finally, effective frameworks are established and supported for ongoing professional development that promotes teacher interaction and student inclusion to result in positive student outcomes for all. For a summary of key features of a collaborative school culture and their implications for English language learners see Table 3.1.

Table 3.1 Features of a Collaborative School Culture

Feature	What It Is	What It Means for ELLs
Shared vision and mission	Clearly agreed-upon desired outcomes, shared values, and goals that focus on all students characterize the vision.	A culturally responsive school in which ELLs are not marginalized is the result.
Curriculum alignment	Through curriculum mapping and coordinated curriculum development programs, coherence is established.	Curriculum changes and modifications consider ELLs' linguistic and academic needs. ELLs are meaningfully included in general-education curriculum learning.
Shared instructional practices	Planning, implementation, and assessment practices are coordinated among all faculty.	Differentiated instruction is designed and implemented with ELLs in mind.
Ongoing shared professional development	Individual teacher learning is integrated into collaborative efforts to enhance all teachers' practice.	All faculty interacting with ELLs understand and implement research-based methods for instructing and interacting with ELLs.
Student-centered approach	Instructional focus is on the needs of the learner; students develop their own understanding through active learning techniques.	ELLs are able to build their background knowledge and complete self-selected projects at their own level of linguistic ability.

Vignette Revisited

Ms. Kovacs realized that her principal, Mrs. Carpenter, was deliberately building a collaborative school culture. Mrs. Carpenter shared with us her version of collaborative leadership using the 3 Hs approach (Head, Hand, and Heart of Collaboration):

As head of this institution, I am responsible for the academic, social, and emotional learning that takes place in the building. I take pride in that most teachers are willing or on their way to embracing the idea of ongoing collaboration. I am a very hands-on principal, involved in activities all day long. When I do my three-minute walk-throughs, I look for examples of successes just as much as areas of concern. I always see myself as a leader who is part of the team and ready to give a hand or lend an ear when needed. I never lose sight that the heart of the matter for me is that we are all here for the children: their success, their development, and their needs define us.

Vignette Reflection

You might wonder, is it only Mrs. Carpenter's and other school administrators' responsibility to promote collaboration? Of all the stakeholders discussed above, who will develop a collaborative school culture? Who will nurture it and help sustain it? A collaborative school culture is a result of shared responsibility and shared leadership, which are equally intertwined with having collaborative classrooms (the microcultures of schooling) and a culture of collaboration in the larger educational community (the macroculture of schooling). School culture as a separate entity is nestled between the unique culture of each classroom and the unique culture of each community (see Figure 3.2).

Figure 3.2 Collaborative Cultures

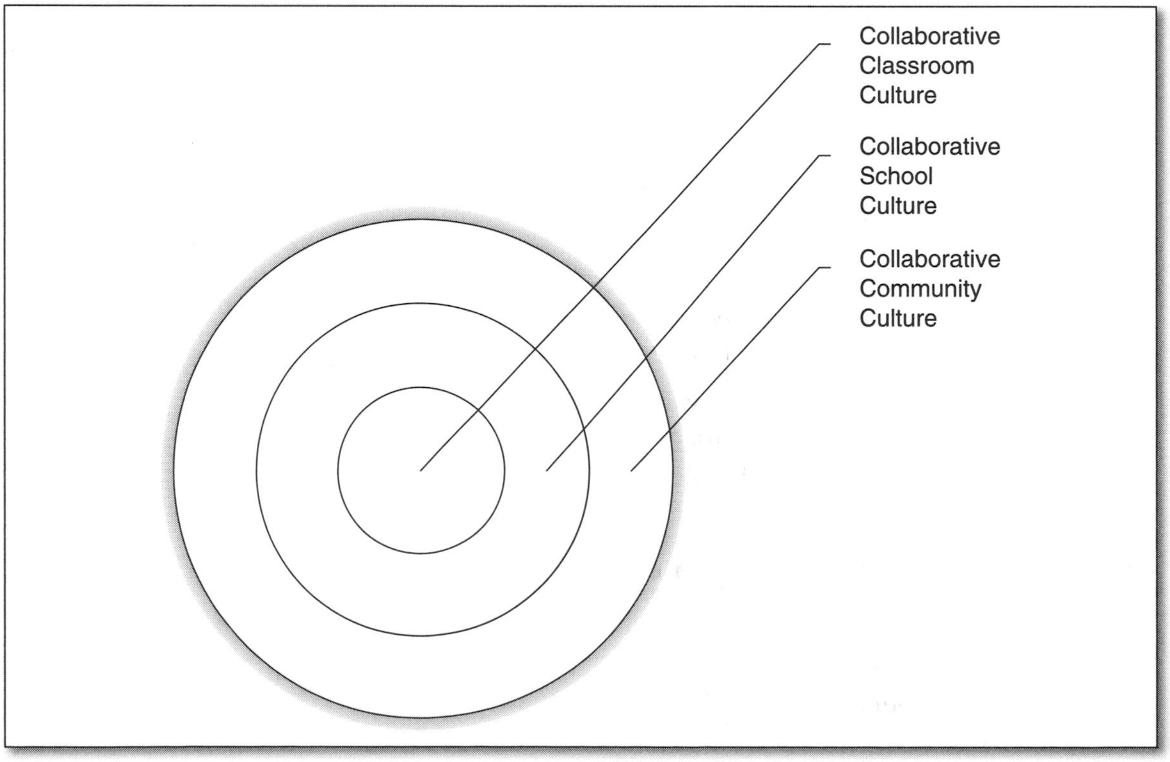

Collaborative
Classroom
Culture

Collaborative
School
Culture

Collaborative
Community
Culture

Creating an inclusive school culture is a complex undertaking. It requires both administrators and faculty to be a part of a community of learners who focus on improving the academic performance and social and emotional development of *all* students. Effective school cultures are collaborative in nature. They have common achievable and measurable goals that are established through a collaborative process. Members of productive school cultures have protocols for clear communication in place and are able to maintain focus over an extended time period. It takes time, patience, and persistence to develop a school culture that supports learning for ELLs.

SUMMARY

All those involved in a child's education will be key stakeholders in a multilingual school community, each with a unique role in helping to shape best practices and educational opportunities for English language learners. A majority of students in the school community will benefit from teacher collaboration and ESL co-teaching, which facilitate instruction in the general-education class and use strategies that benefit all learners. All stakeholders are responsible for developing and sustaining a collaborative school culture in which co-planning and co-teaching can flourish. Frequently, it is the ESL teacher who initiates, designs, and implements co-teaching practices for the sake of ELLs, but support from classroom teachers, administrators, paraprofessionals, as well as parents and community members, is vital.

DISCUSSION QUESTIONS

1. Take an inventory of your entire school community. Who are all the stakeholders in your own community and what is at stake for each constituency?

2. Engage ESL and general-education, or content-area, teachers in a collaborative inquiry project with a focus on ELLs' in-school and out-of-school experiences. Discuss ways in which ELLs' lived experiences are or are not connected to or represented in school activities. Explore possible avenues to introduce, enhance, and validate ELLs' lived realities through either the taught or hidden curriculum or both.

3. Sketch out a case study vignette about one of your ELLs. Briefly discuss his or her background, the home and school context, and the challenges the student faces.

4. Consider the list of demands placed on ELLs as discussed in this chapter and explore your students' specific needs. In collaboration with your colleagues, discuss possible steps you can take to meet those needs.

5. Generate a graphic overview or a summary chart of all existing practices that encourage parental participation and community involvement in your school. Brainstorm ways to involve parents of ELLs more effectively.

KEY ONLINE RESOURCES

Professional Organizations

Association for Supervision and Curriculum Development
www.ascd.org

National PTA
www.pta.org

Teachers of English to Speakers of Other Languages
www.tesol.org

Other Related Resources

National Clearinghouse for English Language Acquisition
www.ncela.gwu.edu

U.S. Department of Education, Office of English Language Acquisition
http://www2.ed.gov/about/offices/list/oela/index.html

4

What Are the Essential Components of an Integrated, Collaborative ESL Program?

Vision is not enough; it must be combined with venture. It is not enough to stare up the steps; we must step up the stairs.

Vaclav Havel
Progressive Czech Author and Politician

OVERVIEW

The goal of this chapter is to explore the collaborative practices that ESL and general-education teachers engage in. We will address the types of collaboration among ESL and general-education teachers that yield effective instruction to meet the diverse academic and language development needs of ELLs. Both formal and informal, as well as instructional and noninstructional, collaborative activities are presented. We will examine seven ESL co-teaching arrangements teachers use and will explore the advantages and challenges of each. Finally, we will identify the steps to creating a collaborative ESL program, including launching a co-teaching program.

Voices From the Field

At a recent TESOL Convention, Janette Cho and Ruth Jensen sat across from one another at a workshop on co-teaching for English learners. Both are experienced ESL teachers; however, Ms. Cho works in an elementary school in Missouri, and Ms. Jensen teaches in a high school in New Jersey. At the beginning of the workshop, the presenters asked teachers to share their own experiences with collaborative planning or co-teaching at their group's table. Ms. Jensen was first to share her formal collaboration routine:

"At the high school where I work, 2,000 students are enrolled, and close to 10 percent of our population are ELLs. It's a huge building with four floors plus a basement where classes are conducted. I'm fortunate to have one planning period per week to meet with core content teachers. The frustrating part is that's the only time we have. Because the building is so large, the other teachers and I hardly ever see each other in the hallway so if there are any lesson changes or any problems with individual students, it's usually put on a back burner until our next formal meeting."

After listening intently to Ms. Jensen, Ms. Cho volunteered to tell her story:

"I always envied teachers who had formal planning time, but I guess every strategy has its shortcomings. Well, my small elementary school over the past few years has had a large influx of Chinese immigrants. At first, most teachers found it difficult not knowing quite how to best help these youngsters if they did not speak Chinese. We knew that one major problem was the lack of continuity between the general-education and the ESL classroom. You see, there was never any time in our schedules to plan. Then, I got an idea. I asked my principal if I could change rooms to be in the primary wing of the building, which housed the majority of the English learners in the school. In that way, I could have access to the teachers with ELLs who were nearby and take a few minutes each morning before the official start of classes to learn what is on their teaching agenda for the day. Although it's just informal planning, it's been quite successful so far. Some of us have even tried to experiment with co-teaching, too, with good results."

Vignette Reflection

As our vignette illustrates, both Ms. Cho and Ms. Jensen take every opportunity to exchange information about their students and those students' instructional needs, including problems and successes with specific children. From our own experiences, informal collaboration takes place at the morning lineup, in the hallway, at recess, in the teachers' lounge, at lunchtime, and at dismissal. It often involves a quick chat to share anecdotal evidence about a student, an update, a question and answer, an opportunity for clarification. Informal occasions as well as formal practices are necessary components of ongoing teacher collaboration.

INFORMAL COLLABORATIVE PRACTICES

Engaging in informal professional conversations with colleagues who share common concerns and experiences is among the most rewarding experiences many teachers report. As Charlotte Danielson (2009) notes, "it's through conversations that teachers clarify their beliefs and plans and examine, practice, and consider new possibilities" (p. 1). Professional conversations may be successfully included in both formal and informal collaborative practices such as collegial circles, critical friend groups, mentoring and peer coaching, and so on. Danielson emphasizes how critical the role of the *other* is in all types of professional conversations: "they supply the mirror, the sounding board, the sympathetic (and indeed sometimes challenging) voice" (p. 6).

At the same time, informal collaboration may also be accomplished through distributing or sharing information via teacher mailboxes or designated folders, school e-boards, e-mail correspondence, blogs, and wikis. (See Chapter 5 for a more detailed discussion of each.)

ISOLATION REPLACED WITH RELATIONSHIPS

If teachers have more opportunity to interact socially, they build friendships.

If teachers have more opportunity to interact professionally, they build partnerships.

FORMAL COLLABORATIVE PRACTICES

Most teachers agree, however, that while informal interactions keep teachers connected, they do not support sustained, professional collaboration. For successful collaboration, formal structures and procedures must also be developed, implemented, and maintained. Such formal collaborative practices may have a more or less direct instructional or noninstructional focus. Instructional activities include (1) joint planning, (2) curriculum mapping and alignment, (3) parallel teaching, (4) co-developing instructional materials, (5) collaborative assessment of student work, and (6) co-teaching.

Noninstructional activities include (1) joint professional development, (2) teacher research, (3) preparing for and conducting joint parent-teacher conferences, and (4) planning, facilitating, or participating in other extracurricular activities. The following section details each of these collaborative activities.

Instructional Activities

1. Joint Planning

When ESL teachers are invited in grade-level meetings (at the elementary school) or team or department meetings (at the secondary level), they are not only included in the planning process but also treated as essential and equal partners. Some teachers we know do not wait for formal invitations; they invite themselves, listen to the discussion, and proactively offer their input. In a different context, team-based, collaborative planning may periodically take place to prepare for special projects such as field trips, school plays, Harvest Festivals, Earth Day celebrations, field days, multicultural events, and more.

The purpose of a more focused joint planning process—also referred to as cooperative or collaborative planning—is to allow ESL specialists and classroom teachers (at the elementary level) or content-area teachers (at the secondary level) to share their expertise as they (a) discuss students' needs and (b) plan lessons and units that they may deliver jointly or independent of each other. Sharing responsibility for ELLs through collaborative planning ensures that a sustained professional dialogue takes place. As a result, instruction offered by the teachers involved is aligned, rather than disjointed or fragmented. Joint planning helps ensure that the curriculum is made accessible to ELLs through scaffolding, tiering, or other differentiated instructional techniques. See Figure 4.1 for critical components of teacher collaborative planning. Joint planning opportunities must be part of the regular school schedule; common preparation time is often the most frequently cited obstacle to successful teacher collaboration (see Chapter 6).

EFFECTIVE CO-PLANNING NEEDS ESCROW

To maximize the effectiveness of collaborative planning, we suggest you build your **ESCROW:**

Establish and stick to set meeting times

Start by discussing big ideas and setting essential learning goals

Concentrate on areas of special difficulty for ELLs: scaffold learning, adapt content, modify assignments, and differentiate tasks

Review previous lessons based on student performance data

Overcome the need to always be in control

Work toward common understanding of ELLs' needs

A unique form of co-planning is when general-education and ESL teachers use the Sheltered Instruction Model (SIOP) (Echevarria et al., 2008) or the Exc-ELL protocol (Calderón, 2007). Content specialists or general-education teachers provide the content goals and objectives and the ESL teacher helps generate appropriately aligned language goals. Similarly, the content teacher or classroom teacher provides the required curriculum along with instructional resources commonly used to teach that curriculum, whereas the ESL specialist provides supplementary materials and helps adapt difficult texts, assignments, or assessment tools based on ELLs' needs.

Co-Planning Basics. Regardless of grade level or instructional program model, key co-planning activities include the following:

- Identifying academic content standards and language proficiency standards for the lesson
- Aligning language objectives to content goals
- Adapting required reading, textbook passages, and assignments to reduce their linguistic complexity
- Selecting supplementary materials that help bridge new content to ELLs' background knowledge
- Developing differentiated, tiered activities that match ELLs' language proficiency levels

- Designing formative assessment tasks and matching assessment tools that will inform you about student progress and lesson effectiveness
- Identifying essential questions that scaffold meaning and clarify information
- Using individual student profiles to differentiate instruction

As suggested by TESOL (2006), ESL teachers are not only encouraged to collaborate and co-plan instruction or other activities with content-area teachers and classroom teachers but with all faculty. They may work with bilingual teachers (to tap into ELLs' first language), literacy or math resource teachers (to share results of diagnostic and formative assessments), or special education teachers (to review student data together, to attend prereferral and individualized education planning meetings, to inform parents about available services). In addition, it is beneficial to collaborate with school administrators (to design, implement, and coordinate the ESL program; to design professional development for the entire staff; to enforce local, state, and national regulations) as well as district level administrators and curriculum directors or coordinators (to align the ESL program with other programs).

When planning time is scarce, teachers need to develop communication strategies that consistently keep all parties informed and allow for shared decision making. Resourcefulness regarding planning and implementing instruction is often supplemented with creative ways to communicate with each other about students, lesson ideas, teaching strategies, and instructional materials. A shared planbook or aligned curriculum maps can serve to frame the major concepts and skills that all students must learn for a particular unit of study and assist the ESL and the classroom teacher to organize lessons. (See Chapters 5 and 6 for more ideas.)

2. Curriculum Mapping and Alignment

Curriculum mapping. Jacobs (1997), Udelhofen (2005), and others agree that curriculum mapping is an effective procedure for collecting data about the taught curriculum in a school or district using a yearly or monthly calendar as the framework. Even when collaboration is the ultimate goal, participating ESL and general-education teachers independently map their own curriculum. Once such overviews of students' actual learning experiences are created in the various content areas, teachers engage in a dialogue to ensure alignment and explore possible misalignments of essential knowledge and skills taught in the general-education and ESL curriculum. As Jacobs (1999) notes,

> The fundamental purpose of mapping is communication. The composite of each teacher's map in a building or district provides efficient access to K–12 curriculum perspective both vertically and horizontally. Mapping is not presented as what *ought* to happen but what *is* happening during the course of a school year. Data offer an overview perspective rather than a daily classroom perspective. (p. 61)

Curriculum planning, mapping, and alignment among ESL professionals are receiving increasing attention. In Table 4.1, we summarize what is targeted and what is to be accomplished when curriculum planning is the focus of collaborative efforts for the sake of ELLs.

Table 4.1	What Is ESL Curriculum Planning?

What Is Targeted?	What Is to Be Accomplished?
Entire district	To establish common goals and a common curriculum framework from pre-kindergarten to high school graduation; the focus is on curriculum mandates, curriculum continuity, and meeting state regulations
Whole school	To plan instruction based on locally defined goals
Multiple grades	To plan a multigrade scope and sequence of the target content area to meet established district and school goals
A grade level	To plan learning experiences within the multigrade scope and sequence of the content
A class or group	To plan differentiated learning activities/resources/assessment tools
An individual	To plan individualized instruction for students by adapting curricula

Most maps reveal four types of information: the content (essential knowledge taught), the processes and skills used to teach the content, the assessment tools, and key resources used. The year-at-a-glance template we like to use allows for differentiation for beginner, intermediate, and advanced ELLs (see Figure 4.1).

Curriculum mapping may be carried out both by looking back (backward mapping) and looking ahead (forward mapping). Table 4.2 offers a useful summary to reflect on the advantages and disadvantages of different types of curriculum mapping from the ESL perspective.

Curriculum alignment. What does the ESL curriculum look like in your district? When we pose this question, the answers vary greatly. We hear anything from "I don't have a set curriculum, I have kids from kindergarten to fifth grade often all at the same time in my class; I have to focus on the four language skills," to "I follow the state standards for ESL," to "I am a content-support ESL teacher, and my job is to support what the students learn in their classes to be able to graduate from high school," to citing a published ESL program as the mandated curriculum.

What are the curricular options?

1. A stand-alone ESL curriculum following a locally developed scope and sequence of language and literacy development

2. A stand-alone ESL curriculum following a statewide ESL curriculum framework

3. A stand-alone ESL curriculum based on a commercially available ESL program

4. A content-support ESL curriculum based on content standards

Carefully conducted curriculum alignment is expected to result in the following:

1. ESL curriculum aligned to grade-level literacy/English language arts program

2. ESL curriculum aligned to grade-level content courses

Figure 4.1 Year-at-a-Glance ESL Curriculum Mapping Template

GRADE: _____ TEACHER: _____

Month	Essential Questions	LANGUAGE SKILLS CONTENT GOALS			Resources	Assessment
		BEGINNER	INTERMEDIATE	ADVANCED		

Table 4.2 Backward (Journal) Mapping Versus Forward (Projection) Mapping

Initial Mapping Format	Advantages	Disadvantages
Backward Mapping (*Sometimes referred to as journal or diary mapping*)	• This type of mapping is less time-intensive; it requires a small amount of time on a regular basis to record the ESL and general-education content, language skills, and assessments taught each month. • When various levels of language proficiency are considered, this type of mapping allows for a more accurate account of what was actually taught to various groups of ELLs.	• It slows the completion of the initial mapping cycle, as teachers cannot proceed to the editing step until maps are completed. • The next steps probably would not occur until the beginning of the subsequent school year. • The curriculum mapping process can lose momentum. • Monthly check-ins must occur with each teacher to keep abreast of everyone's progress.
Forward Mapping (*Sometimes referred to as projection mapping*)	• The initial curriculum maps are completed within a short time frame, enabling teachers to move to the next steps of mapping much faster. • If a district allocates the appropriate amount of time, the initial cycle of mapping can be completed in one academic year.	• It is more time-intensive. • Some teachers may have difficulty projecting future teaching. • It is troublesome for teachers who wish to document their differentiated maps for the three language proficiency levels.

Adapted from Udelhofen, S. (2005). *Keys to curriculum mapping: Strategies and tools to make it work.* Thousand Oaks, CA: Corwin. (p. 19)

If the ESL program does have a strong, purposeful connection to the grade-level content through curriculum alignment, instruction in the content classes becomes more meaningful for ELLs. Without such curriculum alignment, the ESL services may become fragmented, the content delivered in each class may become disjointed, and the skills introduced and practiced may become confusing for ELLs.

Curriculum development to build community. According to Sergiovanni (1994), curriculum development is a potential avenue to building a learning community. Although critical and helpful, no mention of English language learners is made in his work. Thus, we reviewed and adapted his eight platforms to indicate the key questions that need to be considered when curriculum development and community building in linguistically diverse schools are shared goals (see Table 4.3).

Table 4.3	Curriculum Platforms and Key Questions
Platforms	**Key Questions to Consider When Servicing ELLs**
1. The aims of education	What is our goal: English acquisition or bilingual development?
2. Major achievements of students this year	How are students doing? What have they learned? How do we know?
3. The social significance of the student's learning	In what ways do ELLs improve their status in the school and community?
4. The image of the learner	How are ELLs perceived by others?
5. The image of the curriculum	How does the ESL curriculum align to the general-education curriculum?
6. The image of the teacher	Who delivers instructions to ELLs, the ESL specialist or all teachers?
7. The preferred pedagogy	What ESL methodologies are used?
8. The preferred school climate	Do we welcome students and parents from all cultural and linguistic backgrounds?

Based on Sergiovanni, T. J. (1994). *Building community in schools*. San Francisco: Jossey-Bass. (p. 79)

3. Parallel Teaching

ESL services are often implemented in the form of a stand-alone, pull-out program. At the elementary level, ESL specialists often gather the children from one or more classrooms and take them to a designated ESL room. What happens while ELLs are away from their regular classrooms? Their teachers are often puzzled by this challenge: What to teach and what not to teach while ELLs are not in the room? One solution to this dilemma is for ESL specialists and general-education teachers to coordinate the objectives of their lessons by doing the following:

- Focusing on the same theme (In kindergarten, while learning about farm animals at the same time, ELLs will match pictures to animal sounds and learn children's songs and nursery rhymes about farm animals.)
- Addressing the same essential questions (In second grade, while exploring why friendship is important, ELLs will read *My First American Friend* by Sarunna Jin.)
- Studying the same genre (In fourth grade, when reading autobiographies, ELLs will create a timeline of their own lives and create a storyboard of their major life events.)
- Exploring the same topic by either building background knowledge or creating extensions of the shared objectives (In fifth grade, when studying about the Civil War, ELLs create a summary chart of the two sides, while the general-education class analyzes contemporary letters written by soldiers from both sides.)
- Practicing the same or closely related literacy skills (In eighth grade, while enhancing note-taking skills, ELLs receive various levels of modeling and scaffolding.)
- Preteaching or reteaching key concepts and skills (In ninth grade, while preparing to take standardized tests, ELLs review the direction words and explore the language of test questions and prompts necessary to understand what is required of the students.)

At the secondary level, ELLs are typically not pulled from content classes. Since the ESL courses are incorporated into students' schedules by design based on state and local regulations, the ESL program may parallel the general-education classes that help students master the content and skills necessary to earn a high school diploma.

4. Co-Developing Instructional Materials

When teachers collaborate with ELLs' needs in mind, their attention may be focused on not only creating lesson or unit plans together but also developing instructional materials, resources, activity sheets, in-class and homework assignments, and assessment tools. There are many already-available classroom items that can be easily adapted for ELLs. Sometimes, those involved in planning together for ELLs can spend collaborative sessions conducting research on the Internet to gather appropriate information and materials for content, culture, grade level, and language proficiency for ELLs. The following are examples of how ELLs' lived experiences are reflected in the curriculum:

- In kindergarten, when the four seasons are introduced and reviewed, teachers consider each ELL's country of origin and create illustrated diagrams that show how many seasons are in each of those locations.
- In second grade, when the three main types of communities (rural, urban, suburban) are explored, ELLs' lived experiences prior to coming to the United States are recognized. Their countries of origin are featured in photographs, video clips, and other supplementary materials.
- In third grade, when the food pyramid is discussed, teachers locate ethnic food pyramids on the Internet that reflect ELLs' home culture and dietary customs.
- In fourth-grade geography, when the continents and oceans are identified, ELLs can share their experiences living in different parts of the world and discuss the continent they lived on and its adjacent oceans.
- In fifth grade, when the scientific method is introduced, ELLs receive a native-language version of the five-step outline.
- In seventh-grade science, when the digestive system is presented, diagrams, summary charts, and three-dimensional models are made available for the students.
- In 10th-grade world history, when Peter the Great's accomplishments (and atrocities) are explored, authentic documents such as contemporary letters are adapted or excerpted to match ELLs' language proficiency levels.
- In 12th grade, in preparation for standardized tests necessary to earn a high school diploma, teachers collaboratively develop scaffolded essay templates and outlines that are appropriate for ELLs' varied language proficiency levels.

The possibilities of material development are as diverse as lessons taught in the K–12 classroom!

5. Collaborative Assessment of Student Work

A powerful collaborative activity ESL and general-education teachers may engage in is sampling and carefully examining representative work by ELLs. In one recently developed model, *Collaborative Analysis of Student Work: Improving Teaching and Learning,* Langer, Colton, and Gott (2003) suggest the use of rubrics within a framework of collaborative conversations and inquiry. Specifically, they propose that participating teachers focus both on students' strengths and weaknesses and identify appropriate strategies to respond to patterns of learning problems. Using a protocol, members of teacher study groups analyze student work, offer plausible explanations for student performance levels, explore promising strategies to implement, and plan interventions. Once the teacher follows the collectively determined steps, new data are collected from the student, and the performance is assessed. This cycle is repeated, as teachers reflect on their students' learning and their own growth and needs.

Blythe, Allen, and Schieffelin Powell (2008) summarize and compare three different protocols teachers typically follow when they examine student work. Each approach varies based on the answers to the following questions:

1. What is the purpose or goal?
2. What is the purpose of describing, interpreting, and evaluating student work?
3. What is the context in which student work is presented?
4. What kind and how much student work is shared?

See Table 4.4 for possible answers to these four questions in each of the three approaches.

In our work, we found it helpful to customize the protocol of examining student work by focusing on challenges shared by ELLs and their teachers. We call our protocol *Sampling Work by English Language Learners* (SWELL). See textbox below for the entire protocol.

PROTOCOL FOR SAMPLING WORK BY ENGLISH LANGUAGE LEARNERS (SWELL)

As you collaboratively examine student work samples produced by English language learners, consider the following questions organized in four subcategories.

1. Linguistic Development
   a. What stage of second language acquisition is evident?
   b. Which linguistic features has the student mastered and been able to use systematically?
   c. What are two or three prominent linguistic challenges the ELL's work demonstrates?
   d. Other comments:

2. Academic Needs
   a. What are two to three examples of successfully acquired content-based knowledge and/or skills?
   b. What are some noticeable gaps in the ELL's prior knowledge?
   c. What are some gaps in the ELL's new content attainment?
   d. What content-specific skills does the ELL need to work on?
   e. Other comments:

3. Cultural Experiences and Challenges
   a. In what way are the ELL's cultural experiences reflected in his or her work?
   b. Is there any evidence that the ELL was struggling with cultural misunderstandings or misconceptions?
   c. Other comments:

4. Social-Emotional Aspects of Learning
   a. Is there evidence of motivated, self-directed learning in the ELL's work sample?
   b. Has the ELL been engaged in the task?
   c. Is there evidence of task persistence?
   d. Is there evidence of being engaged in cooperative learning (peer editing, etc.)?
   e. Other comments:

Table 4.4 Three Processes for Looking at Student Work

	Tuning Protocol	Collaborative Assessment Conferences	The Consultancy
Purposes	• To develop more effective assignments and assessment tasks • To develop common standards for students' work • To support teachers' instructional practice	• To learn more about students' goals and interests • To learn more about the strengths and needs of a particular student • To reflect on and gather ideas for revising classroom practice	• To gain insight into teachers' and administrators' dilemmas or "burning questions" arising from their practice • To open up the thinking about problems of teaching and learning
Role of description, interpretation, and/or evaluation	*Primarily evaluation:* The process asks participants to provide warm and cool feedback on student work samples, teachers' assignments, and so on.	*Primarily description, with some interpretation:* The process asks participants to describe the student work, to ask questions about it, and to speculate about the problems or issues in the work that the student was most focused on.	*Primarily interpretation:* The process asks participants to interpret the presenter's dilemma, to raise questions, offer hypotheses about the essence of that dilemma, and to offer other perspectives on the dilemma.
Presentation of the context for the student work	*Context presented initially:* At the beginning of the session, the presenting teacher typically provides descriptions of the assignment, scoring criteria, and so on.	*Context withheld until middle of process:* The presenter does not describe the context for the work until after participants have looked carefully at it and formulated questions about it.	*Context presented initially:* The protocol begins with the presenting teacher's description of the dilemma and the context that gives rise to it.
Kinds and amount of student work typically shared	*Kinds of pieces:* There is a single assignment, task, or project. *Number of pieces:* There is work from several students, often at different levels of accomplishment. May also be used with a single sample.	*Kinds of pieces:* Student work is generated by an open-ended assignment (as opposed to worksheets). *Number of pieces:* One or two pieces of work from a single student are shared. May also be used with multiple samples from a single student.	*Kinds of pieces:* The process does not require student work samples; they may be included to illustrate the dilemma or classroom context. *Number of pieces:* When student work is shared, the number of pieces varies from one to a few, depending on the point the presenter is trying to illustrate.

Adapted from Blythe, T., Allen, D., & Schieffelin Powell, B. (2008). *Looking together at student work* (2nd ed.). New York: Teachers College Press. (p. 34)

6. Co-Teaching as a Framework for Sustained Teacher Collaboration

Co-teaching frameworks have been presented for special education inclusion models by several authors. Most experts on co-teaching to support students with special needs talk about four to six possible co-teaching arrangements: In *A Guide to Co-Teaching: Practical Tips for Facilitating Student Learning,* Villa et al. (2008) identify four predominant approaches to co-teaching: Supportive, Parallel, Complementary, and Team teaching.

They define supportive co-teaching as that in which "one teacher takes the lead instructional role and the other(s) rotates among the students to provide support" (p. 20). In parallel co-teaching "two or more people work with different groups of students in different sections of the classroom" (p. 20). When complementary co-teaching is used, "co-teachers do something to enhance the instruction provided by the other co-teacher(s)" (p. 20). Lastly, "team teaching is when two or more people do what the traditional teacher has always done—plan, teach, assess, and assume responsibility for all of the students in the classroom" (p. 21).

Vaughn, Schumm, and Arguelles (1997), as well as Murawski (2009) in *Collaborative Teaching in Secondary Schools: Making the Co-Teaching Marriage Work!,* outline five common approaches for co-instruction (One teach, one support; Parallel teaching; Station teaching; Alternative teaching; and Team teaching). Friend and Cook (2007) and others discuss six co-teaching models in their work, including the following: One teach, one observe; One teach, one drift; Parallel teaching; Station teaching; Alternate teaching; and Team teaching. When six models are considered, the supporting role is more distinguished. This approach results in two different models, indicating whether one teacher takes on the support role of making observations or helping around the room as needed.

According to Conderman, Bresnahan, and Pedersen (2009), the goal of purposeful co-teaching is student achievement, which is supported by several key factors or co-teaching components, such as interpersonal skills, content knowledge, teaching behaviors, philosophy of teaching, and co-teaching stage. Inspired by Conderman and his colleagues' model, we have designed a visual representation of key factors that are necessary to address the unique academic, cultural, and linguistic characteristics and needs of ELLs in an ESL co-teaching context (see Figure 4.2).

- *Shared Philosophy of Teaching:* Teachers must reflect on and share their fundamental beliefs about learning and teaching all children, and more specifically, about how ELLs can acquire a new language and learn challenging academic content best.
- *Collaborative Practice:* Teachers must willingly and voluntarily engage in all three phases of collaborative practice: planning, implementing, and assessing instruction.
- *Cross-Cultural and Interpersonal Skills:* To effectively co-teach, all involved must pay special attention to and further develop their cross-cultural understanding, communication, and interpersonal skills.
- *Bridging and Building Content Knowledge:* Teachers must recognize that ELLs may bring both limited prior knowledge of the target content areas and a wealth of life experiences and other information to their classes. The challenge is to activate such prior knowledge, successfully connect it to new learning, or, when needed, effectively build background knowledge so students can understand the new content.
- *Consistent and Supportive Teacher Behaviors:* Teachers must recognize that they are role models to their students and are constantly being observed by them. So modeling consistent behavior sends a clear message to all students: Two teachers are in charge and are sharing equal responsibilities.

- *Linguistic Adaptations:* The greatest challenge ELLs face in any K–12 classroom is the linguistic complexity in spoken and written communication. Thus, collaborating teachers must purposefully work on adapting the difficulty level of tasks.

Co-Teaching Models

In our work with ESL teachers and their general-education colleagues, we observed the following seven co-teaching arrangements. In the first three cases, the teachers work with one large group of students. In the next three models, there are two groups of students split between the two cooperating teachers. In the final model, multiple groups of students are engaged in a learning activity that is facilitated and monitored by two teachers. Each of these configurations may have a place in any co-taught classroom, regardless of the grade level or the content area taught. We encourage our readers to consider both

| Figure 4.2 | How to Create a Blossoming Co-Teaching Program |

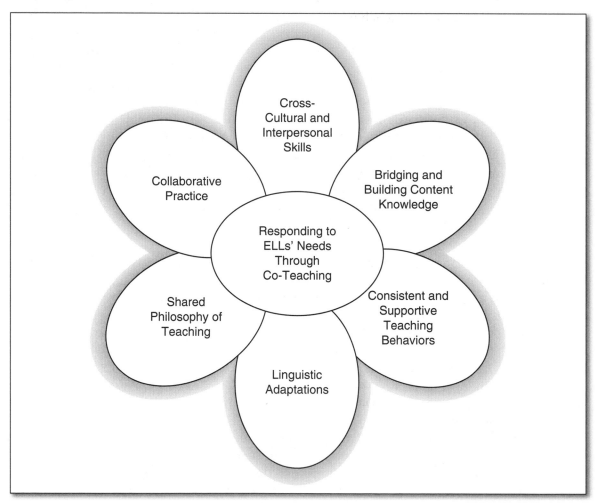

Adapted from Conderman, G., Bresnahan, V., & Pedersen, T. (2009). *Purposeful co-teaching: Real cases and effective strategies.* Thousand Oaks, CA: Corwin. (p. 16)

the advantages and disadvantages of each and pilot various models in their classes to see which ones allow them to respond best to the students' needs, the specific content being taught, the type of learning activities designed, and the participating teachers' teaching styles and own preferences.

1. One Group: One Lead Teacher and One Teacher "Teaching on Purpose" (Table 4.5 and Figure 4.3)

2. One Group: Two Teachers Teach Same Content (Table 4.6 and Figure 4.4)

3. One Group: One Teaches, One Assesses (Table 4.7 and Figure 4.5)

4. Two Groups: Two Teachers Teach Same Content (Table 4.8 and Figure 4.6)

5. Two Groups: One Teacher Preteaches, One Teacher Teaches Alternative Information (Table 4.9 and Figure 4.7)

6. Two Groups: One Teacher Reteaches, One Teacher Teaches Alternative Information (Table 4.10 and Figure 4.8)

7. Multiple Groups: Two Teachers Monitor and Teach (Table 4.11 and Figure 4.9)

1. One Group of Students: One Lead Teacher and One Teacher "Teaching on Purpose"

The general-education teacher does not always assume the lead role, nor does the ESL teacher solely serve in the role of "teaching on purpose," which refers to giving short, focused mini-lessons to individual students, pairs of students, or a small group of students. Teaching on purpose might involve a follow-up to a previous lesson or a check and extension of what is presently being taught based on a teachable moment. Teachers who implement teaching on purpose may also keep a written log of information for each ELL who needs follow-up.

Table 4.5 Model 1: One Group: One Lead Teacher and One Teacher "Teaching on Purpose"

Advantages	Challenges
The curriculum is accessible to everyone.	If not enough planning time is given, one teacher might take all the responsibility for teaching.
All students receive equal benchmark instruction.	
Formative data may be produced via logs (for follow-up).	The ESL teacher and teacher teaching on purpose feel like well-paid teacher aides.
Constant monitoring of ELL understanding is possible.	If the ESL teacher is the one taking responsibility, the general-education teacher might treat the co-taught time as a "break."
Personal, individualized attention may be given to students in need.	

Figure 4.3 What Does Model 1 Look Like?

One Group: One Lead Teacher and One Teacher "Teaching on Purpose"

2. One Group: Two Teachers Teach Same Content

Two teachers are directing a whole class of students. Both teachers are working cooperatively and teaching the same lesson at the same time. For example, a general-education teacher presents a lesson, and the ESL teacher interjects with examples, explanations, and extensions of the key ideas. The ESL teacher can provide strategies to assist the students in better remembering and organizing the information that was presented.

Table 4.6 Model 2: One Group: Two Teachers Teach Same Content

Advantages	Challenges
There is more extensive modeling.	It needs a good amount of planning.
It allows collegial observation.	It requires time to get a smooth back and forth, to gain comfort with material.
It provides immediate reinforcement/remediation.	It may be challenging for the ESL teacher to become thoroughly familiar with the general-education studies.
It allows the ability to take notes; offers authentic modeling.	It is like a marriage—some work and others don't.
It adds clarity to the lesson.	
It is very effective when done well.	

Figure 4.4 What Does Model 2 Look Like?

One Group: Two Teachers Teach Same Content

A,B,C

3. One Group: One Teaches, One Assesses

Two teachers are engaged in conducting the same lesson; however, one teacher takes the lead, and the other teacher circulates the room and assesses targeted students through observations, checklists, and anecdotal records. The observing teacher may also take notes on which activities successfully engaged students, caused confusion, and so on.

Table 4.7 Model 3: One Group: One Teaches, One Assesses

Advantages	Challenges
There is opportunity to carefully observe students in action.	One teacher is responsible for the instruction of the entire class.
There is opportunity to collect a large amount of authentic data.	The observing teacher might not be perceived as equal by students.
The observing teacher can focus on specific subskills.	The observing teacher needs to be able to move into other models of co-teaching as needed.
The observing teacher may offer peer feedback on what worked and what did not for individual students to the colleague who teaches.	It is not an effective model if used too frequently.

Figure 4.5 What Does Model 3 Look Like?

One Group: One Teaches, One Assesses

4. Two Groups: Two Teachers Teach Same Content

The students in the class form two heterogeneous groups, and each teacher works with one of the groups. The purpose of using two smaller groups is to provide additional opportunities for the students in each group to interact, provide answers, and to have their responses monitored by the teacher.

5. Two Groups: One Teacher Preteaches, One Teacher Teaches Alternative Information

Teachers assign students to one of two groups, based on their readiness levels related to a designated topic or skill. Students who have limited prior knowledge of the target

Table 4.8 Model 4: Two Groups: Two Teachers Teach Same Content

Advantages	Challenges
It decreases class size (small groups). • Individualizes instruction • Safe environment/able to take risks	Teachers will need a lot of time to plan.
You can swap groups to allow for fresh perspective. • Alternative way to learn same content • Automatic differentiation	A lack of willingness to share the teaching/planning process and resources might sabotage this model.
There is more interaction due to a lower student-teacher ratio.	It could result in *two* separate classes pulled aside.
There is consistency with particular groups.	It might not work for all teachers; selected content might be more challenging for some ESL teachers to present.
Two brains are better than one!	The noise level might be distracting.

Figure 4.6 What Does Model 4 Look Like?

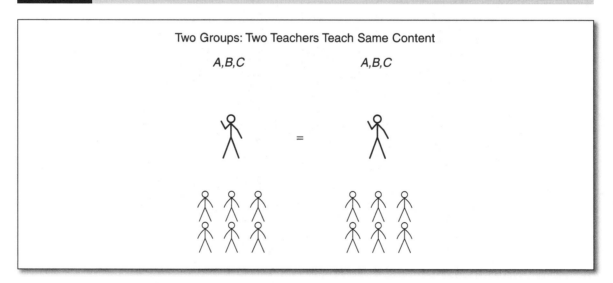

content or skill will be grouped together to receive instruction. The teacher working with that group will have the opportunity to prepare students to bridge the gap in their background knowledge.

6. Two Groups: One Teacher Reteaches, One Teacher Teaches Alternative Information

Teachers assign students to one of two groups, based on their levels of knowledge and skills regarding the designated topic. One teacher will focus on previously presented material and offer the group an opportunity for reinforcement. In this flexible grouping arrangement, the group to which students are assigned is temporary and relates solely to their knowledge and skills regarding the designated topic. As the topic and skills that are addressed change, so does the group composition.

| Table 4.9 | Model 5: Two Groups: One Teacher Preteaches, One Teacher Teaches Alternative Information |

Advantages	Challenges
Focused attention may be given to subgroups' unique needs.	It may appear as if two separate classes are being run in the same room.
It is ideal for tiered lessons and tasks or other forms of differentiated instruction.	The noise level might interfere with information processing.
It allows for building vocabulary for one group of students and expanding the vocabulary of another.	There are concerns that the time allowed for preteaching information might cause some students to have a less rigorous curriculum.
It allows for building background knowledge.	

| Figure 4.7 | What Does Model 5 Look Like? |

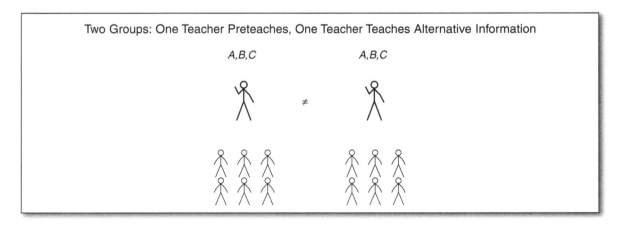

Two Groups: One Teacher Preteaches, One Teacher Teaches Alternative Information

| Table 4.10 | Model 6: Two Groups: One Teacher Reteaches, One Teacher Teaches Alternative Information |

Advantages	Challenges
It is ideal for differentiating.	You may need more than two groups.
It is flexible—only students who need reteaching or reinforcement will get it.	It is challenging to stagger the reteaching with the enrichment to stay at the same pace.
It provides enrichment for a higher level.	Students may quickly differentiate between "smart students" and "others."

Figure 4.8	What Does Model 6 Look Like?

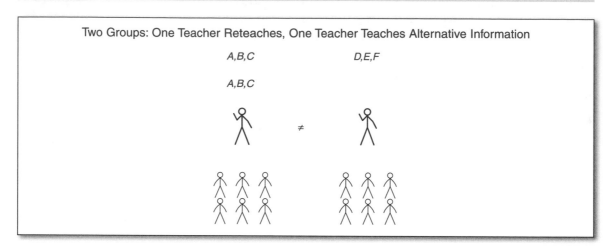

7. Multiple Groups: Two Teachers Monitor and Teach

This multiple-group format allows all or most students to work in either heterogeneous or homogenous groups, with selected students grouped for specific, skills-based instruction. This model can be particularly effective in language arts at the elementary level when students with specific reading difficulties require specific and intensive small-group instruction or at the middle school level when students participate in literature circles. Science or computer labs may also easily lend themselves to such instruction. It is also conducive to learning centers or learning stations, where students rotate from center to center (in the elementary classroom) or from station to station (in the secondary classroom) while two teachers monitor the learning.

As Nathaniel Raynor, an ESL co-teacher, pointed out to us, "although it requires much planning, teachers can focus on introducing one new center or skill every once in a while (especially for young learners who need lots of repetition!). So, if you phase out and replace one station or center per month, you really only had to create one new thing. Many others remain the same. After its initial 'start-up cost,' it does not really require an onerous amount of planning."

Table 4.11	Model 7: Multiple Groups: Two Teachers Monitor and Teach

Advantages	Challenges
There is total engagement due to movement.	Students may be distracted or confused.
More individualized attention is offered.	Students can get off task.
There is increased student participation and engagement.	Grouping can result in a division within the class.
Co-teachers can cover more of the curriculum if the jigsaw technique is used.	• Segregation • Labeling
It lends itself to multicultural interaction.	
There is extensive opportunity for peer learning.	It demands a lot of preplanning and organization.

| Figure 4.9 | What Does Model 7 Look Like? |

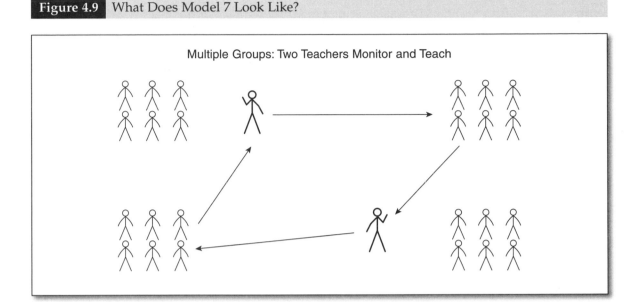

What Is Unique About ESL Co-Teaching?

During any of the above co-teaching configurations, the partnering teachers will share the responsibility for planning instruction, implementing the lessons, and assessing student performance and outcome. In a co-taught classroom, ELLs learn general-education content along with their monolingual peers. When learning groups remain heterogeneous, ELLs have the opportunity to work with students who have various academic capabilities and English language fluency. This is in contrast to remedial or ESL pull-out programs, in which ELLs are either grouped with youngsters who are struggling readers and writers or have no English language proficiency.

ELLs have different needs than remedial students. An ESL program should enhance students' understanding of English while learning classroom content as well as offer English-proficient peers to serve as language models. In our view, these are some of the basic ingredients of a successful ESL co-teaching model. Within a general-education classroom, an ESL teacher can demonstrate strategies during a co-taught lesson, and the classroom teacher can continue to use the same strategies with ELLs when the ESL teacher is no longer present. Very often, the exchange of ideas between both teachers allows for more risk taking and the use of innovative strategies on the part of each teacher to benefit all students in the classroom.

Noninstructional Activities

1. Joint Professional Development

ESL and classroom teachers or content-area teachers may benefit from participating in joint professional-development activities either at their school, within their district, or outside their own professional environment. If they attend external, off-site training programs together, they have an open forum to share their experiences, voice their concerns, and get feedback and responses both from colleagues from other school districts and from the course leader or workshop facilitator. Upon returning to their schools, teachers have the opportunity to share the information they gained both formally and informally with their colleagues. When they transfer the new information to their own practice and implement the new strategies in their own teaching, not only are they obtaining new skills, but they can also share these skills collaboratively with folks who did not attend the same training. When teachers train together, the benefit is even greater since they are able to support each other in their endeavors.

The collaborative professional-development practices that yield the most effective partnership and team building between ESL teachers and their general-education colleagues have the following common elements:

1. Regular, work-based opportunities to reflect on and improve instruction

2. Shared topics of interest

3. Team membership and participation based on self-selection

4. Focus on teachers' instructional practices and students' learning

A. Collegial Circles. Collegial circles are small groups of teachers who meet on a regular basis to discuss common questions, share concerns, offer solutions to common problems, and discuss appropriate instructional techniques. In a classic educational resource, *Looking in Classrooms*, Good and Brophy (2000, p. 490) suggest moving through three stages when designing a group discussion. To transfer this model to the current ESL context, we renamed the stages, adjusted the goals, and gave ESL-specific examples for each stage, as seen in Table 4.12.

Table 4.12 Phases of Group Discussions

Phases	Types of Knowledge	Goals	Examples
Phase 1	External Knowledge: ⬇ Review and Discover	• Explore existing, research-based information • Find out what experts say about the topic	• Find recently published articles on a shared topic of interest, such as co-teaching
Phase 2	Personal Knowledge: ⬇ Reflect and Relate	• Engage in active listening • Share personal experiences related to the topic or problem • Connect and compare external knowledge to group members' own experiences	• Discuss the pros and cons of each co-teaching model • Invite everyone to share his or her personal experiences • Compare own challenges and successes to those documented in the literature
Phase 3	Future Actions: ⬇ Revise and Devise	• Internalize new knowledge about the topic • Review and revise prior understanding of the problem • Develop a plan of action	• Decide on the feasibility of the various models for one's own context • Develop a plan to experiment with and implement new models

B. Peer Observations. One powerful school-based professional-learning opportunity for ESL and general-education teachers is created by visiting each other's classes. When observing the teaching-learning process and monitoring student outcomes in a classroom where ELLs are placed, teachers may focus their observation on the following:

> *Kid watching:* What are some of the observable challenges ELLs face as the lesson unfolds? How do they respond to the tasks and activities presented by the teacher? How do they interact with their classmates? What opportunities do they have to meaningfully use and, thus, develop their English language skills? What do ELLs do differently in the observed class?

> *Teacher watching:* Are both content and language objectives implemented? If so, what are the language and content goals for the lesson? How clearly are they communicated? How does each teacher approach the varied needs of ELLs? What types of adaptations are used? In what ways are the assigned texts, tasks, homework assignments, and assessment practices modified (if at all)?

Allen and LeBlanc (2005) promote a simple yet effective collaborative peer coaching system they call the *2 + 2 performance appraisal model.* The name suggests that teachers who engage in this form of peer support offer each other two compliments and two suggestions following a lesson observation. Figure 4.10 is our adapted version of the observation form that may be used by either the ESL or general-education teacher. We suggest several general and ESL-specific key areas to consider when offering each other feedback as summarized in Table 4.13.

C. Collaborative Coaching/Mentoring. When teachers participate in a mentor/coaching program either as a mentor/coach or as a mentee, opportunities to improve or learn new techniques for ELLs abound. Collaborative coaching and peer mentoring imply that teachers support each other's practice beyond conducting peer observations. Through a framework of coaching, teachers learn from each other, model effective instruction for each other, and provide sustained, job-embedded, and student-centered classroom assistance to each other. Collaborative coaching requires a more equal relationship between the two partners, such as the relationship between co-teachers or those who collaborate formally in other ways to provide instruction to ELLs. It is effective (a) when both participants possess knowledge about the topic or issue, such as high-stakes testing and test preparation for ELLs or (b) when the coach understands one part of a problem (content requirements for all students to pass a state exam) and the partner understands another part (ELLs' linguistic development) (Dunne & Villani, 2007). Thus, collaborative coaching becomes a vehicle for professional growth both for the novice and experienced teacher.

2. Teacher Research

When teachers engage in classroom-based practitioner research, they may do so individually or collaboratively using a number of different formats. Working in research and development (R&D) teams, participating in collaborative inquiry groups, and engaging in collaborative action research or lesson studies are briefly described below.

A. Research and Development Teams. Research and development (R&D) teams are formed by small groups of teachers who more formally decide on a particular instructional

Figure 4.10	2 + 2 Classroom Observation Form

Teacher: _____   School: _____

Observer: _____   Date: _____

Grade: _____   Subject: _____

Number and Level of ELLs: _____

1. *Compliments:*

   a.

   b.

2. *Suggestions:*

   a.

   b.

Reflections:

Adapted from Allen, D. W., & LeBlanc, A. C. (2005). *Collaborative peer coaching that improves instruction: The 2 + 2 performance appraisal model.* Thousand Oaks, CA: Corwin. (p. 27)

Table 4.13	Target Areas of Feedback in the 2+2 Model

General Feedback	Feedback Specific to Working With ELLs	Comments
Clarity of lesson objectives	Language and content objectives	
Motivation	Connection to ELLs' prior knowledge and experiences or building background knowledge	
Lesson sequence	Lesson accessibility	
Differentiated activities	Scaffolded and tiered activities	
Student engagement	ELL participation	
Questioning techniques	Questions matched to ELLs' language proficiency levels	
Grouping techniques	Using heterogeneous and homogenous groupings with the purpose of bilingual peer bridging	
Assessment techniques	Differentiation of assessment for ELLs	

Adapted from Allen, D.W., & LeBlanc, A. C. (2005). *Collaborative peer coaching that improves instruction: The 2 + 2 performance appraisal model.* Thousand Oaks, CA: Corwin.

approach that they study collaboratively. In some districts, R & D projects and accompanying teacher portfolios that document teachers' success with the target strategy may be used in lieu of more traditional teacher evaluations (which are often based on observations by an administrator and may only yield limited data on the teacher's performance).

After collaborating teachers review research related to the selected instructional approach, they collaboratively plan and implement lessons based on the approach, assess their own (and each other's) growth, and evaluate the student outcomes. In New York State and some school districts around the country, a similar activity is called the Annual Professional Performance Review (APPR). Tenured (or even untenured) teachers may choose to participate in it. The ultimate goal is to improve the quality of instruction and learning in the classroom while assessing and documenting teacher learning.

B. Collaborative Inquiry Groups. When teacher discussion groups or collegial circles elect to engage in more in-depth explorations, they may decide to form collaborative inquiry groups. They may decide to investigate an overarching concept (such as the teaching-leaning process or second language acquisition patterns) or choose more specific topics that deal with ELLs' instructional needs (such as using effective note-taking strategies). A form of collaborative inquiry is conducting teacher research or action research. We use Johnson's (2008) definition of *action research* as "the process of studying a real school or classroom situation to understand and improve the quality of actions and instruction" (p. 28). Berger, Boles, and Troen (2005) identify the following six paradoxes that are inherently present in teacher research or practitioner research:

1. It must be mandated; it can't be mandated.

2. It must be championed by a strong principal; it can't be owned by the principal.

3. There must be an outside actor; the outside actor's role is questionable.

4. Teachers must learn research skills; teachers must trust their own knowledge so as not to be overwhelmed by the things they need to learn.

5. Teachers' teaching changes profoundly; teachers say their research confirms things they already knew.

6. For it to work as a whole-school reform, teacher research must be woven into the fabric of the school culture; teacher research is contrary to the culture of schools. (p. 103)

Despite the obvious challenges noted by Berger et al. (2005), when collaborative action research is woven into the school culture and supported strongly by both the administration and the faculty, it allows teachers to examine their practice systematically and participate in the highest level of professional learning by conducting authentic, classroom-based research (Cochran-Smith & Lytle, 1999). See the action-research planning template we use with teachers in the following textbox.

ACTION-RESEARCH PLANNING TEMPLATE

Action Research Outline

Background

Give a brief description of the educational issue.

Research Questions

Generate questions that are researchable, answerable, and relevant to the students' needs.

Participants

Describe the community, school, and classroom in which the study will take place.
Describe the students (ability levels, language backgrounds).

Data Sources

Identify the purpose of each data source (instrument) and how it will help answer one or more of the research questions.

Data Collection Procedures

Describe week-by-week (if applicable, day-by-day) sequential steps for both instructional and research (data collection) activities.

Data Analysis

Plan how you will analyze and interpret the data in order to answer each research question.

Anticipated Outcomes

Identify some desired or anticipated outcomes.

Action Plan

Outline a possible action plan following the study.

C. Lesson Study Teams. The lesson study concept originated in Japan as a professional-development movement for experienced inservice teachers who wanted to regularly engage in examining their teaching practices to improve their effectiveness (Lewis, 2002). In the classic format, participating teachers jointly plan a lesson in response to a preestablished study question or goal. One teacher teaches the lesson while others observe. Next, teachers discuss the lesson, revise it, and another team member teaches the lesson in a new class. This process of observation and discussion is repeated and ends with a written report (Fernandez & Chokshi, 2002). Yoshida (2004) emphasizes that "lesson study helps to make teachers into lifelong learners. It is especially important to think of lesson study as a professional development activity, not as teacher training and lesson development. It creates opportunities for teachers to think deeply about instruction, learning, curriculum, and education" (par. 5). Among many others, Jalongo, Reig, and Helterbran (2006) reported on how to transfer the Japanese lesson study to the U.S. context. Teachers we worked with used the SIOP model and the lesson study approach in a modified framework (Cohan & Honigsfeld, 2006; Honigsfeld & Cohan, 2007). We found that sustained lesson study projects need considerable outside support. These activities are not supported by most schools' current professional-development structures. Time, resources, incentives, and opportunities to share the group's findings are all necessary components.

3. Preparing for and Conducting Joint Parent-Teacher Conferences

When ESL teachers and their general-education colleagues compare ELLs' behavior, attitudes, and overall academic performance in their respective classes, they may observe that the same child acts quite differently in two different settings. Use the blank note-taking template in Table 4.14 to generate a list of observable behaviors in various instructional settings.

Table 4.14	Compare ELLs' Observable Behavior

Observations Notes (Setting 1 _____)	Observations Notes (Setting 2 _____)

When ESL specialists and general-education teachers write progress reports and quarterly, semiannual, or annual report cards based on collaboratively reviewed student work samples, portfolios, and test scores, multiple perspectives are included. Such collaborative effort is beneficial in assessing students' linguistic and academic progress since it leads to providing a clearer picture of areas of strengths and needs for both teachers and families.

4. Planning, Facilitating, or Participating in Other Extracurricular Activities

Jointly preparing and facilitating parent outreach and family involvement programs, as well as other community-based activities, also enhances collaboration. What are some common and uncommon collaborative practices?

1. Parent Teacher Association (PTA) meetings

2. Parent Information or New Family Orientation Night

3. Parent Workshops

4. Family Game Night

5. Cultural Events

6. Collaborative Class, Grade, or School Newsletters

7. Family Field Day

8. Class and School Plays, Concerts, Talent Shows

ADMINISTRATORS' ROLE: CREATING COLLABORATIVE OPPORTUNITIES AND SUPPORTING COLLABORATIVE EFFORTS

Administrators play a critical role in providing the human and material resources necessary for teacher collaboration and co-teaching practices to develop and thrive. We propose that administrators consider the key components of an integrated, collaborative model for ESL service delivery as outlined in the following textbox.

AN INTEGRATED, COLLABORATIVE MODEL FOR ESL SERVICES

What are the components of an integrated, collaborative model to serve ELLs?

1. Interdisciplinary, cross-department (cross-specialization) conversations

   a. To discuss students and their ongoing linguistic and academic development

   b. To consider ELLs' changing curricular needs and appropriate adaptations

   c. To explore extracurricular opportunities for ELLs and to enhance parental involvement

(Continued)

(Continued)

2. Common Planning Opportunities
   a. To align curriculum
   b. To adapt curriculum
   c. To modify instructional materials
   d. To vary instructional strategies

3. Shared Classroom Experiences
   a. Classroom visits to observe each other's best practices
   b. Classroom visits to observe ELLs' participation in various instructional settings
   c. Classroom visits to peer coach (2+2 model)
   d. Co-teaching to deliver instruction collaboratively

4. Individual and Shared Reflection and Inquiry
   a. Based on teachers' experiences with students
   b. Based on teachers' best practices
   c. Based on a shared professional reading of emerging literature on collaboration and ESL strategies

5. Administrative support and feedback
   a. Establishing logistical support for all levels of collaboration
   b. Offering instructional leadership (being knowledgeable about both ESL and collaborative practices)
   c. Creating a professional learning community through the integrated, collaborative model to serve ELLs and improve instruction for all students

WHAT ADMINISTRATORS NEED TO CONSIDER

DuFour (2005) claims that "the powerful collaboration . . . is a systematic process in which teachers work together to analyze and improve their classroom practice. Teachers work in teams, engaging in an ongoing cycle of questions that promote deep team learning. This process, in turn, leads to higher levels of student achievement" (p. 36). In his essay "Masters of Motivation," Saphier (2005) offers a simple yet profound formula to help administrators establish a shared understanding of a critical belief.

If you believe that teacher collaboration is critical to your school's success, then undertake the following actions:

- Say it
  - Talk about it with conviction and passion but without stifling critical questions
- Model it
  - Show its importance by practicing collaboration
- Organize it
  - Create opportunities that value, encourage, and reward collaboration

- Protect it
  - Stand behind teachers who exemplify collaboration despite difficulties by allocating resources
- Reward it
  - Recognize and reward teachers who practice collaboration on a daily basis both privately and publicly

SUMMARY

Woodrow Wilson once said, "I not only use all of the brains I have, but all I can borrow." His acknowledged reliance on others may fit the topic of teacher collaboration as well. We are confident that once they have tried it, many teachers will welcome the opportunity to regularly collaborate or co-teach and to be able to borrow from each other. When teachers collaborate, they share their wisdom about teaching, experience complex situations together, and reveal insights about instructional planning. When teachers successfully share their skills of delivering a lesson, or meet the challenges and enjoy the rewards of helping a new generation of ELLs, their students become integrated into the fabric of the classroom, the school community, and, ultimately, into the larger society of the United States.

DISCUSSION QUESTIONS

1. In *Building Community in Schools,* Sergiovanni (1994) said, "If we are interested in community building, then we, along with other members of the proposed community, are going to have to invent our own practice of community" (p. 5). With your colleagues, validate or refute this statement by exploring the extent to which your school is engaged in inventing its own practice of community for the sake of ELLs.

2. In all collaborative contexts, the distribution and control over power plays an important role. In his book, *The Three Faces of Power,* Kenneth Boulding (1989) argues that change is a difficult process in all institutions. Since schools are no exception, we invite you to consider the three forms of power Boulding suggests that advocates and leaders can use to initiate change:

   a. "Stick power" is the power of threat.
   b. "Carrot power" is the power of incentive.
   c. "Hug power" is the power of shared vision, values, and beliefs.

   Discuss what *stick power, carrot power,* and *hug power* look like in your school and explore ways in which they have impacted the implementation of collaborative practices and co-teaching (if applicable). Have the outcomes been positive or negative?

3. List all the formal and informal, as well as instructional, noninstructional, and collaborative, activities that you engage in during any given day. Consider the effectiveness and importance of each of these activities as they relate to the impact on student learning.

4. Review the seven co-teaching arrangements outlined in this chapter and discuss appropriate teaching scenarios that may be aligned to each model.

KEY ONLINE RESOURCES

Action Research
www.alliance.brown.edu/pubs/themes_ed/act_research.pdf

Annual Professional Performance Review (APPR) Guidelines
www.nysut.org/files/bulletins090225appr.pdf

Curriculum Mapping (Virtual Workshop)
www.educationworld.com/a_curr/virtualwkshp/virtualwkshp004.shtml

Interdisciplinary Learning on Thirteen.org
www.thirteen.org/edonline/concept2class/interdisciplinary/index.html

Internet Projects Registry (for Global Collaborative Projects)
www.globalschoolnet.org/gsh/pr

Making Family and Community Connections
www.thirteen.org/edonline/concept2class/familycommunity/index.html

Professional Learning Communities (Virtual Workshop)
www.educationworld.com/a_curr/virtualwkshp/virtualwkshp005.shtml

Sheltered Instruction
www.siopinstitute.net

5

How Do Teachers Plan, Instruct, and Assess ELLs Collaboratively?

Without leaps of imagination, or dreaming, we lose the excitement of possibilities.
Dreaming, after all, is a form of planning.

Gloria Steinem

OVERVIEW

Carefully coordinated planning, instruction, and assessment are integral parts of a successful collaborative program to teach English language learners. This chapter will outline the necessary organizational techniques for ESL specialists, general-education teachers, and school administrators to implement collaborative practices and, more specifically, co-teaching strategies effectively. We will offer several frameworks for (a) creating collaborative teams, (b) engaging in collaborative planning, and (c) initiating, maintaining, as well as refining co-teaching practices. We offer suggestions on how to assess ELLs cooperatively and also discuss the role technology tools play in teacher collaboration.

Voices From the Field

The late bell rings as students at a small suburban elementary school clamor toward their classrooms. In the hallway, Ms. David, a novice ESL teacher assigned to her first teaching job, weaves through a sea of young students. She reaches Mr. Jay's third-grade classroom door just in time to slip inside behind the last student. Ms. David is eager to discuss her teaching plans with Mr. Jay, her general-education colleague, to

(Continued)

(Continued)

coordinate the third-grade's social-studies curriculum with her ESL lessons for the mutual benefit of their ELL students. While Mr. Jay is busy settling his students down and taking attendance, Ms. David attempts to get his attention. Unfortunately, her natural smile is met with an icy stare from across the room. The classroom teacher, annoyed with her intrusion, curtly tells her that he cannot speak with her now. As she exits the classroom, Ms. David feels somewhat disconcerted and confused. Although she may not have chosen the most opportune time to speak with Mr. Jay, she concludes that this particular classroom teacher is not interested in collaborating with her, and her ELL students will surely suffer the educational consequences.

Vignette Reflection

This chapter's vignette represents how well-meaning teachers can be misguided by their honest enthusiasm to communicate with other faculty members. Ms. David's interest in helping her ELLs coupled with her inexperience with a classroom teacher's morning routine caused her to enter Mr. Jay's classroom unexpectedly. This event resulted in miscommunication and injured feelings. This unfortunate exchange could have been prevented if a framework had been established for ongoing communication and teacher collaboration to take place.

THE NEED FOR COLLABORATIVE EFFORTS

A common complaint among ESL teachers is that they lack time to conduct collaborative activities with other educators in their schools. Very often, teachers substitute genuine collaboration for brief hallway conversations in an attempt to isolate broad content-area topics that may be covered in class during a particular lesson. These conversations frequently take place moments before the lesson occurs. Although short-lived discussions only provide some congruence between general-education and ESL lessons, they do not address the many issues that underlie best practices to help ELLs achieve academic success.

Setting the Collaboration Stage

Teachers often say they collaborate, but the term means different ideas to different educators. Teachers often use the term to refer to the informal discussions regarding school issues they have with friends and colleagues. Serving on committees or grade and subject meetings are other situations that are often a part of faculty members' collaborative activities. It appears that any situation in which teachers are not working in isolation and working in tangent with others might be deemed collaboration.

Friend and Cook (1992) define *collaboration* as "a style of direct interaction between at least two co-equal parties voluntarily engaged in shared decision making as they work toward a common goal" (p. 5). They identify several features that can be used to clarify the meaning of collaboration. Among these features are the sharing of goals, decision making, responsibilities, resources, and accountability of outcomes.

Collaboration for the instruction of ELLs in its many forms encompasses teaching teams sharing their expertise, equipment, materials, skills, strategies, time, and physical classroom space to enhance student learning. Each teacher brings to the planning table a wealth of knowledge about appropriate resources to meet individual student needs. Whether ESL lessons are being co-taught in the general-education classroom or conducted in a separate setting, collaborative planning is essential to meet the unique needs of diverse groups of learners.

Building Collaborative Planning Teams

In order to restructure your school and initiate a co-planning ESL delivery system, the members of the co-planning partnership first must be identified. Will your team consist solely of an ESL teacher and a general-education teacher or will it involve administrators, other faculty specialists, and paraprofessionals? How might the organization of the team affect the students you wish to support?

A common practice is to develop a core team, which generally involves the classroom teacher and the ESL teacher. This partnership provides the backbone for the co-teaching/ collaborative plan. In order to form a core team partnership, we recommend the following strategies:

- Establish regular avenues of communication from the onset in order for the core team to practice ongoing collaborative activities
- Identify leadership roles and individual responsibilities
- Outline decision-making strategies such as which decisions can be made individually and which should be made in consultation with one another
- Review available co-teaching models and make decisions as to whether lessons will be conducted in the same or separate classroom settings

Other faculty members such as literacy or special education specialists may provide additional support to enhance the collaborative efforts of the core planning team depending upon each ELL's individual learning needs. Literacy specialists may be able to offer insight into appropriate reading programs or present ongoing assessment information for individual students. Special education consultants may also provide guidance for instruction regarding learning issues that go beyond second-language learning.

Paraprofessionals such as teacher assistants and classroom aides can be an important part of a co-planning team. These team members often have a working knowledge of individual students' abilities and skills and can provide important insight during the planning process. In addition, bilingual paraprofessionals can be invaluable to the success of some ELLs who need native-language support.

Administrators need to be kept informed and may choose to participate in regular team meetings depending upon their individual leadership styles. Some administrators prefer to be involved in the day-to-day planning by offering feedback on weekly written lesson plans. Others would rather be an integral part of the overall team process (see Figure 5.1).

Figure 5.1 Flexible Co-Planning Team Configuration

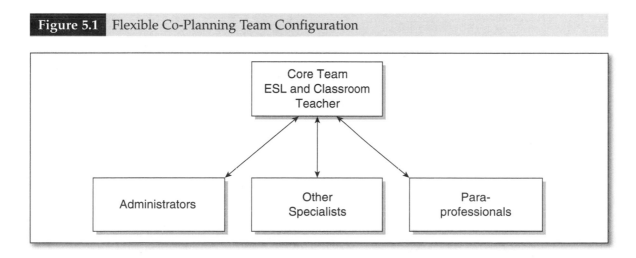

LAUNCHING THE CO-PLANNING TEAM: TOP DOWN OR BOTTOM UP?

An important matter to consider is who is initiating the co-teaching and co-planning strategy. If it is a top-down decision set into motion through an administrative directive, to what extent will administration play a part? In general, administrators may require teachers to use co-planning strategies but may themselves have limited experience implementing and using such strategies. Teachers in turn may be asked to work under the mandates established by the top-down approach without adequate support on how collaborative planning and co-teaching will be accomplished. It is important to consider what strategies are necessary for a collaborative team's success, and administrators can be a powerful resource to provide appropriate support to institute a co-planning team.

An alternative to a top-down directive is a bottom-up approach, which may be prompted by an individual teacher who establishes a cooperative plan with one or more colleagues. ESL teachers, to support their ELLs in learning grade-level curriculum, are the ones who sometimes make the first move toward developing a collaborative or co-taught plan. Teachers taking leadership roles at the grassroots level may face many challenges and should have a detailed plan for successful implementation.

A Grassroots Approach to Collaborative Planning and Co-Teaching

Collaborative planning and co-teaching can enhance the skills and strategies teachers use for instructing ELLs in the general-education classroom. Collaborative planning helps general-education and ESL teachers adapt content and establish language learning objectives. It can be a means for developing necessary supplementary materials that differentiate instruction for ELLs and increase the odds of learning successes. Co-planning also furnishes information regarding students' cultural backgrounds as well as their individual physical and psychological needs. So how might teachers initiate the collaborative planning process to accomplish these ends?

As teachers start rethinking collaboration, we often recommend the following easy-to-follow start-up steps:

- Start small while considering the *BIG* picture
- Begin with a simple dialogue among teachers
- Choose *one* teacher with whom to collaborate
- Think creatively!

While most teachers welcome these recommendations, they point out that they need more specific guidelines (see Figure 5.2).

Figure 5.2 Collaborative Planning: What to Do and How to Do It

Collaborative Planning	
What to Do	**How to Do It**
Start small while considering the *BIG* picture	• Identify one or two major goals and objectives • Have realistic expectations for yourself and your colleagues • Share a favorite lesson plan or a sure-fire activity • Share a very effective resource only you have access to • Offer to co-teach part of a lesson

What to Do	How to Do It
Begin with a simple dialogue among teachers	• Take an informal step toward discussing ELLs' needs • Follow up with some great resources • Invite colleagues to see ELLs in your classroom
Choose one teacher with whom you could collaborate and co-teach	• Make friends—there are lots of potential friends in the teachers' lounge • Get to know colleagues who seem to have teaching philosophies similar to yours • Decide who is most likely to work with you
Think creatively	• Look for "found time" for planning • Explore electronic means of communication

COLLABORATIVE TEAMS IN ACTION

Examining Student Data

The first step toward a successful collaborative ESL program is to consider ELLs' individual needs by reviewing available student assessment data to establish goals and objectives for each student. Mandated state assessment scores often do not provide adequate information to guide general-education teachers or ESL teachers. Faculty members involved in co-planning efforts need to establish goals according to other available data or criteria. These may include local school district assessments, class assessments, observations, and other formal and informal assessments to determine individual student needs.

Identifying Educational Objectives

Once individual needs have been established, decisions must be made as to the source from which lesson objectives are developed for ELLs. Will objectives be based on the specific academic subject matter or on broader objectives such as those stated in the state standards? In addition, how will language learning objectives be addressed? A template in Figure 5.3 helps teachers co-plan: The general-education teacher primarily provides the content objectives, and the ESL teacher supports the lesson through language objectives.

General-education teachers, and all experts in grade-level content area, are able to guide ESL teachers to adapt content for their ELL students by distinguishing salient facts and material the students are expected to learn (Crandall, 1987; Echevarria et al., 2008; Freeman, Freeman, & Mecuri, 2003). Lesson objectives may encompass both specific academic features or incorporate basic target vocabulary and concepts depending upon the language proficiency of the individual student. In contrast to identifying specific academic objectives, co-planning teams may identify broader concepts to be addressed and choose different academic subject matter to meet students' needs. For example, a math lesson focusing on converting improper fractions to mixed numbers may pose challenges for ELLs on multiple levels. In addition to the math concepts needed for the lesson, ELLs will have to understand the math-specific vocabulary use (*improper* and *mixed*) as these terms differ in meaning from their everyday usage. Figure 5.4 illustrates how content and language objects can be designated using each teacher's expertise.

Thus, ESL teachers share information about ELL students' language proficiency and guide classroom teachers to set appropriate expectations for ELL students' in-class activities. ESL teachers need to set specific language learning goals for their students and

Figure 5.3 | Co-Planning Form for Classroom and ESL Instruction

ESL Teacher: _____ Classroom Teacher: _____ Grade: _____

For the Week of: _____

Weekly Overview
What is the focus for the week? What content-area topics will we address?

	Content-Area Objectives Language Objectives What are we going to teach?	Teacher/Student Activities What will each teacher do? What will students do?	Resources/Materials What materials do we need?
Monday			
Tuesday			
Wednesday			
Thursday			
Friday			

	Figure 5.4 Sample Matched Content and Language Objectives	

	Content Objectives	**Language Objectives**
ELA	Students will define and explain the concept of cultural diversity through a read-aloud of the book *People* by Peter Spier and a class comparison activity of similarities and differences.	Students will read for detail, take notes, and create a graphic organizer by discussing personal similarities and differences in groups of four. Each group will then share what they have found to create a class comparison chart depicting the diversity within the class.
Social Studies	Students will explore how the world is made up of major geographical and cultural differences, with a focus on the geography, climate, and culture of each student's native country or region through the creation of posters and culture boxes.	Students will write about their native country's geography, climate, and culture on a poster board. Students will also create a culture box, which contains five items paired with a tiered activity. Depending upon proficiency level, the student should (a) only label the items, (b) write one descriptive sentence for each item, or (c) write a descriptive paragraph for each item. Students will present their board and box to small groups. Students will complete outcome sentences as a culminating activity.
Mathematics	Students will estimate, measure, and record specific body parts in nonstandard units of measure, such as the length of their foot using paper clips.	Students will discuss and create written notations for their estimates of nonstandard units of measurement on a worksheet and whiteboard to later compare and contrast the lengths of their own body parts and other common objects.
Science	After observing and participating in a hands-on sensory activity, the students will identify and differentiate the five senses.	Students will discuss in groups the experience of the workstations while completing a worksheet consisting of observations and recordings. Students will also complete a KWL chart that records what the students *know,* what they *want* to know, and what they *learned.*
ELA/Technology	Students will master the proper format of letter writing and apply it to the task of writing friendly letters to e-pals who are pen pals via the Internet. Students will also use the computers to type, spell check, and prepare their letters in proper form.	Students will label the parts of a letter with the correct terminology. Students will write their first letter to their e-pal and then maintain open communication via the Internet throughout the school year.

Collaboratively developed by Lucia Posillico and Andrea Honigsfeld.

encourage general-education teachers to incorporate language learning into their daily lessons for ELLs as well. This may be accomplished by preteaching the necessary vocabulary in small-group instructional settings, in which the two teachers work with children on the specific skills necessary for (a) basic comprehension, (b) on-grade-level understanding, or (c) above-grade-level enrichment activities.

Sharing Cultural Information

ESL teachers furnish information regarding students' cultural background, which can provide insight into problems or difficulties a student is having in the general-education classroom. Students from other countries have different expectations and concerns as far as what a school environment should be and how teachers and students should act. They often struggle to adapt their own behaviors and adjust their expectations. These youngsters may be reluctant or unable to ask their teachers questions.

Family constellations, religious identities, socioeconomic status, and race or ethnicity can play major roles in how students are accepted and treated by others in school. Certain cultural groups might be devalued or accorded a lower status in the greater community (Marshall, 2002). ESL teachers can provide insight to both teachers and students to understand the unique features of different cultural backgrounds and how to best work with these youngsters and their families.

Understanding Students' Social and Emotional Well-Being

In addition to teachers conveying ideas and resources on academic subject matter for ELLs, sharing information regarding ELL students' social and emotional needs is vital to understanding their particular learning challenges. Many newcomers experience culture shock and need time to adjust to a new culture, the norms and expectations of the society, and, more specifically, the norms and expectations of the school itself. Many youngsters living in the United States are separated from their parents and siblings. They may suffer from a number of maladies and negative repercussions including post-traumatic stress syndrome, separation anxiety, and physical illness. Though creating a sensitive, nurturing, and culturally responsive learning environment is the responsibility of all teachers, ESL professionals are more extensively prepared in cross-cultural awareness and more knowledgeable about the twenty-first-century immigrant experience. With these considerations in mind, ESL teachers can guide general-education teachers on what expectations they should hold for their newcomer students with respect to their class participation, homework completion, and attendance.

Table 5.1 summarizes some key tips we have to offer as you embark on collaborative endeavors.

Table 5.1 What to Do and What Not to Do When You Collaborate

DO	DON'T
Focus on all aspects of ELLs' development: academic, linguistic, social, cultural, and emotional	Blame or scapegoat anyone, especially the parents
Document both the process and outcome of collaborative activities	Think you need to do it all on your own
Request administrative support; find and create time to collaborate	Be dissuaded by lack of time
Share information, resources, and ideas	Withhold information or resources
Ask questions, listen carefully, and offer your input	Put yourself or anyone down—ever!—or say "It's a stupid question . . ."
Expect conflicts and resolve them professionally	Allow collaborative practices to dissolve due to different points of view

A FRAMEWORK FOR EFFECTIVE COLLABORATIVE INSTRUCTION

Setting a framework to organize what and when content material will be taught is a tremendous asset for collaborative teams to have as an overall resource. This strategy can assist ESL teachers in assuring lessons are congruent with classroom instruction and can relieve classroom teachers of the anxiety of releasing their ELLs for ESL instruction. In co-teaching arrangements, ESL and general-education teachers need to share common guides to content-area curricula, scope and sequences, and core texts that are vital to the planning of collaborative instruction.

Before the School Year Begins

Inviting collaborative teachers to meet over the summer months allows you to plan for the coming year, both formally and informally. Formal planning includes the use of *curriculum maps,* which may be arranged monthly, yearly, or by marking period. Once you and your collaborating teachers establish content-area goals and standards-based skills and concepts, formative and summative assessments should be identified along with major and supplementary resources for instruction. Informal planning can also play an important role at the beginning of the school year. It might include a simple invitation to visit each other's classrooms to browse available resources. You will be surprised by the hidden treasures you will find down the hall!

During the School Year

Establishing routines and responsibilities is most effective early in the year. Planning sheets such as the one in Figure 5.3 can aid in this process. When ongoing communication and co-planning seems to be an insurmountable challenge, experiment with electronic methods of communication to inform each other about lesson ideas and student needs. Once you are comfortable, go beyond the routine and try jointly planning brief activities and then full lessons with teachers not involved in your regular collaborative planning team.

At the End of the School Year

We recommend that you pilot your collaborative activities for one entire school year. At the closure of the pilot year, and each year thereafter, set aside time to evaluate all your collaborative efforts. This can be accomplished periodically by sharing reflective journals that each team member personally keeps. In addition, plan on showcasing your success stories to your administrators, fellow faculty, parents, and school board members. Find the time to spend with your collaborative partners to reflect on the challenges of the coming school year.

TECHNOLOGY AND COLLABORATION

Technology can play an important role in establishing ongoing collaboration among educators who, for whatever reason, are unable or for whom it is difficult to meet face-to-face. Telecommunication can alter the way in which teachers participate in shared decision making with their colleagues regarding lesson planning, curriculum selection, and instructional strategies. Teachers may no longer be thwarted from conversing with their colleagues due to inadequately scheduled time throughout the regular school day. Electronic media can provide an avenue for educators to correspond with others in the same school and even explore how teachers provide instruction in other areas of the world. Blogs, wikis, online communities, and social networks have redefined communication and interaction in the twenty-first century (Langer de Ramirez, 2009). The Internet is one of the most important innovations of our time, bringing substantial benefits to economies and societies, but also driving change in the way we live and work. As the Internet is not confined to national borders, these changes need to be managed at European and global levels. What are the choices teachers have to communicate with each other more effectively?

E-Mail

E-mail is a simple form of Internet use. Since many teachers have made the leap to planning their weekly lessons by computer, they may simply share lesson plans via e-mail or propose activities and ideas to each other—even from their portable or handheld devices. If necessary, teachers may identify and set parameters for certain times during the week in which e-mail can be sent, received, responded to, and so on. Conversely, they can use this form of communication in the most informal, ongoing fashion.

Blogs

Blogs, short for *Weblogs,* can take many forms, including personal online journals as well as platforms for the greater world community to post opinions and share commentary via the Web. Teachers use blogs to exchange ideas regarding a variety of educational matters, to share their personal knowledge, to assist in instructional problem solving, and to network with educators regardless of geographic location. Blogging is particularly useful for those ESL teachers who feel isolated in their school or district and would benefit from the support of other ESL teachers.

Wikis

One of the best-known online encyclopedias, Wikipedia, defines a *wiki* as an accumulation of information on the Web designed to allow anyone to contribute or modify its content. Invented by Ward Cunningham in 1995, a wiki is a collection of Web pages in which its members often are encouraged to add or modify information. Wikis may be used to construct collaborative Web sites and frequently are implemented in businesses that use similar features on their networks for company employees to communicate and collaborate. In education, teachers can use wikis to collaboratively work on curriculum content or lesson planning instead of e-mailing and attaching documents back and forth. A wiki can serve as a collective of grade-level or subject-level materials and provide necessary curriculum maps and information for all teachers to use in their planning for ELLs. There are ready-to-use, easy-to-implement wikis available for teachers who might hesitate to use new technology.

Vignette Revisited

Before the commencement of a recent faculty meeting, Ms. David noticed Mr. Jay using smartphone technology to send a text message to someone. She gathered up the courage to approach Mr. Jay and complimented his choice of phone. To her amazement, a broad smile appeared across Mr. Jay's face. He began to relay to Ms. David all the interesting features that he regularly uses on his phone. After the meeting, Ms. David asked Mr. Jay if he would mind if they communicated by text message in order to coordinate instruction for their mutual ELLs. Mr. Jay thought it was a great idea, and together they set a weekly time to text one another.

CO-TEACHING FOR POWERFUL INSTRUCTION

Co-teaching is a dynamic component of teacher collaboration that employs its own special set of teaching competencies. Its major goal is to merge ESL and general-education instruction to increase the time ELLs are exposed to general-education curriculum and thereby strengthen their overall academic achievement. Co-teaching often requires a restructuring of the school environment, a shift in ways to not only collaborate with other teachers but also to emphasize learning for all students; establish high standards for ELLs; share responsibility for planning, instruction, and assessment; and take on new roles within the classroom.

Roles and Responsibilities

In practice, some co-teaching partners may appreciate the naming of individual tasks and the delineation of responsibilities each teacher will have in order to create successful classroom experiences for all students involved. The roles may be perceived as flexible and interchangeable to ensure parity and coordinated support for ELLs. Some of these teacher functions can be identified as follows:

- The *leader* keeps the lesson's pace, allows enough time for task transitions, and makes suggestions about how to reorganize lessons due to time constraints.
- The *supporter* considers directions from the leader, follows the leader's cues, and supports spontaneous lesson changes.
- The *techie* takes charge of technology and prepares and sets up presentations from online, video, DVD, or teacher-made resources.
- The *scribe* writes spoken information, provides bulleted lists on chart paper, and copies directions on the board.
- The *illustrator* identifies information for students through simple board sketches, graphic organizers, or downloaded photographs off the Internet.
- The *evaluator* uses a co-teaching journal to jot down a lesson's strengths and challenges for future discussion in collaborative team sessions.

Some of these identified roles are decided according to the co-teaching team's chosen model of instruction (see Chapter 4) for particular lessons. By determining each team member's tasks for each lesson, teachers can prepare instruction more effectively and be better able to obtain the materials necessary to meet their students' needs. When lessons are carefully orchestrated and teaching roles clearly established, what would otherwise be awkward or confusing instruction can be executed seamlessly. In this way, classroom activities are more likely to be of maximum benefit to ELLs.

Co-Teaching Competencies

Each person on the co-teaching team must have a thorough understanding of the selected co-teaching model. As previously discussed in Chapter 4, some teaching teams prefer to use one model consistently while others enjoy the flexibility of using different co-teaching models at different times or on different days. In addition, not all collaborative planning results in the use of co-teaching. Regular co-planning sessions establish important curriculum continuity even when teachers deliver instruction in separate class settings.

Although there may be little time for ESL and general-education teachers to meet face-to-face, the need to collaborate is too important an issue to be hindered by inadequately scheduled planning time. Innovative planning methods need to be devised to ensure collaborative objectives are met.

ESL Co-Teaching 101: A Quick-Start Guide

From our discussions with ESL and general-education teachers, we often are asked how to get started with co-teaching. We offer the following guidelines to jump-start your program.

First Steps

1. Start by doing what you know best! Think of your favorite, most successful lessons, activities, and tasks that always worked in a one-teacher classroom. Be ready to try those out in a co-taught setting.

2. Make sure that common grade-appropriate, content-based objectives are identified for each lesson. Your ELLs will learn the same content material in an adapted format.

3. Start the lesson together standing in front of the class. In this way, you establish parity—you will have equal roles in the eyes of all students.

   The following are lesson starters that can be used based on your lesson objectives:

   a. Use a graphic organizer, advance organizer, or some visual aid to offer an overview or introduce a concept.
   b. Role-play for your students (frequently taking advantage of the fact that two adult English language models are available).
   c. Read aloud (Teacher 1) and think aloud (Teacher 2), commenting on what Teacher 1 just read.
   d. One teacher introduces information; the other teacher clarifies, illustrates, writes key words on the board, shows related pictures, *realia* (real-life object), and/or asks questions of key points.
   e. Teach a rhyme, use poetry or finger plays, sing a song or play music, or involve everyone in a game.
   f. Take turns talking (learn to take signals from each other).

4. Consider student grouping configurations for the next section of your lesson.
   a. Split the class into two, approximately even homogenous groups.
      i. Group A: current ELLs, former ELLs, and other learners who need extra support, scaffolding, preteaching, reteaching, etc.
      ii. Group B: more proficient native speakers

- Each teacher stays with his or her group for a set period of time working in a parallel teaching mode using differentiated instructional techniques.
- The ESL group focuses on language and content that is needed to reach general-education goals.

b. Split the class into three, approximately even homogenous groups.
   i. Group A: ELLs
   ii. Group B: learners who need extra support
   iii. Group C: highest-performing group working on advanced tasks independently
      - Teacher 1 takes Group A, Teacher 2 takes Group B, and Group C works independently for a set period of time. Each teacher stays with his or her group for a set period of time working in a parallel teaching mode using differentiated instructional techniques.

c. Feel free to experiment with other models of instruction, such as setting up and monitoring four to five learning centers.

5. In the last section of the lesson, bring the entire class together for debriefing.
   a. Groups take turns sharing ideas and products, outcomes of learning, answers to worksheets, results of problems solved, etc.
   b. Teachers take turns asking review questions.
   c. Teachers play a closure game (an example is Wonder Ball, where you toss a koosh ball to students and have them finish sentence starters such as *I wonder, Today I learned, I liked,* etc.).
   d. Teachers use some type of exit activity together. (Students respond to one of several possible summary questions on "exit cards," or "tickets to leave," slips of paper, or index cards. The ESL teacher or general-education teacher collects the "tickets" and uses them for assessment purposes.)

6. Remember to reflect daily (jointly or individually) on the co-teaching experience. Keep a simple "2+2" log: jot down two things that worked and two things that could be done differently next time.

Date	Two Things That Worked	Two Things to Work On

Other Tips

1. Look for opportunities to create your unique set of co-teaching routines or rituals early on. Your students will notice and be able to anticipate the sequence of activities.

2. Bring your own talent forward. If you are a singer, introduce the topic through songs (www.songsforteaching.com). If you are artistic, illustrate key concepts for your students as the other teacher explains them.

3. Don't be afraid to think creatively and try new ideas.

4. Visit inclusive classrooms where colleagues have been co-teaching for many years.
   a. Ask them for their favorite techniques to collaborate.
   b. Visit them to watch a lesson they co-teach.

5. Be spontaneous; co-teaching does not have to be scripted.

6. Respect each other's comfort zones but encourage each other to be adventurous.

7. Show your enthusiasm for being with the whole class together and for working with each other. Students always pick up on nonverbal signals.

8. Enjoy the experience.

How to Manage a Co-Teaching Situation

Conderman et al. (2009), Dieker and Murawski (2003), Fattig and Taylor (2007), and many others offer effective strategies for purposeful co-teaching in the inclusive classroom setting. As previously stated, ELLs have very different needs than students with special needs. Expanding on Conderman et al.'s (p. 31) approach, we created a summary chart to represent the ESL perspective (see Table 5.2). What could each teacher do as he or she engages in the various stages of a co-taught lesson?

Table 5.2 Teacher Activities During the ESL Co-Teaching Process

When the Classroom Teacher Is Doing This . . .	The ESL Teacher Is Doing This . . .	Benefits of Collaboration
Taking attendance	Collecting or reviewing homework or introducing or reviewing a social or study skill	Instruction time is increased. Skills-based instruction is integrated into lessons.
Distributing papers or other resources	Reviewing directions or rules or modeling the first problem in the assignment	Instruction time is increased. Examples promote student understanding.
Presenting information through lecture or media (PowerPoint, video, or audio clip)	Modeling note taking on the board or overhead or filling in a graphic organizer	Content is accessible for all students. Strong connections are made between new and previously learned content. Student understanding is facilitated.
Giving instructions orally	Writing down instructions on the board or overhead or repeating or clarifying any difficult concept	Content is accessible for all students.
Checking for understanding with large heterogeneous groups of students	Checking for understanding with small, homogeneous groups	Reteaching can occur without delay.

When the Classroom Teacher Is Doing This . . .	The ESL Teacher Is Doing This . . .	Benefits of Collaboration
Circulating; providing one-on-one support as needed	Providing direct instruction to ELLs one to one or in small groups	Learning is not merely incidental.
Prepping half the class for one side of a debate	Prepping ELLs for the opposing side of the debate	Instruction time and student engagement are increased.
Facilitating independent, silent work	Circulating and checking for comprehension	Reteaching can occur without delay.
Providing large-group instruction	Circulating, clarifying key concepts or cultural information	Culturally challenging information is made understandable.
Monitoring the large group as students work on practice material	Preteaching or reteaching challenging concepts to a small group of ELLs	Student language learning is enhanced.
Facilitating sustained silent reading	Reading aloud quietly with a small group or previewing upcoming information	Students are exposed to or internalize language structures they will need to apply to independent reading.
Creating basic lesson plans for standards, objectives, and content curriculum	Providing suggestions for language objectives, scaffolding activities, adapting instructional materials	Student needs are met through differentiated instruction. Lessons are created to meet the needs of student subgroups.
Facilitating stations or groups	Facilitating other stations or groups	Instructional materials can be tailored to the needs of ELLs.
Explaining a new concept	Conducting a role play, modeling a concept, or asking clarifying questions	Students' interest and motivation are increased. ELLs are engaged in varied activities.
Considering enrichment opportunities	Considering reinforcement opportunities	Everyone works toward essential understanding and skills. More options are available to meet student needs.

Adapted from Conderman, G., Bresnahan, V., & Pedersen, T. (2009). *Purposeful co-teaching: Real cases and effective strategies.* Thousand Oaks, CA: Corwin. (p. 31)

How to Achieve Co-Teaching Success

Co-teaching can be accomplished through a variety of approaches and contexts. ELLs can be well served when co-teachers acquire effective skills and generate lessons through collaboration. Here are some strategies for initiating your co-teaching programs.

1. Initiate a pilot program; secure administrative and peer support for piloting co-teaching in one class.

2. Engage in informal and formal explorations of co-teaching with colleagues who might be potential co-teachers.

3. Request formal training in co-teaching practices from your administrators.

4. Following initial training, secure ongoing support in the form of mentoring, coaching, or establishing a collegial circle.

5. With your co-teaching partner, agree upon a feasible model and experiment with its practicability. For example, choosing a model of instruction in which one teacher leads and the other assists, or *teaches on purpose*, may prove to be an effective approach to exploring co-teaching.

   a. When one teacher leads and the other assists students during a lesson, it requires less planning time and coordination between the teachers involved.

   b. As trust and mutual respect for each teacher's ability builds, this model can be executed simply with rewarding results for both students and teachers. It is most successful when both the ESL teacher and the classroom teacher share the responsibility of taking the lead role. In this way, both teachers' individual talents can be used to benefit the students.

6. Establish routines and clearly defined expectations. Always talk about differences, work to prevent potential problems before they arise, and resolve conflicts professionally and in a timely fashion.

7. Once you have an established co-teaching relationship, experiment with an eclectic model of instruction. This works best when the ESL and general-education teacher have an established rapport with one another and their teaching styles are able to accommodate much flexibility.

   a. Teachers who have similar instructional and disciplinary styles are likely to select certain co-teaching arrangements.

   b. On the other hand, teachers who have differing styles—perhaps complementary styles—will use co-teaching arrangements that allow for each teacher's individual strengths to receive a more pronounced focus.

8. Document and share your successes.

COLLABORATIVE STUDENT ASSESSMENT

Stiggins and DuFour (2009) suggest engaging in collaborative assessment practices to maximize the power of formative assessments:

> In professional learning communities, collaborative teams of teachers create common assessments for three formative purposes. First, team-developed common assessments help identify curricular areas that need attention because many students are struggling. Second, they help each team member clarify strengths and weaknesses in his or her teaching and create a forum for teachers to learn from one another. Third, interim common assessments identify students who aren't mastering the intended standards and need timely and systematic interventions. (p. 641)

Collaborative assessment for ELLs' linguistic, academic, and social development incorporates the use of a variety of data to determine student progress. Collaborative partners and co-teachers use ongoing, informal classroom assessment techniques, adapted formal assessment tools, and teacher-created, differentiated standardized-test preparation materials. Consider the following recommendations for student assessment:

- Use multiple, varied assessment measures to show student competence of a skill or content knowledge or language and literacy development
- Develop a portfolio assessment system that allows including student work samples from a variety of content areas
- Scaffold assessment tasks by incorporating visuals, graphic organizers, reduced linguistic content, and simplified directions
- Permit students to use dictionaries, glossaries, and, if feasible, teacher and student notes and other resources
- Schedule extra time for students to complete assessment tasks
- Plan opportunities for individual student conferences and small-group assessment techniques
- Keep teacher observation notes and periodically compare them with your colleagues
- Offer students opportunities to reflect on and evaluate their own content-based and linguistic performance and progress
- Develop tools such as checklists, rubrics, and rating scales for teachers to gather ongoing student assessment data and for students to self-assess

ADMINISTRATORS' ROLE: EFFECTIVE MANAGEMENT OF RESOURCES

Although program administrators in charge of services for English language learners often understand the benefits of teacher collaboration and advocate its use, they are unable to schedule adequate time for general-education teachers and ESL specialists to meet and plan activities on a regular basis. However, for successful implementation of educators' collaborative efforts, the following recommendations should be considered:

- Establish common planning time
- Use staff development days to evaluate progress and establish long-term goals
- Hire substitute teachers to provide release time for teachers to collaborate during the school day
- Allow teachers time to plan during faculty meetings
- Schedule meetings for collaborative partners during special student programming (e.g., assemblies)

SUMMARY

A combined team effort is necessary for effective co-planning of instruction for English language learners. A core pair of educators, such as the ESL teacher and the classroom teacher or content-area specialist, act as a base for the co-planning team, which also may include administrators, paraprofessionals, and other teacher specialists. A commitment to using a variety of planning, instruction, and assessment strategies will yield the most effective instruction to meet the academic needs of ELLs. Teachers have no choice but to explore new options in order to find the time to plan cooperatively if they are to co-teach or co-plan with colleagues successfully. Administrators can support co-teaching and collaborative teams by providing the time, money, and staff development activities that ensure program success.

DISCUSSION QUESTIONS

1. In your current teaching situation, what personal and institutional roadblocks prevent teacher collaboration, co-planning, or co-teaching from taking place (effectively)? What recommendation do you have to remove those roadblocks?

2. How does a school commitment to equitable education for English language learners affect teacher collaboration, co-planning, or co-teaching efforts?

3. How do standards and standardized assessments affect the type of collaboration that teachers engage in?

4. How does teacher collaboration or co-teaching benefit general-education students and ELLs in terms of (a) linguistic and literacy skills, (b) interpersonal and cross-cultural development, and (c) overall academic achievement?

KEY ONLINE RESOURCES

Blogs in Plain English
    www.teachertube.com

Creating a Wiki
    http://pbworks.com
    www.wiki.com/startyourown.htm

Education Alliance at Brown University
    www.alliance.brown.edu

Electronic Forum
    www.teachade.com

ESL Science
    www.larryferlazzo.com/eslscience.html

Jill Mora
    http://moramodules.com

Jim Cummins
    www.iteachilearn.com/cummins

Learn the Language
    http://blogs.edweek.org/edweek/learning-the-language

SIOP Model
    www.siopinstitute.net

6

When Do Teachers and ESL Specialists Collaborate and Co-Teach?

A single conversation across the table with a wise person is worth a month's study of books.

Chinese Proverb

OVERVIEW

The benefits of collaborative practices are well established, yet impediments to consistent and meaningful professional conversations and other collaborative opportunities regarding instruction for ELLs persist. Lack of time is often cited as a major factor, which prevents teachers from exchanging ideas, jointly planning lessons, evaluating individual student progress on a regular basis, and discussing appropriate interventions. This chapter will identify time frames in which collaboration among teachers can take place successfully. We will examine favorable occasions already built into current schedules as well as offer sample templates to consider and schedules for a range of collaborative practices including co-teaching. We will conclude with suggestions on how to ensure adequate time for collaboration and co-teaching.

Voices From the Field

On a Wednesday afternoon, the clock in the main lobby of De Salle Middle School strikes three as the dismissal bell simultaneously rings. Swarms of young teenage students file out the lobby doors and climb onto school buses for their short journey home. In the midst of the clamor, Mr. Timothy, a veteran ESL teacher, makes his way toward the school library where he will join his colleagues for their usual Wednesday afternoon grade-level meetings.

Mr. Timothy finds the table where his fellow ESL colleagues are seated and sits down just in time to hear his new principal outline what needs to be accomplished at this afternoon's meeting. The principal directs grade-level teams to set their own agendas, record their meeting's minutes, and submit their minutes directly to her by week's end. After she assigns subject specialists to grade-level teams, the principal wishes everyone a good afternoon and makes a hasty retreat.

Groups of teachers file out of the library and settle into separate meeting spaces throughout the building. Mr. Timothy joins a sixth-grade interdisciplinary team that has entered a small classroom across the hallway. Immediately, the English language arts teacher takes charge and suggests topics that should be covered. Several people nod their heads in agreement, and the discussion begins.

The group exchanges ideas about standardized-test preparation, parent-teacher conference schedules, and report card comments. When report cards are discussed, Mr. Timothy takes the opportunity to speak up about the lack of grading policies the school has for ELLs. His concerns stem from the inconsistent manner in which ELLs are assessed and their progress is reported to parents. It seems as if some students are graded with their current language-proficient abilities in mind while other ELLs' progress is reported using the same criteria as the general-education students in their classes.

As Mr. Timothy begins to outline some of his ideas for improvements in the grading system, the science teacher quickly interrupts him. She notes that grading policies are beyond the scope of their meeting. Although she and others on the team sympathize with Mr. Timothy's concerns, the science teacher refocuses the discussion on the next agenda item.

Vignette Reflection

As our vignette illustrates, in order to accomplish effective communication among its members and make the most of available time, collaborative teams need to establish goals, a clear purpose, and guidelines for their operation. Agendas need to be set with all members in mind and conversation protocols developed so that member focus remains on the issues. These groups also need administrative support to schedule the necessary time to accomplish their objectives in order to produce the intended outcomes.

TIME AND STRUCTURE FOR TEAMWORK

The setting of interdisciplinary teams for the purpose of collaboration is a worthwhile goal for schools and districts to pursue. These cross-subject collaborators generally consist of teams who teach the major content areas of the school curriculum or are a combination of grade-level teachers and subject specialists (ESL, literacy, technology, etc.). Teachers working in these groups share essential information about their teaching craft along with skill and content objectives that can be carried across the curriculum to enhance the continuity of instruction. In this way, ELLs can be exposed to a wide range of educational experiences all aimed at the same objectives.

Members of any collaborative team need to develop cooperation and a shared interest in the group's collective purpose. Participants, be they core-subject, general-education classroom, or special-subject teachers, should be on an equal footing when it comes to agenda setting and group discussions. When given the opportunity to meet, administrators and collaborative teams must pay careful attention to how meetings are structured in order to make the best use of allotted time and to ensure that all members have an equal say in sharing their concerns, ideas, feelings, and personal beliefs.

Creating Teams for Collaboration

In our opening vignette, Mr. Timothy and his fellow subject specialists did not have the same status as the other members of the interdisciplinary team. Core members of each team had already been established and were permanent members of a collaborative group, whereas subject specialists were *just visiting* respective teacher groups.

It is a common occurrence for special-subject teachers not to be included as permanent members of interdisciplinary teams. Administrators view this practice advantageously; it allows various teams the time and opportunity to have the counsel of different specialists that rotate in and out of different team meetings throughout the school year. Besides, the number of ESL teachers per school is often small, which creates challenges for administrators when assigning them to permanent interdisciplinary teams. A critical recommendation we have is to make sure ESL specialists are accepted and valued as contributing members of all school-based teams and professional groups and, as such, are fully included in collaboration at an established time and place. Several issues arise from the practice of assigning nonpermanent members to teams. First and foremost, it does not allow teacher specialists to bond with other members of the team. According to Levi (2007), participants in any collaborative effort need to develop some level of personal relationship with each other in order for good communication and trust to occur. When social relationships are lacking between group members, communication can break down. Rotating between teams does not allow specialists to form strong relationships or afford the opportunity to develop trust. In turn, communication is negatively impacted and specialists' ideas and concerns minimized.

When special-subject teachers float between teams, they are perceived as guest participants and not as full members of the team. Teacher specialists may be marginalized in these collaborative meetings. The regular group members may use teacher specialists as a resource for information when they need clarification about a discussion issue, yet they do not expect them to fully participate as other members of the group do.

Another problem that arises from this scheme is that rotating team members may be underused. The valuable expertise of ESL teachers and other specialists regarding youngsters with exceptional needs may not be not given a voice during team meetings, which leaves classroom teachers, already challenged with the education of these pupils, without needed support. Additionally, when the knowledge of specialists is not shared, teachers restrict the scope of their collaborative meetings and reap fewer benefits from their teams. It is important to establish equal status among all participants and to give their ideas and opinions equal weight.

SETTING A PURPOSE FOR COLLABORATION

Before administrators can plan sufficient time for teachers to meet, the purpose of collaboration must be identified and carefully discussed. Most often, teachers cite the need to exchange their views on the *nuts and bolts* of lesson planning and student instruction with each other, as well as day-to-day organization and classroom management they commonly share. However, collaborative topics are much broader than classroom practices. They encompass a whole host of educational objectives that can be used as building blocks to transform a school culture. Before setting time frames for collaborative work, the rationale for collaboration must be identified. Once the purpose is set, a time frame for collaborative activities can be established.

Finite Collaboration

Certain collaborative activities easily lend themselves to having a set beginning and end. These types of collaborative practices are for the purpose of establishing a basis for an overall shared mission or vision for ELLs, to develop a common understanding of general information about English learners, or to decide the future goals for particular content curriculum, grade levels, program models, or school resources. These collaborative activities may involve the whole faculty as well as the support staff so that everyone can have a common perception of instructional data regarding the education of ELLs.

Finite collaborative practices may include broad topics such as the following:

- Brainstorming ideas to facilitate ESL and general-education teacher collaboration
- Curriculum mapping to align ESL and content-area instruction
- Defining the collective purpose for the education of ELLs
- Designing a plan for staff development
- Examining beliefs and assumptions about the abilities of ELLs
- Identifying state and local standards for ESL instruction
- Providing professional-development activities that promote a better understanding of a specific subpopulation of ELLs

Finite collaborative activities also may include small-scale ideas such as the following:

- Classroom seating to assist English learners' comprehension
- Customs and observances of different cultures to be included in the curriculum or to bring relevance to classroom instruction
- Identification of students' language proficiency levels
- Interpretation of student assessment data
- Reviewing, locating, or developing online resources for ELLs to learn specific skills
- Developing or enhancing instructional strategies for teaching beginning-level ELLs

Small-scale information usually is shared during teacher preparation periods, lunchtime meetings, or brief hallway conferences. In contrast, broad-based finite collaboration often is accomplished during general faculty meetings or days specifically scheduled for staff development. An outside expert may even be invited to conduct a series of workshops for a large-scale or select group of faculty to outline and clarify collaborative practices. Targeted professional development for specific purposes can be the stimulus for meaningful change in teaching and learning if the right approach is taken.

AN EXAMPLE OF FINITE COLLABORATION

Collaborative Task: ESL Program Revision in a K–12 District

Who is involved?
An eclectic team consisting of building and central-office administrators, elementary classroom and special-subject (art, music, etc.) teachers, ESL specialists, middle and high school content-area teachers, special education professionals, social workers, and outside consultants will participate and contribute ideas regarding programs for ELLs.

What are the team's short-term goals?
The team will strive to understand the challenges of ELLs in the general-education classroom, identify the district's current programs for ELLs, review assessment and other pertinent data to outline the strengths and limitations of the district's programs, and identify programs and broad-based strategies to help meet the needs of the ELL population. The following are the team's guiding questions:

- What beliefs govern the way programs are devised for ELLs?
- What factors affect the academic progress of ELLs?
- How can the district improve its policies and programs for ELLs?

What are the desired outcomes?
Through collaborative efforts, the team will decide on three long-term goals for the coming school year, determine how each goal will be evaluated, and identify any necessary professional development or resources to accomplish established goals.

When and where do meetings take place?
Meetings are scheduled when school is not in session. Approximately 20 hours of commitment is necessary to accomplish the task. Participants are remunerated for their time.

Ongoing Collaboration

The characteristics of ongoing collaboration require continuous and planned opportunities for teachers and administrators to engage in meaningful dialogue about instruction and student learning. The need for this type of consistent practice is embedded in the nature of the perceived or desired outcomes. Whether teachers are engaged in co-teaching ELLs, in-class coaching, mentoring new teachers, reciprocal classroom observations, or specific teacher study groups to increase understanding of ELLs, continuous collaborative effort is necessary to implement these innovative practices successfully.

The main challenge of this kind of collaborative effort is that a great deal of time is needed to plan and share with colleagues, much more so than with finite collaboration. Some schools have built time for collaboration into daily class schedules. Teachers are grouped into teams, often in one of the following configurations[1]:

- *Grade-level planning teams:* General-education and ESL teachers are the core members who may be joined by literacy specialists, speech pathologists, special education teachers, and other faculty or support staff. These teams may meet daily or weekly to discuss core curriculum, planning, and student assessment data and work to facilitate co-teaching for ELLs.

---

1. Adapted from *Schools as Professional Learning Communities* by Roberts & Pruitt, 2009 (p. 16).

- *Content-area planning teams:* ESL teachers meet on a weekly or monthly basis with specialists segregated by subject (English language arts, mathematics, science, social studies) to align curriculum and standards for ELLs and share instructional strategies in their areas of expertise.
- *Cross-grade planning teams:* The main focus of multigrade team meetings is for all teachers to be aware of grade-level expectations both above and below their curriculum level and to better understand the demands of upcoming standardized assessments for ELLs. Cross-grade planning may occur once per month or at specific intervals throughout the school year.
- *ESL planning teams:* ESL specialists meet weekly or biweekly to discuss their successes and challenges with co-teaching, meeting curricular demands, specific issues regarding student learning difficulties, and the use of innovations and techniques with English learners.

The following are various types of information teams may share about co-teaching, curriculum, and instructional strategies for ELLs in collaborative groups:

- Adaptation of materials
- Alternative instructional resources
- Assessment data
- Cultural norms
- Family history and issues
- Language proficiency levels

- Learning style preferences
- Native-language literacy skills
- Referrals for special education services
- Reporting progress
- Student motivation
- Student work

Contractual issues prevent some school districts from altering teachers' schedules in order to produce effective ongoing collaboration. Other districts do not want to change the amount of teacher contact time with students in order to schedule collaborative team meetings; administrators often are concerned with not having community support for this practice. Yet, schools that value collaborative practices find creative ways to schedule meetings in already overburdened schedules. Whatever the case, a specific framework for structured and reoccurring meetings allows teachers to engage in dialogue in the most meaningful ways for their students. Table 6.1 illustrates the key components of an ongoing-collaboration framework.

Table 6.1 Framework for Ongoing Collaboration

Identify the participants	• Grade-level teams • Content-area teams • Interdisciplinary teams
Set the purpose	• Data review • Lesson planning • Material adaptation • Reflection • Student learning • Study of specific content • Sharing strategies and best practices

Framework for Ongoing Collaboration	
Establish required time frame and scheduling logistics	• Before or after school • Scheduled congruence period • Lunchtime • Online
Determine needed resources	• Shared values • Supportive leadership • Protocols for conversation

Time for Reflection

Ongoing collaboration should encourage teachers to reflect upon their current practices. The process of reflection allows teachers to revisit what they have learned, share their experiences with their colleagues, and obtain insight into their own teaching (practices) by continually evaluating what is done in the classroom to assist English learners.

Teams involved in collaborative practice should include periodic reflection. This type of evaluative process can be accomplished through developing, discussing, and answering key questions regarding classroom instruction for ELLs. Some questions that may be helpful for reflection are as follows:

- How have we provided a low-anxiety, stress-reduced learning environment for our ELLs?
- How have we successfully differentiated instruction to meet the needs of English learners?
- What are the overall successes ELLs have had in learning academic content?
- What issues need to be addressed to improve instruction for our ELLs?
- How can we improve our collaborative efforts to make instruction more meaningful for our English learners?

Since reflection is an essential component of both self-assessment practices and formative assessments, we will more fully explore it in Chapter 8.

AN EXAMPLE OF ONGOING COLLABORATION

Collaborative Task: Planning Interdisciplinary Instruction for ELLs in Grade 6

Who is involved?
An interdisciplinary team consisting of core content-area teachers (English language arts, math, social studies, and science) and an ESL specialist plan thematic units to benefit ELLs.

What are the team's prevailing goals?
The team's purpose is to plan interdisciplinary instruction on an ongoing basis. Necessary goals will focus on the following:

- Identify curricula elements that are conducive to thematic instruction
- Outline components of each identified theme
- Share strategies for individual lesson plans
- Determine evaluation of interdisciplinary thematic units

(Continued)

(Continued)

What are the desired outcomes?

Considering thematic instruction is an important key to English learners' academic success (Freeman & Freeman, 2003). An increase in English learners' adequate yearly progress (AYP) is desired. Additionally, the ability to identify successful units and retain them for future use is a suitable aim.

When do meetings take place?

Meetings are scheduled during a weekly congruent planning period. School schedules should be devised so that all ELLs in Grade 6 are able to work with the interdisciplinary team creating thematic units.

TWO OBSERVATIONS OF ONGOING COLLABORATION

Effective Ongoing Collaboration: Teachers Plan Instruction for ELLs

We have observed numerous groups of teachers working collaboratively to plan lessons for ELLs. One group of third-grade teachers in cooperation with their shared ESL teacher had a unique way of developing instruction for their students. They formed a group that met during a specially scheduled time for one period each week with the expressed purpose of planning differentiated learning for all their students.

This team of teachers arranged themselves in front of a bank of computers. A five-minute brainstorming session elicited numerous topics and a theme was chosen by consensus. At that point, the members of this group assumed different roles. The classroom teachers took on the positions of leader, reporter, and clarifier of content-area instruction. The ESL teacher acted as the in-house expert on materials and strategies for ELLs.

The lead teacher used a checklist of the different elements necessary for the selected theme, the reporter keyed the information on the computer, and the clarifier identified standards, literature, and other materials as possible resources. The ESL teacher took notes, suggested ways to organize the theme components, determined activities that were appropriate for the different language proficiencies of the group of third-grade ELLs, and explained that she would need more time to devise some activities according to specific content.

These collaborative partners seemed to take their job seriously. They remained focused on their lesson-writing task and used a common lesson plan format. This team complained little, refrained from personal discussion, and incorporated humor to keep their spirits up. Each team member carefully debated how to present the theme's topics using appropriate strategies and resources for ELLs. These teachers actually engaged in conversations about their students' abilities, tried to match activities that were appropriate to each level of instruction, and remained on task until the lesson plans were completed.

Collaboration Pitfalls: When Time to Collaborate Fails to Yield Desired Results

We observed a second group of teachers faced with the same task, to develop lessons that incorporated differentiated instruction for their students. This group of teachers included three kindergarten teachers, an ESL teacher, and a student teacher. The teachers also began by sitting at a bank of computers while the student teacher sat apart from them. They both individually and collectively looked through various file folders, and they expressed their concerns about duplicating copies of student handouts for future class activities while engaging in various discussions other than lesson planning.

The teachers' topics of conversation ranged from housekeeping issues such as "Healthy Snacks Week" to curriculum activities such as events for Dr. Seuss's birthday. They rapidly moved from topic to topic, and their conversations thoroughly engaged everyone in the group. During a brief pause, one teacher turned to us and said, "Now this is collaborating." After approximately 15 minutes, the teachers focused on creating the differentiated lessons they were charged to do.

The group tried to search for previously written lessons, but after another 15 minutes had passed, they could not find them and decided to proceed without them. One teacher commented, "Lessons in math are already differentiated in the math text." The teachers moved forward in the planning process by individually searching through the math text for possible lessons to adapt.

The teachers engaged in personal discussions about other faculty members. They used an established format for writing collaborative plan summaries on the computer to copy a lesson from the math book. With 10 minutes left in the session, the teachers shared with each other ways to differentiate the established math lesson. As the session ended, the teachers' discussions again steered away from lesson planning. A variety of topics captured their individual attentions and amused them: from the way one eats a Reese's Peanut Butter Cup to what is entailed in incubating eggs in the classroom.

Time to Meet: Not the Only Issue

In both the kindergarten and third-grade groups, the teachers had established strong relationships among their peers. Each teacher seemed to accept the other for her contributions and role in the process. These teachers had the ability to console and amuse one another, and each exhibited trust in her colleagues. Yet, one set of teachers was better able to focus on its intended planning task while the other eventually accomplished its prescribed goal but in a more superficial way.

Although it appears that collaborative conversations may be effective in some situations, one cannot suppose that just providing the necessary time for professional discourse leads to desired outcomes. The problem some teachers face with the collaborative process may stem from the manner in which collaboration itself has been implemented. Change is a complicated issue, and although the purpose for collaboration may be set, the means for accomplishing its intended outcomes often are not. According to Fullan (2007), teachers not only need to understand the need for improved practices, they must also have a clear understanding of the beliefs and practices they are asked to implement. Participation in the collaboration process is no different. Without a clear understanding and a strong buy-in to its purpose and beliefs, teachers will focus on superficial goals to satisfy an administrative directive instead of engaging in activities that are meaningful to the group as a whole.

There may be many obstacles to overcome to ensure teacher collaboration yields desired results. Some of these barriers have to do with a teacher's status in the school community. Inger (1993) discusses how teaching certain disciplines—such as core academic content—commands greater respect in the school community compared with others who are less valued because they work with special student populations. Other barriers that impede collaboration include departmental walls, physical separation due to allocated space or program scheduling, and concepts of teacher autonomy (Inger, 1993). How then do we identify the qualities that take these collaborative conversations to the desired level of transformative learning for teachers and thereby their students? And what if time *is* the major obstacle to effective communication among teachers?

A REMEDY FOR TIME LIMITATIONS: CONVERSATION PROTOCOLS

Engaging in productive conversations with colleagues can be frequently hindered by time. One way to make the best use of allotted time to discuss workplace issues is to use specific formats for structured conversations that allow for a clear, common focus of discourse and provide guidelines for all members' participation. These conversation protocols facilitate a balanced approach, allowing all members to be actively involved in the decision-making process by bringing a diversity of voices and opinions to bear on issues that require it (Garmston, 2007).

Conversation protocols can be very specific in how they guide the course of a discussion by identifying each group member's time frame for speaking and the precise subject matter to be addressed. Staying within the protocol's framework can help assure collaborative partners that each member will be heard and prevent conversations from going off on tangents. Various types of structured conversations can help generate ideas and provide a means for collaborative groups to interact and reflect on their practices. Table 6.2 is an example of a conversation protocol that can be used for co-teaching partners to reflect on their classroom practices.

Even if you have been a collaborating partner, or co-teaching for a long time, each new school year brings its new and unique challenges. Teachers change grade levels, retire, are reassigned to other schools, or are no longer employed with the district due to budget cuts. New curriculum and special programs are adopted or assessment/evaluation methods, government standards, and state regulations are revised. These events and policies lead ESL teachers to forge new relationships or begin needed conversations with additional colleagues to strategize and plan for ELL instruction. Conversation protocols can be a useful tool to further the progress of these important dialogues. Table 6.3 illustrates the many conversation topics that can be facilitated by conversation protocols for newly formed or ongoing collaborative or co-teaching partners.

Table 6.2 Protocol for Collaborative Professional Conversations on Co-Teaching

1. Co-teachers set aside 20 minutes for this activity. They agree to a set of accepted parameters for this professional conversation.

2. One co-teacher offers his or her account of successful aspects of the shared co-teaching experience. The other co-teacher is silent and takes notes. (3 minutes)

3. The same step is repeated with the second co-teacher. (3 minutes)

4. Each teacher takes a turn to clarify one key element in the other's presentation. (3 minutes total)

5. Co-teachers start an open discussion to analyze the reasons for their successes and/or identify any other contributing factors that hindered the success. (8 minutes)

6. The session is concluded with each co-teacher reflecting on the conversation and identifying one specific goal or step for the future. (3 minutes)

Adapted from Easton, L. B. (February/March 2009). Protocols: A facilitator's best friend. *Tools for Schools, 12*(3), 6.

Table 6.3	Conversation Protocol Topics to Enhance Instruction for ELLs

Categories	Subareas
1. Use of Teaching Strategies	Lesson structure Questions Examples Teaching aids Group learning Reinforcement
2. Engagement	Learner attention Learner background knowledge and life experiences Learner interest
3. Lesson Content	Clearly identified concepts Clear distinction between concepts and illustrations Appropriate level of complexity
4. Classroom Management	Variety of control techniques • Positive and negative • Verbal and nonverbal Efficiency of class administration Use of students in administrative tasks
5. Trial-and-Error Learning	Appreciation of mistakes Openness to student correction Sufficient repetition
6. Classroom Environment	Joy Order Best use of facility
7. Language Skills	Clear pronunciation Appropriate vocabulary level Effective communication
8. Evaluation	Modification in lessons based on real-time experience Awareness of learners' success or failure Assistance to weak students Interventions
9. Administrative Issues	Record keeping

Adapted from Allen, D. W., & LeBlanc, A. C. (2005). *Collaborative peer coaching that improves instruction: The 2 + 2 performance appraisal model*. Thousand Oaks, CA: Corwin. (pp. 76–77)

WHEN *DO* COLLABORATIVE TEAMS MEET?

According to Love (2009), teaching can be divided into three parts—lesson planning, delivery, and personal reflection. However, time for planning and reflection, as a part of ongoing practices with colleagues, is minimally scheduled into the school day. Administrators as well as other stakeholders view student-teacher contact time to be the key for increased academic success among pupils and believe "if teachers are not in front of students, they are not doing their job" (Love, 2009, p. x). Yet, a growing number of research studies indicating positive relationships between teacher collaboration and increased student achievement (Goddard, Goddard, & Tschannen-Moran, 2007; Louis, Marks, & Kruse, 1996) are beginning to lay the foundation for a change of attitude toward collaborative practices.

In our own discussions with a variety of educators, teachers frequently reported that the regular school day is the best time to collaborate with their fellow teachers and that their teaching schedules should reflect formal opportunities to work together. ESL teachers throughout the United States have shared with us that they conduct most of their planning with classroom teachers informally—in the hallway, in the classroom when children are engaged in an activity, while warming lunch in the teachers' lounge, or waiting to use the rest room. They have also revealed that when they have had formal opportunities to collaborate, their efforts have resulted in more successful lesson delivery in a variety of classroom settings for English learners.

Finding Time During the School Day

Although several obstacles can challenge teachers who are interested in coordinating their instruction or developing co-teaching lessons for ELLs, the most pressing one is a lack of time to implement collaboration and co-teaching schemes. When administrators do offer teachers time for collegial conversations, these discussions usually occur at the end of the school day when most faculty meetings are scheduled. Not only are teachers tired from their day's work, but most people's energy levels are the lowest in the late afternoon (Dunn & Dunn, 1999). This causes many participants to have a *let's just get this over with* attitude, and the overall quality of planning for ELLs can be greatly reduced. Not having planned time during the school day can soon quell teacher enthusiasm and prevent the enhancement of instructional routines, settings, resources, and strategies to benefit ELLs. Table 6.4 suggests ways to facilitate scheduled time for collaborative teams to meet.

Table 6.4 Creating Opportunities for Teachers to Meet During the School Day

Adjust School Schedules	• Establish one period per week at the beginning or end of the school day in which students are engaged on the playground or in the auditorium so teachers can meet
	• Devise a common planning period for teachers
	  o Employ substitute teachers to cover classes
	  o Reduce number of periods teachers have contact with students
	  o Schedule special subjects (art, music, etc.) during same time block
	• Modify the school schedule to add 15 minutes per day for four days with early dismissal on day five, leaving one hour each week for collaboration

Provide Incentives	• Provide extra pay for teachers who formally collaborate during their lunchtime • Employ school aides to release teachers from lunch or recess duty • Offer teachers rewards, for example, for the first to obtain the latest technology or for collaborating during personal preparation time
Use Resources More Efficiently	• Have certain teachers (literacy, gifted and talented, etc.) provide special lessons in classrooms to free up general-education teachers • Redistribute students for one period so that three classes become two • Invite community members to demonstrate their talents for students to free up teachers • Consider funding sources and available grant money to fund a collaboration initiative
Find Time During Class Hiatus	• Employ staff development days for teaching teams to conduct long-term planning • Increase days teachers work or decrease days school is in session • Use faculty meetings before and after school • Engage students in community service or in-school tutoring for younger pupils to free teachers to meet

Sources: Love, 2009; Villa, Thousand, & Nevin, 2008

EXPECTATIONS FOR TEACHER COLLABORATION

Vignette Revisited

Mr. Timothy sits quietly for the remainder of the meeting with his colleagues. After the meeting ends, the science teacher approaches him and begins to apologize for her earlier interruption. She says she understands his concerns and frustrations, but she and her fellow teachers who must instruct students in the content areas where state assessments are an issue must discuss many other matters. Unfortunately, the time they have together is short, and their agenda usually is too long.

Vignette Reflection

It is apparent that Mr. Timothy is not considered an equal partner during this group's collaboration time. This problem may stem from his purpose being finite in a collaborative effort that is ongoing. Because specialists are rotated between different interdisciplinary teams, this ESL specialist is not perceived as a vital contributing member. Since Mr. Timothy is not a constant factor in the group, the team still functions more or less with or without his input.

Equity in Collaboration

In order to improve the equity in collaborative practice and to solidify both general-education and ESL teacher expectations for its practice, all participants must have the *DESIRE* to make collaboration work.

- *Define each member's purpose as finite or ongoing.* Ongoing members can avail themselves of professional-development opportunities when specialists and outside experts are incorporated into their collaborative practices.
- *Explore topics that meet the needs of marginalized students.*
- *Share your personal expertise with one another.*
- *Identify the desired outcomes.* Partners in the process should have a clear focus on the purpose of both finite and ongoing collaboration.
- *Recognize each member's role in the collaborative process.* Content-area specialists need to understand the unique language demands of their teaching curriculum for ELLs and use the expertise of ESL teachers to monitor their classroom practices and obtain necessary feedback.
- *Evaluate your efforts.* Let all who have been a part of the collaborative group offer their observations and evaluations of the process to improve collaborative efforts.

When the purpose and expectations for collaboration are set, administrators and teachers can develop time frames for collaboration to take place. Table 6.5 illustrates various topics for teacher collaboration accompanied by possible time frames to accomplish the task.

Table 6.5 Identifying Time Frames for Teacher Collaboration

Sample Time Frames for Collaborative Purposes		
Purpose	**Type of Collaboration**	**Time Frame**

Examine beliefs and assumptions about ELLs	Finite	• Single-meeting framework after school
		  o Full-faculty meetings
		  o Department meetings

Improve instructional planning for ELLs	Ongoing	• Team meetings during the school day • Voluntary in-person meeting after school • Use of online or Web-based resources beyond the school day
Adapt resources for test preparation	Finite or Ongoing	• Congruent preparation periods
Lesson preparation and planning for co-teaching	Ongoing	• Scheduled collaboration period during the school day • Use of online or Web-based resources beyond the school day

Identifying obstacles to collaboration scheduling	Finite	• Single-meeting framework after school
		  o Full-faculty meetings
		  o Department meetings

Resolving issues in collaborative practices	Ongoing	• Team meetings • Scheduled collaboration periods

Roadblocks to Establishing Time Frames for Collaboration

At times, administrators who want to foster collaborative environments will elicit from their faculty ideas to produce the needed time frames for collaborative practices. Unfortunately, not all teachers view collaboration in a positive light, and some may seek to create impediments to prevent the establishment of specific schedules for meetings to take place. Based on our conversations with both ESL and classroom teachers, the following are some of the possible roadblocks to setting collaborative time frames:

1. The idea that the school community does not recognize the value of collaboration between ESL and general-education teachers during the school day

2. The belief that administrators will not provide the necessary time during the school day for ongoing collaboration

3. The existence of a school culture that overvalues autonomy, individualism, and personal space, time, or possessions

4. The lack of continuous professional development that not only demonstrates the benefits of teacher collaboration but also provides clear instruction with respect to how to effectively collaborate

5. The acceptance of diverse beliefs and opinions regarding educational practices and how this diversity can benefit the instruction of ELLs and support the overall ESL program

TIME FRAMES FOR CO-TEACHING

For a growing number of ESL and general-education teachers who co-teach or would like to adopt a co-taught or inclusion model of instruction, scheduling is one of the many variables to be addressed for the successful development of language acquisition, literacy, and content-area subjects with English learners. Adequate time must be designated during the school day to accomplish co-teaching goals. Furthermore, if ESL classes are to be taught using co-teaching models, administrators and teachers must take into account the age of the students, the set-up time each lesson entails, and the time of day for instruction that would most benefit ELL students.

Scheduling begins with the building administrator creating a master plan, and the rest often depends upon the grade level of the students. For elementary-level teachers, time frames for ESL classes are organized around general-education class schedules that frequently include block time for literacy and mathematics as well as lessons outside the regular classroom in music, art, technology, etc. Many ESL teachers are responsible for setting up their own schedules and must navigate within the confines of each class's program timetable to arrange their own ESL sessions.

For middle and high school classes, separate ESL instructional periods are usually written into the overall master schedule. However, if co-teaching models are used exclusively, there is no longer a need to schedule separate periods for ESL. Table 6.8 illustrates a sample schedule on the middle-school level for an ESL teacher to co-teach core subjects in general-education classrooms without separate periods designated for ESL. In any case, whether or not ESL co-teaching is conducted throughout the day or used on a part-time basis in combination with a pull-out or regularly scheduled period of ESL instruction, administrative support is essential for co-teaching schedules to be established.

Facilitating Factors for Scheduling Co-Taught Classes

When organizing ESL lessons or activities in general-education classrooms, the following ideas should be considered before scheduling takes place:

1. *Student clustering.* Co-teaching programs for ELLs benefit from thoughtful student placement in general-education classrooms. If ELLs are clustered or grouped together into fewer classrooms, more students can be provided extended ESL services in their regular classrooms.

2. *General-education teacher volunteers.* When general-education teachers are enthusiastic about co-teaching, minor scheduling glitches and adjustments do not overwhelm willing faculty members.

3. *Class configurations to use co-teaching models.* Adequate classroom size and flexible furniture arrangements assist in successfully accommodating co-taught lessons. These all-important spaces must be available when ESL co-teaching is scheduled.

4. *Full- or part-day ESL co-teaching.* Decisions must be made in terms of whether the ESL teacher will

   • remain in one general-education classroom the entire school day,
   • follow the ELL group from classroom to classroom and co-teach with various content-area teachers,
   • co-teach in more than one grade level, or
   • provide ESL services through a combination of co-teaching and pull-out programs.

Part-Day ESL Co-Teaching

ESL co-teaching can be successfully accomplished using a part-day schedule. In this teaching scenario, the ESL teacher spends part of the school day co-teaching with one or more general-education teachers, and the rest of the day is devoted to pull-out or regularly scheduled instruction for ELLs. Table 6.6 identifies a combination co-teaching/pull-out schedule for an elementary ESL teacher who is responsible for ELLs in Grades 3 and 4.

In our illustrated schedule (Table 6.6), the first period is set aside for collaboration with the different Grade 3 and Grade 4 team levels on alternate days (Monday–Thursday) before the start of daily instruction; the fifth day (Friday) is designated for departments such as ESL or grade-level teachers to meet as separate teams. Each morning is divided into two periods of back-to-back instruction for each grade level serviced. The afternoon hours are designated for small-group instruction in a separate classroom setting with a select group of ELLs. The last period of the day is an individual preparation period for the ESL teacher.

Some ESL teachers co-teach specific academic subjects in general-education elementary school classes for part of the school day. Table 6.7 on page 128 outlines literacy activities that can be co-taught in Grades K–3; it specifies a double, 45-minute period for each ESL co-teaching session; yet individual literacy activities are not 45 minutes long. The schedule additionally suggests co-teaching models to be used by cooperating teachers.

Another part-day schedule configuration involves the ESL teacher providing instruction by accompanying English learners to their core-subject classrooms. In essence, the ESL teacher spends most of the days with his or her ELLs but co-teaches with different content-area teachers. Table 6.8 on page 128 identifies a sample middle-school schedule.

Table 6.6	Sample Elementary School Schedule: Part-Day Co-Teaching				
	Monday	**Tuesday**	**Wednesday**	**Thursday**	**Friday**
8:10–8:50	ESL Collaborative Team Meeting Grade 4	ESL Collaborative Team Meeting Grade 3	ESL Collaborative Team Meeting Grade 4	ESL Collaborative Team Meeting Grade 3	Department and Grade-Level Meetings
8:50–9:35	Grade 3 ESL Co-Teaching	Grade 3 ESL Co-Teaching	Grade 3 ESL Co-Teaching	Grade 3 ESL Co-Teaching	Grade 3 ESL Co-Teaching
9:35–10:15					
10:15–11:00	Grade 4 ESL Co-Teaching	Grade 4 ESL Co-Teaching	Grade 4 ESL Co-Teaching	Grade 4 ESL Co-Teaching	Grade 4 ESL Co-Teaching
11:00–11:45					
11:45–12:45	LUNCH AND RECESS				
12:45–1:30	Grade 3 Pull-Out Beginning-Level ELLs	Grade 3 Pull-Out Beginning-Level ELLs	Grade 3 Pull-Out Beginning-Level ELLs	Grade 3 Pull-Out Beginning-Level ELLs	Grade 3 Pull-Out Beginning-Level ELLs
1:30–2:15	Grade 4 Pull-Out Beginning-Level ELLs	Grade 4 Pull-Out Beginning-Level ELLs	Grade 4 Pull-Out Beginning-Level ELLs	Grade 4 Pull-Out Beginning-Level ELLs	Grade 4 Pull-Out Beginning-Level ELLs
2:15–3:00	Prep Period	Prep Period	Prep Period	Prep Period	Prep Period

Time Management in a Co-Taught Classroom

Co-taught lessons may require additional planning time initially. ESL and classroom teacher teams may spend many hours planning content, creating materials, identifying models of instruction, and selecting learning strategies. However, it is as valuable a part of overall planning to jointly develop guidelines for classroom time management to ensure co-taught lessons run smoothly.

Teaching teams must estimate the time planned-learning activities will take and adhere to identified time frames as best as possible. There should be adequate time set aside for instruction, group and individual learning, student evaluation, and debriefing. It also is necessary to be flexible if certain activities take longer than originally anticipated or vice versa and alter allotted time *on the spot.*

Table 6.7 Part-Day Co-Teaching Schedule for Specific Content: Literacy

ESL Co-Teaching General Schedule for Basic Literacy: Grades K–3					
	Monday	**Tuesday**	**Wednesday**	**Thursday**	**Friday**
Class Activity I	Introduce New Word, Wall Words	Reader's Workshop	Word Wall Activity	Writer's Workshop	Word Wall Activity
Time Frame	40 minutes	40 minutes	30 minutes	40 minutes	30 minutes
Co-Teaching Model	One Group: One Lead Teacher and One Teacher *Teaching on Purpose*	Multiple Groups: Two Teachers Monitor and Teach	One Group: One Lead Teacher and One Teacher *Teaching on Purpose*	Multiple Groups: Two Teachers Monitor and Teach	Two Groups: One Teacher Reteaches, One Teaches Alternative Information
Class Activity II	Shared Reading	Guided Reading	Writer's Workshop	Guided Reading	Reader's Workshop
Time Frame	30 minutes	30 minutes	40 minutes	30 minutes	40 minutes
Co-Teaching Model	Two Groups: Two Teachers Teach the Same Content	Multiple Groups: Two Teachers Monitor and Teach	Multiple Groups: Two Teachers Monitor and Teach	Multiple Groups: Two Teachers Monitor and Teach	Multiple Groups: Two Teachers Monitor and Teach
Class Activity III	Debriefing				
Time Frame	20 minutes				
Co-Teaching Model	One Group: Two Teachers Teach the Same Content				

Table 6.8 Middle School ESL Team Teaching Schedule: Core Subjects

Seventh-Grade ESL Team Teaching Schedule Monday–Friday	
Period 1	Science/ESL Team Teaching
Period 2	Social Studies/ESL Team Teaching
Period 3	Interdisciplinary Team Meeting: ELA, ESL, Mathematics, Science, and Social Studies Teachers
Period 4	ELA/ESL Team Teaching
Period 5	Lunch
Period 6	Lunch/Hallway Duty
Period 7	Mathematics/ESL Team Teaching
Period 8	Preparation and Planning

Co-teaching partners must identify specific time management parameters and classroom procedures to facilitate co-taught lessons. Some potential topics for discussion with fellow co-teachers are the following:

- Punctuality regarding starting and ending co-taught sessions
- Respect for each other's time by following already-agreed-upon and planned activities and procedures
- Routines and rituals for beginning, transitioning in and out of, and ending activities
- Classroom rules and classroom management
- Student mobility about the classroom
- Appropriate time and procedures for students to take breaks, retrieve materials, sharpen pencils, etc.
- Strategies for reducing transition time from one activity to another
- Ways and means of offering timely feedback to students and managing student discipline

ADMINISTRATORS' ROLE: SCHEDULING AND SUPPORTING COLLABORATIVE AND CO-TEACHING PRACTICES

When we have questioned ESL teachers regarding the need for administrative support, time and again we have heard the same concerns from many different voices:

- "I need my administrators to recognize the benefits of co-teaching and to provide the necessary time for collaboration between ESL and classroom teachers."
- "Administrators need to make collaboration a priority and find planning time for us."
- "My administrators are aware of our need to collaborate and have committed to make the necessary scheduling changes *next* year."

Scheduling collaborative practices must begin with identifying an overall plan for collaborative initiatives to take place. Although the majority of teachers may be requesting time to have professional conversations with their colleagues on an ongoing basis, a building principal may not be able to meet that particular request immediately. Additionally, the desire to implement co-teaching as an innovative school practice may exist; yet, administrators may not have all the necessary resources (money, personnel, professional development, time) available to commit to such a long-term plan.

Issues beyond the control of an individual school might first need to be resolved in order for ongoing collaboration to be a part of the regular school day. Contractual and union issues are likely to be negotiated. However, several essential opportunities for collaborative practices can be put into place immediately while other initiatives are developed and implemented over time. It may take years for the desired collaborative practice to be fully developed and instituted. Nevertheless, the most important concerns for administrators to address are the focus on collaboration as a priority, the need to keep the faculty informed, and the necessary efforts to move forward with an overall plan that considers teachers' need for time. The key features for establishing the collaboration time frame for the benefit of ELLs are as follows:

1. A strong, articulated commitment to the practice of schoolwide collaboration by establishing, through conjoined efforts, a timeline for the initiative

2. A comprehensive plan with clearly identified incremental goals for both finite and ongoing collaborative practices to take place

3. Continuous professional-development activities on teacher collaboration for both administrators and teachers to build capacity by expanding the scope of collaborative activities and to improve the quality of teacher collaboration or co-teaching practices

4. Time devoted to evaluate established collaborative practices as they unfold

SUMMARY

In this chapter, we have discussed challenges and presented possible solutions to find the necessary time for establishing effective collaborative practices. We have outlined specific strategies to manage time constraints by identifying the purposes for collaboration and their related time frames, creating strong team partnerships, and establishing scheduled time for both collaboration and co-teaching activities. We concluded that determining specific time demands along with accompanying resolutions will ensure the institution of regular collaborative practices and co-teaching instruction.

DISCUSSION QUESTIONS

1. With your colleagues, generate a list of ideas detailing when and how you can find time to collaborate and how you can use the time most effectively.

2. Reflect on all the finite and ongoing collaborative practices that you are engaged in this year. Discuss with your colleagues how to enhance your use of the available time frame for each activity.

3. Develop an ideal co-teaching schedule for the grade level(s) you teach. Support your plan with arguments from this chapter or other sections of this book. Present your plan to a colleague or administrator and negotiate the schedule for the upcoming school year.

4. Lisa Dieker's (2001) study on special education co-teaching practices concludes that most teams needed a minimum of three common preparation periods a week to be effective. Whether you have that time available or not, carefully outline how common preparation time could be used most effectively.

KEY ONLINE RESOURCES

Center for Multilingual Multicultural Research
   www-bcf.usc.edu/~cmmr/BEResources.html

The Internet TESL Journal
   http://iteslj.org

TESL-EJ Electronic Journal
   www.tesl-ej.org/wordpress

The University of California Linguistic Minority Research Institute (LMRI)
   www.lmri.ucsb.edu

7

Where Do Teachers and ESL Specialists Collaborate and Co-Teach?

New frameworks are like climbing a mountain—the larger view encompasses rather than rejects the more restricted view.

Albert Einstein

OVERVIEW

Collaborative practices require teachers to share space both inside and outside of the classroom. With twenty-first-century technology, many practitioners also make use of virtual space with online and networked tools for ongoing professional discourse. This chapter will describe the different physical and virtual environments that general-education and ESL teachers use in order to enhance the collaborative process. Our discussion of collaborative space will be placed within the framework of establishing and maintaining a positive, inclusive school culture. We will explore the possibilities of using formal and informal shared spaces for instructional planning and offer strategies to maximize shared classroom space for co-teaching purposes. Organizational tips and suggestions for creative classroom design and classroom management are also presented.

Voices From the Field

Sara, a veteran ESL teacher, steps into her first classroom of the morning. She is quietly yet warmly greeted by Christine, a fifth-grade teacher who is wrapping up a test prep lesson. Sara makes eye contact with two of her ELL students as she squeezes past a few seated youngsters and maneuvers to the back of the room where she stands and waits for the lesson to end. Slung over her shoulder is a large canvas bag filled with materials and supplies—pencils, scissors, glue sticks, sticky notes, mini whiteboards, erasable markers, paper, and guided reading books—to carry out the day's lesson. Sara is also carrying her daily lessons plans, attendance logs, several teacher editions, and resource guides.

The classroom teacher, Christine, ends up going longer with her lesson than either teacher had anticipated, and Sara stands in awkward silence, not wanting to interrupt yet not knowing where to set up for the next lesson. The table and surrounding chairs that Sara is sometimes able to use are filled with students' poster projects. But she is hesitant about rearranging another teacher's classroom. In front of the room, Christine wonders why Sara is still standing until she notices her students' projects spread all over the back table. She interrupts a student who is speaking and races to the back of the room, apologizing profusely while she scoops her students' projects off the table and puts them on the windowsill. Christine's lesson abruptly ends, and the class begins to noisily transition to the next activity (a jointly planned social studies lesson).

Vignette Reflection

Even when teachers have the best of intentions, proper organization and space management are necessary for successful collaborative partnerships. Sara and Christine's situation is an example of what might occur when teaching teams do not share the same classroom space or when teachers have not adequately planned how they will use the space they share. Other issues involving space include arranging available meeting space outside the classroom to ensure ongoing collaborative efforts. Whether it is classroom space or a place to plan collaboration, ESL and general-education teachers need to have designated areas, set meeting places that each can count on to be available for collaborative purposes.

REEXAMINING THE IMPORTANCE OF A POSITIVE SCHOOL CULTURE

We strongly believe that teacher collaboration is essential to all schools' general success and especially for their English language programs that serve ELLs. Apart from careful planning to orchestrate the use of available meeting places and to organize classrooms for collaborative or co-teaching teams, schools may wish to start by examining their school culture (see Figure 7.1).

Collaboration provides teachers with a common ground for meeting the needs of ELLs. It also becomes the vehicle for change and an effective process within a school culture that supports all learners' academic success. Moreover, teachers must believe they each have some input and influence on what is important, useful, and valued within their school organization. In this way, the school culture will reflect not only the common goals of administrators but of teachers as well. If teacher collaboration is

Figure 7.1 Elements of a Positive School Culture

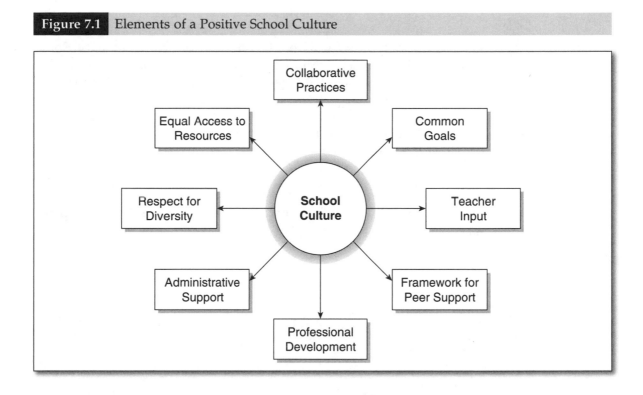

recognized as a valuable practice, the necessary resources will likely be made available to make it a reality.

Another concern is that ELL populations may be marginalized by the school culture along with the very programs that are designed to meet their educational needs. In fact, some ESL teachers have reported that they also feel marginalized and that they wish their students would have access to resources such as classroom aides, suitable textbooks, and supportive technology that are available to other student populations.

At times, a school culture may need to be revitalized in order for teacher collaboration to take place most effectively. This most certainly will not happen overnight. It takes much time, patience, and nurturing to develop the necessary trust, understanding, and acceptance for quality teacher collaboration to occur.

COLLABORATING OUTSIDE THE CLASSROOM

Teacher collaboration takes many forms, and within a week's time in any school building, teachers will be involved in a number of different collaborative practices. Some of these practices represent the de facto, on-the-fly type. One teacher might see another in the hallway or have a quick chat between regular class sessions. Although a hallway is not the ideal setting for collaborative conversations, informal spaces can play an important role in the overall collaborative process.

Formally planned meetings will require a different type of meeting space. Will grade-level meetings, structured department meetings, professional development or technology workshops, and faculty meetings that provide whole-group or small-group discussion all be held in the same place?

Physical Spaces

Schools across the country vary in size, shape, layout, and building capacity. Some school campuses have the capability of accommodating large student populations, which often translates to having the facilities that enable faculty and staff members to meet regularly. Faculty rooms, staff cafeterias, all-purpose rooms, and department offices can all be put to good use for collaboration. Unfortunately, some schools are overcrowded and have difficulty supporting their student populations let alone being able to provide readily available meeting space for teachers.

Informal Spaces

The following spaces are usually available for casual conversations that take place throughout the school day:

- School entrance and exit areas
- Hallways
- Main office
- Playground
- Recess area
- Water cooler or coffee pot
- Teachers' lounge
- Teachers' cafeteria

These informal areas limit the types of professional conversations that can take place. One must be careful when discussing individual students or confidential matters in public or shared spaces. In addition, the physical size of the school building may be a deterrent to informal conversations between faculty members. Large urban schools that house several thousand students generally have multiple floors and hallways in which some pairs of teachers would rarely meet.

Formal Spaces

Areas of school buildings that do not house students are precious commodities. How these faculty-only spaces are used often indicates what is valued by the school culture. One school whose administrators and staff are concerned with health and well-being may have a fitness room occupy an available space while another may have a teachers' lounge filled with comfortable sofas, a lending library of popular novels, and a seemingly bottomless pot of coffee. Similarly, if members of a particular district value collaboration, mechanisms will be in place for it to occur regularly. One such way to provide access to teacher collaboration is through formal meeting spaces.

One School's Vision: The Literacy Suite

At Shaw Avenue School, new building principal Ms. Angela Hudson had a particular vision for a specialized literacy location where teachers would be able to find classroom resources to assist their literacy lesson planning and be able to have regular meetings with the district's literacy coach. Both her vision and the hard work of several teachers produced the Literacy Suite, a room filled with leveled, guided reading material, big books, reader's theater scripts, and professional literature. However, the Literacy Suite not only became an excellent place to find classroom resources, it blossomed into a centralized meeting place for teachers to collaborate.

The Literacy Suite is half the size of a regular classroom, and it originally housed the office of the school's superintendent. In more recent years, it served as two small classrooms for the school's remedial reading program. Its renovation into a teacher meeting spot was realized through numerous donated items and time spent planning. For its décor, items such as window curtains added visual appeal. Teachers also contributed materials for student learning in the form of class packs of novels, expository text sets, professional books and journals, and portable technology. Other materials for the lending library were purchased with budgeted funds. In addition, school personnel chipped in to buy a state-of-the-art beverage maker that brews individual servings of coffee and tea.

Whether it's during their prep periods, lunch breaks, or time before and after school, teachers frequent the Literacy Suite to "shop" for new materials, get quick advice from the literacy coach, or grab their favorite hot beverage. It is a place where groups of teachers eat lunch together, share ideas, and help each other plan lessons.

Another School's Vision: The Book Room

The Cordello Avenue School in Central Islip, New York, has a special place called the Book Room. As Yanick Chery-Frederic showed us around, she explained, "When you peek in, you see neatly organized floor-to-ceiling book shelves all around the perimeter of the room. The shelves contain literacy, content-based, and ESL resources on all grade levels taught in the building. The Cordello Book Room was established in 2001, as a mandate of our Literacy Collaborative Initiative."

The Book Room is accessible to all teachers and has an organized policy for borrowing books. Specific needs of the ELL community are addressed via a book selection that simultaneously acknowledges language needs as well as the importance of providing culturally rich and diverse literature.

There are numerous volumes of leveled books for implementation of small-group instruction. There is a large selection of shared reading books and recommended read-alouds for beginner ELLs. Grade-appropriate texts of different genres are also available. In addition, a variety of teacher resources that support ELL curricula occupy a section of the Cordello Book Room. Also obtainable are units of study for different writing genres—including poetry, personal narratives, how-to writing, nonfiction, fiction, memoirs, essays, and more. These units invariably consist of components that can be differentiated to specifically target ELL student writing curricula. The resources have been carefully collected, organized, and reviewed over the years by a committee to make sure all subject matter content and essential skills are supported with multiple and varied instructional resources. The Book Room is not just a professional place for teachers to pick up workbooks or browse teacher guidebooks; it is also a meeting place where important professional conversations about students' needs and best practices to respond to those needs may take place.

A Third Example of Shared Space: A High School Study Center

Susan Dorkings, the study skills/ESL department chairperson at the William A. Shine Great Neck South High School in New York, describes a unique place for ELLs and teacher collaboration. Over 10 years ago, the administrators of South High School decided to create a Study Center where various academic labs throughout the building were centralized in one location. Over the years, the Center evolved to a program staffed by 11 qualified teachers and teaching assistants. The teachers rotate through a schedule designed to provide support in math, science, social studies, and English each period throughout the day and before and after school. In addition, two reading teachers and two ESL teachers are part of the team. They share the same work space with students, creating an atmosphere where serious academic work takes place. For this reason, collaboration among Center teachers and communication with classroom teachers, guidance counselors, administrators, and other support staff is an ongoing process. This collaboration, both formal and informal, is key to the success of this program.

Many students are assigned to the Study Center program as part of their schedules. Others take advantage of the support provided and drop in for help when needed. During a period, students can receive help in one academic area or in multiple subjects. Study Center teachers, who have access to students' progress reports and grades, direct students to the teacher who can best address their needs.

Study Center teachers collaborate formally and informally to develop strategies that engage all students in the school—including the ELL population. Although the focus of instruction is directed toward each student's course work, teachers are aware that many students need to build their basic skills in reading, writing, listening, speaking, and studying. Therefore, the collaboration of academic specialists with reading, ESL, and special education teachers allows for a team approach toward the development of strategies that address those skills. Each member of the department brings his or her expertise, experience, dedication, and enthusiasm to the Center each day. Students respect the knowledge of the teachers and feel welcomed and supported.

Virtual Spaces

Faculty members who do not have the time or the available space to meet with each other during the school day are learning how to collaborate using virtual meeting spaces. Technology is enabling teachers to collaborate from different locations, even from the comfort of their home office or living room sofa. There are Web sites where you can access virtual tools to conduct meetings on the Web; some are available at no cost. Anyone with access to a desktop computer easily can connect to a virtual meeting location. Some Web sites even offer secure meeting sites so that confidentiality is assured. These virtual meeting spaces allow participants to present information, share documents, and collaborate in a way that can be equally as effective as a face-to-face meeting.

A quick search for free Web-based chat software will yield many options for teachers to explore. The "Messenger" feature of numerous Internet service providers also provides chat rooms for group discussions, file transfers, photo sharing, and even audio and video capabilities to enhance the online collaborative experience. Colleagues can identify a convenient time to conduct their meetings from their desktop. Another online tool, Google Docs, allows groups to collaborate and share their work online. Documents such as lesson plans, curriculum maps, and student reports can be uploaded to a secure location on the Internet. Anyone with permission may access the documents from any computer as well as edit and share changes to the documents in real time.

Apart from general apprehension about, or lack of experience with, new technology, there are other difficulties teachers may face when trying to engage in collaborative conversations using Web-based tools. Although most educators have a personal computer in their home, many of these collaborative Web sites require certain computer specifications for them to work effectively. In addition, in spite of being sufficiently computer savvy, some teachers resist scheduling meetings, even virtual ones, outside the school day. They may feel these meetings intrude on their own personal time, while others are obligated to follow local teacher-union guidelines regarding contractual work hours and extracurricular activities. See Table 7.1 for a summary of some of the most prevalent advantages and disadvantages of using Web-based technology for teacher collaboration.

Table 7.1	Pros and Cons of Virtual Collaboration

Collaboration and Web-Based Technology	
Pros	**Cons**
• Teachers can collaborate from separate locations. • Virtual environments allow real-time communication. • Meaningful interactions such as idea sharing and problem solving can occur between participants. • Collaborative writing projects can be facilitated. • Collaborative learning and professional development can take place.	• Teachers sometimes resist using new technology. • Technology tools may be unreliable or difficult to use. • There may be resistance to scheduling regular group meetings outside the school day. • A lack of up-to-date home computer technology may be an issue.

Virtual Meetings Without Technology

Another type of virtual meeting can be conducted without the benefit of large blocks of time, meeting space, or technology. It can be accomplished by the use of a simple paper form and interoffice mail. Table 7.2 outlines how to establish technology-free, virtual collaborative opportunities.

Virtual meetings of this nature require little time and commitment on the part of group members, yet most participants can contribute to the process within the confines of the school day. It provides opportunities for a variety of staff members to offer their suggestions and advice to those who may have special concerns and can engage faculty members who are only available on a part-time basis. See Figure 7.2, which offers a sample template for preparing for or documenting the outcomes of virtual meetings.

Table 7.2	Steps to Create Technology-Free Virtual Meetings

Technology-Free Virtual Meeting	
Step 1	Faculty and staff join a collaborative team. Teams may consist of administrators, general-education and content-area teachers, ESL and bilingual specialists, psychologists, social workers, special educators, and support staff.
Step 2	A single team member selects a topic for discussion. It may be a grade-level, content-area, or special-subject concern. The issue also may focus on classroom and behavior management or a problem with a particular student.
Step 3	One team member starts the virtual meeting process by filling out a summary of the issue on a standard form developed specifically for this purpose. The same team member duplicates the form and sends it to all team members via interoffice mail.
Step 4	All team members return their forms to the person who initiated the process by the date indicated. All forms are then duplicated and copies of each participant's comments are sent to all group members.

Figure 7.2	Virtual Meeting Form

Virtual Meeting Form

Your input is valuable to our school. Please take a few minutes to share any ideas, suggestions, or advice about the following concern.

Team members' names:	
Date:	Team member initiating discussion:

Concern:

Summary of the issue:

Your feedback:

Please return this form by _____ to _____ .

You will receive a copy of all team members' feedback. Thank you for your time and attention to this matter.

Whether Web-based or technology free, meetings that do not require a face-to-face presence by their participants can be an essential form of collaboration to benefit ELLs. General-education teachers with little or no experience with the special needs of ELLs can ask for help and receive advice within a short period of time from a variety of practitioners. ESL teachers who are struggling to find solutions for ELLs who have difficulties outside second language learning can seek help from their colleagues specializing in K–5 classroom teaching, content-area subject matters, or special education.

In the past, the responsibility of assisting the classroom teacher or problem solving for ELLs rested solely on the shoulders of the ESL teacher. However, through virtual meetings and other forms of collaborative practice, classroom teachers can be guided by the expertise of different members of the school community, of which the ESL teacher is an essential member. In addition, ESL teachers will be more capable of remedying the situation at hand with the assistance of their general-education peers. Virtual meetings can assist all school community members to move in the direction from a "your kids" to an "our kids" mentality.

Virtual Meetings via E-Mail

If your school is involved in an initiative to "go green," a paperless version of the virtual meeting can be accomplished in a low-tech fashion by simply using interoffice e-mail protocols. A standard meeting form can be sent electronically to all team members following steps that are similar to the paper version. The member who initiates the meeting writes one e-mail message with the completed form attached and sends it to the multiple team recipients. Team members may return their feedback electronically to all participants, eliminating the need for duplicating feedback messages. This version is only useful for schools in which all collaborative partners have easy, in-school access to a personal computer. Everyone involved should also have an official school e-mail address because some faculty and staff may not want to provide information regarding their personal e-mail accounts. If computer access is difficult, or if the school culture is one in which e-mail is not frequently used, this electronic version of the virtual meeting will be less effective.

COLLABORATION INSIDE THE CLASSROOM

The school day begins with most teachers entering the school building, visiting the main office, performing a few clerical duties, offering some brief morning greetings, and proceeding to their separate hallways. From the moment the morning bell sounds, these practitioners remain isolated in their classrooms away from their peers, left alone with the students in their charge to meet the day's challenges.

Teachers, generally speaking, are accustomed to having their classrooms as their sole domains and take comfort in the modicum of control they hold in their workspace. They set their own class routines, arrange student seating to suit their own lesson ideas, and decide what to teach, where to teach it, and when activities will take place within school policy guidelines. However, when ESL and general-education teachers work together and share the same classroom, there is a different dynamic. Deciding where and how instruction occurs involves careful planning, negotiation, practice, assessment, reflection, and adjustment between those responsible for a co-taught classroom.

Sharing Classroom Space

Teacher collaboration can have a tremendous influence over the way instruction is delivered for ELLs and a great impact on how these students are regarded. It involves sharing student information, lesson ideas, teaching strategies, and, with certain ESL programs, sharing classroom space. Yet, many factors must be considered when two teachers work so closely together.

Co-teaching requires many teachers to move out of their comfort zones and into unknown territory. Space is not only the final frontier, as a voice from a popular 1960s television series told us, but for some teachers, it is the only frontier. Classroom space is a closely and carefully guarded commodity. Some people, generally speaking, need more control over personal space than others in order to feel sufficiently relaxed and confident to meet the school day's challenges. Concerns about classroom space and how it is best used can bring about a great deal of anxiety and cause conflict between those who must share it.

Examine the behavior of colleagues when they hear someone is changing their position in the district or retiring, and you will observe many of them vying for the soon-to-be vacated space, particularly if it is a plum spot. With overcrowded classrooms and schools bulging at their seams, no wonder general-education teachers need all the courage they can muster to open their doors and share their classrooms. On the other hand, ESL teachers do not always understand what the fuss is all about. Most of their careers are spent in small, divided classrooms, shared office spaces, all-purpose rooms, borrowed classrooms, hallways, or spare closets next to gymnasiums or music rooms. Most ESL teachers have never had the joy of classroom "ownership," and so they may not understand a classroom teacher's concerns over the matter.

One Classroom Versus Two Classrooms

ESL programs generally are established on the K–12 level according to ELL student population, assessed needs, available faculty and personnel, funding, and resources. Some ESL teachers have the flexibility to select from a variety of program models to deliver instruction while others are restricted to one particular model. The choice of model may have been determined by a program coordinator, building principal, or an administrator at the district level. Some programs establish separate classroom settings for ESL instruction while others prescribe a shared environment. Let's take a look at some program models that incorporate collaborative practices to enhance instruction for ELLs.

- *Pull-out programs:* Even though general-education and ESL teachers maintain their own separate rooms, co-planning efforts and the use of a parallel teaching model can yield positive learning environments for ELLs in both class settings. The ESL teacher incorporates grade-level curriculum with language acquisition instruction in the ESL classroom while the general-education teacher is teaching the same content material in the general-education classroom. Collaboration efforts can also help general-education teachers identify and include language objectives for ELLs to teach alongside curriculum content when these students are learning in their general-education classrooms.
- *Push-in programs:* ESL teachers provide instruction for a group of ELLs by pulling them aside yet remaining in the general-education classroom. This shared-space arrangement can benefit ELLs with the right amount of joint planning and the use

of a parallel teaching or a multiple-group model, which uses small groups and learning centers. Two teachers can teach the same content to two different groups of students, or multiple groups can be assigned to centers, with the ESL teacher assisting ELLs to complete various center activities. Having established a common set of learning objectives, each teacher has the freedom to choose the best resources to meet all students' needs.

- *Co-teaching programs:* Both the general-education and ESL teacher carefully coordinate instruction for ELLs and determine which co-teaching models will provide the best lesson delivery for all students. Some co-teaching teams may settle on one or two service-delivery models to incorporate into their teaching routines, whereas others prefer to select co-teaching models according to what is being taught. Co-taught classrooms require a great deal of cooperation as well as careful planning not only of lesson content but also of classroom management and use of available space for student learning to take place.

Shared Space Versus Personal Space

Every teacher needs his or her own personal space. In a co-teaching situation, classroom space needs to be carefully planned and negotiated. A good place to start is to have a conversation with your co-teaching partner or team in order to answer the following general and specific questions:

1. What will our co-teaching arrangement look like inside the classroom?

2. Which co-teaching models will we use to meet the needs of our students and match our own teaching styles?

3. If we use multiple models for instruction during one teaching session, how will the classroom's overall design accommodate their use?

4. Where will teaching resources be kept for easy access for all co-teaching partners?

5. Which areas of the room will be designated as shared spaces?

6. How will one classroom accommodate each individual's need for personal space?

The Importance of Personal Space

When ESL teachers enter a general-education classroom for one class period or part of the school day, it is important that they have a "go to" area as soon as they walk in the door. It may be a table in the back of the room, a small desk set aside for their own use, or a designated wall space with their own materials and supplies and an adjacent chair. Having a specific spot for the ESL co-teacher when she or he arrives will lessen classroom interruptions, keep students who are already engaged in learning on task, and prevent awkward moments that can occur. When the co-teacher's entrance is smooth, it eliminates the feeling that one is an "intrusion" teacher instead of an "inclusion" teacher.

Benefits of Shared Space

The benefits of sharing classroom space are endless. It not only benefits students and teachers, but it can also send subtle messages about the school's learning culture to the community at large. Here is a sample of the possible advantages and ideas brought about by ESL teachers who share classroom space with general-education teachers:

- All students are a part of the same learning community.
- Students can learn from the experience of two or more teachers.
- Students can gain different perspectives and guidance.
- Low-achieving general-education students and former limited English proficient (FLEP) students all benefit from the use of ESL strategies.
- The use of various co-teaching models helps to meet individual students' learning style needs.
- Teachers learn different techniques by observing each other's teaching.
- Staff development through in-class coaching or mentoring can readily be addressed in a co-taught classroom.

CLASSROOM DESIGN FOR CO-TAUGHT LESSONS

In your mind's eye, travel back in time to the middle of the twentieth century and enter a classic American schoolroom. What you most likely are picturing is a large teacher's desk sitting front and center, accompanied by rows of stationary, wooden student desks. The classroom walls are covered with chalkboards and bulletin boards. There is little room for students to move about the classroom if they were allowed to do so. Now in the same way, picture the twenty-first-century's typical classroom. What do you see? Apart from movable furniture, maybe a bit more space, and a computer tucked in the corner, classroom design has not changed very much (Dunn & Honigsfeld, 2009).

Get Organized

Anxiety may often be the first reaction some ESL teachers feel when they must leave their personal class domains and enter another teacher's space in order to deliver instruction for ELLs. They wonder how they will be able to conduct lessons when their materials and resources are housed elsewhere. Being organized is essential for ESL teachers to successfully meet the needs of ELLs in general-education classrooms. There are several ways to arrange the necessary resources so that they are readily available. The following steps should be considered when getting materials organized for co-taught lessons:

Step 1: Establish Where Your Materials Will Be Housed

This will depend on the amount of space available in the general-education classroom and the willingness of the classroom teacher to share his or her space. From our own teaching experiences, there is generally little, if any, classroom space available to share. Classrooms are usually overcrowded with students and further crowded with textbooks, reference materials, classroom libraries, and computer stations. Most ESL teaching material will be kept elsewhere and transported to the general-education classroom.

Try to use nearby spaces creatively to house materials if there is no other option available in the co-taught classroom. An ample-sized hallway might hold a tall cabinet where materials can be kept. In addition, storage closets, hidden nooks under stairways, or extra shelf space in the school library might just do the trick.

Step 2: Determine How ESL Materials Will Be Transported

There are a variety of ways that materials can be transported to and from the general-education classroom. One of the best ways is to have a set of wheels that can move ESL resources from place to place. Teacher carts, commercially available in a variety of shapes, sizes, and styles, can provide more than adequate transport.

The goal of using a cart is to create a mobile ESL classroom. In order to make sure the cart is functional, the following planning and preparation is needed:

- At the beginning of each school day, the cart should be reviewed and materials matched with planned lessons.
- Checklists can be developed to aid with the cart's organization.
- When preparing traveling carts, consider how many classrooms will be visited within a single school day.
- Always include complete class rosters, individual ELL student folders, and student assessment information on the cart for reference.

When a cart is not available or a school has multiple floors that would make a cart impractical, a large, sturdy bag can be used to carry materials. Totes, canvas carryalls, or even backpacks with various pockets and slots to separate items can be a portable solution for getting materials to and from different classrooms. Some teachers even have converted rolling suitcases into efficient, organized, and easily portable containers for ESL materials.

Step 3: Negotiate Who Will Provide the General Classroom Supplies

Most classroom teachers are allowed a limited number of supplies—chart paper, erasers, markers, pencils, etc.—and as the school year comes to a close, those items become in short reserve. Yet, ESL teachers cannot always carry all the needed materials from class to class. It would be most wise for the ESL and general-education teacher to discuss which classroom materials can be used by all and what additional materials are needed. For special projects, the ESL and general-education teacher can pool their resources in order to provide the required materials.

Step 4: Predict "Teachable Moments" and Have ESL Resources Available

This step is a tall order and one that requires a good deal of practice. When ESL teachers co-teach, they may not have their instructional resources at their fingertips—as they would if they were in their own classroom. When students ask questions that create opportune teaching moments, ESL teachers like to rely on certain materials to enhance their explanations: bilingual dictionaries, calculators, globes, literature, manipulatives, maps, photographs, textbooks, and workbooks.

ESL teachers often need to travel light and cannot depend upon having all the necessary resources handy for teachable moments. However, most classrooms have a computer available for use, and ESL teachers can avail themselves of the Internet, which can be a great virtual substitute for traditional resources.

Becoming technologically savvy is imperative. ESL teachers should practice searching for general Web sites that contain maps, photographs, and other useful information for ELLs. It can be helpful to maintain a list of suitable sites to use in the general-education classroom. As teachers become more adept at surfing the Web, they will be able to retrieve information on the spot without prior planning, allowing them to make the most of teachable moments. We certainly recognize that despite security measures, teachers still need to be wary about the appropriateness of the information retrieved from the Internet "on the spot" and make sure unsuitable websites are not used for instructional practices.

Rethinking Teaching Spaces

A classroom designed for one instructor might not be adequate for co-teaching situations. Both the ESL and general-education teacher must plan and manage the teaching space in a way that enhances lesson instruction and corresponds with the selected co-teaching model. (See Table 7.3 for a summary of the seven co-teaching models we introduced in Chapter 4 aligned to specific space requirements and recommended suggestions.)

Table 7.3 Co-Teaching Models and Organizing Classroom Space

Co-Teaching Models	Space Requirements	Suggestions to Consider
One group: one lead teacher and one teacher teaching "on purpose"	Space for students to work in small groups	• Desks or tables arranged in clusters • A carry-all bag for resources and supplies for "on-purpose" teaching
One group: two teachers teach the same content	Room sufficient to divide students into two groups	• Separate teaching spaces • Chart easel, whiteboard, etc. • Place to house resources and materials • Seating arranged in horseshoe or circle • May be situated in different rooms
One group: one teaches, one assesses	Area for whole class to gather together	• Carpeted area • Chart easel, whiteboard, etc. • Place to house resources and materials
Two groups: two teachers teach the same content	Whole-group seating area	• Carpeted area • Chart easel, whiteboard, etc. • Interactive whiteboard • Computer with projector • Seating arranged in horseshoe or circle
Two groups: one teacher preteaches, one teacher teaches alternative information	Small- and large-group seating arrangements	• Separate teaching spaces • Hands-on materials • Computers/interactive whiteboards • May be situated in different rooms
Two groups: one teacher reteaches, one teacher teaches alternative information	Small- and large-group seating arrangements	• Separate teaching spaces • Hands-on materials • Computers/interactive whiteboards • May be situated in different rooms
Multiple groups: two teachers monitor and teach	Areas designated for small groups and center or station learning	• Establish areas of the room for each learning station • Have baskets for needed materials • Provide portable box or folder-type centers that can be easily adapted to different classroom spaces

> ### Vignette Revisited
>
> Let's revisit our two teachers, Christine and Sara, from the opening vignette. They spent much time planning their co-taught social studies lesson. Together they reviewed the learning standards, explored the grade-level curriculum maps, examined Web sites, and planned a detailed project that included both language and social studies content objectives for their ELLs. Both Christine and Sara need to plan their use of space in a way that will appropriately address their co-taught lesson objectives as well as make both teachers more comfortable in their shared classroom.

THE IMPACT OF CLASSROOM DESIGN

What Research Says

Tanner and Lackney (2006), Uline, Tschannen-Moran, and Wolsey (2009), and many others have been investigating the impact of school facilities on student learning. When classroom design is the specific focus, many educational facility planners, architects, and school administrators note the trend of replacing individual student desks to create new opportunities for learning. The following elements are frequently identified features of a well-designed classroom that accommodates a range of varied learning needs:

- An individual space or research space where students complete individual work without being distracted by the rest of the class
- A reading nook or learning center where one-to-one instruction and make-up work can be scheduled; it may feature a bookcase, comfortable chairs, and a rug
- Common areas where presentations and community meetings may take place
- A cooperative learning space where various small-group instructional activities occur
- A teacher center where individual testing, conferencing, or meetings are scheduled to take place

Building on social cognitive theorists, Van Note Chism (2006) suggests that "environments that provide experience, stimulate the senses, encourage the exchange of information, and offer opportunities for rehearsal, feedback, application, and transfer are most likely to support learning" (p. 2.4). When two or more teachers share the responsibility for creating such a stimulating learning space for their students, they have the opportunity to do the following:

- Redefine the teaching-learning process: break the mold of the one-teacher-one-class model and allow for multiple educators to interact with students
- Promote student engagement through varied approaches to teaching
- Reduce the teacher-student ratio and increase attention given to individual students
- Foster both collaborative learning and student independence: based on the lesson goals, design activities that invite students to work cooperatively or independently while teachers monitor and facilitate such learning

What Practitioners Suggest

In addition, learning-styles researchers and practitioners also addressed the importance of classroom design to better respond to varied learning needs of students. Irvine and York (1995) state that "all students are capable of learning, provided the learning environment attends to a variety of learning styles" (p. 494). Dunn and Honigsfeld (2009) suggest that teachers create separate classroom sections in which students may work

1. in almost complete silence or by softly discussing the content together;

2. in bright versus subdued lighting;

3. with layered versus lightweight clothing;

4. at desks or on the carpeted floor or pillows;

5. alone, in a pair, in a small group, or with their teacher;

6. passively at specific stations or their desk, or while moving from one area to another as they complete mini-assignments; and

7. snack while concentrating if it helps them complete assignments. (pp. 27–28)

Tomlinson (1999) also recommends that flexible grouping arrangements allow teachers to move away from creating tracks (separating students into low- and high-achievement groups) within the class, but rather group students in different ways at different times. In such a differentiated classroom, ELLs are sometimes grouped together for instruction, whereas at other times they are placed with their more proficient English-speaking class-mates. As Tomlinson proposes, teachers should consider differentiating for content, process, and product based on their students' readiness level, interest, and learning profile.

When you are deciding on grouping configurations, use the following guiding questions:

1. Which students are ready linguistically to work with the target content and language objectives?

2. Which students are ready academically (have solid background knowledge) to work with the target content and language objectives?

3. Which students share common interests (or shared background experiences) regardless of their academic readiness or language proficiency levels?

4. Which students share similar learning-style strengths or multiple intelligence profiles?

5. Which students share similar work habits or other learning tendencies (source of motivation, need for adult guidance, tendency to get distracted if not supervised, etc.)?

6. Which students are able to complete the task independently, with peer support, with written teacher scaffolds, or with direct teacher assistance?

7. Which students work well together for no particular reason?

What All Teachers Need: Classroom Management

To be successful in redesigning the traditional, transmission type classroom model—in which one teacher spends much of his or her instructional time in front of the entire class—it is important to establish class routines and rules of behavior that both teachers in the co-taught classroom adhere to and enforce. These rules and behavior management strategies can change from classroom to classroom and between different co-teaching teams. There are some basic guidelines that should be followed when establishing classroom management practices.

Rules and Routines

Here are some tips for jointly establishing an effective learning atmosphere:

1. With the students, create a set of written class rules that are easily visible. Add visuals or bilingual translations so ELLs clearly understand expectations.

2. Keep students engaged via classroom activities that are meaningful and accessible to them.

3. Be consistent with both praise and necessary consequences.

4. ESL teachers may defer to general-education teachers in all matters that have not been previously negotiated.

ADMINISTRATORS' ROLE: SCHOOL ORGANIZATION AND LOGISTICS

The building administrator's role is to create physical and virtual spaces that support the collaborative team's planning and instruction for ELLs. This can be accomplished in a variety of ways.

Focus on Sustained, High-Quality, Meaningful Teacher Collaboration

1. Secure and create inviting, functional, professional rooms as places for teacher collaboration, including spaces for small- and large-group meetings.

2. Establish and continuously update the school's professional library, where teacher resources may be stored, reviewed, and discussed.

3. Create and support physical and virtual spaces for teachers to share their lesson plans, teacher-created instructional materials, and assessment tools.

4. If feasible, enhance opportunities for collaboration by placing ESL teachers' desks in a teachers' workroom (if they share one).

5. If feasible, set up ESL offices and ESL classrooms in close proximity to those of their general-education colleagues.

Focus on Teacher Assignments and Student Placement

1. Carefully develop ELL placement policies and consider their implications. Cluster ELLs based on your local population and demographics.

   - Saint Paul Public Schools (SPPS) uses the following formula (available at www.spps.org):

o Cluster ELLs in one or two classrooms, when less than 30 percent of students are ELLs

o Cluster, but be sure ELLs do not exceed 50 percent of any class roster, when 30–50 percent of students are ELLs

o Distribute ELLs among all classrooms, but group by need or language level, when 50 percent or more of students are ELLs

- Fearon (2008) reports a similar ratio developed for a team teaching pilot program in a New Jersey public school:

o The number of ELLs should not exceed nine students or 50 percent of the class.

2. Assign ELLs to general-education classroom teachers at the elementary level and content teachers at the secondary level who demonstrate the highest levels of knowledge and skills regarding second language acquisition, cultural responsiveness, ESL methodologies, and who volunteer to be selected for such a task (thus also demonstrating the necessary professional dispositions and positive attitudes toward linguistically and culturally diverse student populations).

3. Assign teachers to work together who complement each other's knowledge base, skills, competencies, and who are willing to engage in collaborative practices.

Overall Recommendation for School Administrators

Most of all, create a school culture that respects both an inclusive and safe learning space for all ELLs and teacher collaboration spaces that inspire and support teachers in their efforts to work together.

SUMMARY

Creating and sustaining real and virtual spaces for teachers to collaborate responds not only to the essential Maslowian (1970) need for "shelter" but also for the need for "safety and security." Despite the critical shortage of available space in many schools, ESL and general-education teachers will only be able to collaborate and co-teach successfully if real and virtual space is provided for planning, delivering, and assessing effective instruction and for being engaged in job-embedded, continued professional development.

DISCUSSION QUESTIONS

1. Sarah Elmasry (2007) claims that "learning environments are directly correlated with the pedagogical practices taking place within them; patterns of space are driven by patterns of events" (p. 28). What are the patterns of spaces and events in your own professional life?

   a. Reflect on the patterns of instructional and noninstructional events that keep happening in your classroom or school. What teaching model is adapted? What are the most common teaching-learning activities that recur?

   b. Review the patterns of space in your classroom or school building: In what way do the patterns of space impact upon the patterns of events?

2. Revisit Figure 7.1 depicting the elements of a positive school culture. With your colleagues, discuss which of the elements presented in this figure have appeared to be most essential to support the education of ELLs.

3. What are the attributes of a collaborative school environment? Consider both what you have read in this chapter and your own experiences. Generate a list of key characteristics you would like to see further developed in your school.

4. How does the teaching-learning environment help teachers develop collaborative practices? In what ways may it hinder such practices?

5. Sketch a floor plan of an ideal classroom where co-teaching could take place most effectively. Consider the need for changing the floor plan to accommodate various co-teaching models. Draw in as many details as possible. Share and discuss your drawing with your co-teacher or other co-teaching teams for additional input.

KEY ONLINE RESOURCES

Association for Supervision and Curriculum Development
www.ascd.org

Classroom Design
http://classroom.4teachers.org

Classroom Management
www.thecornerstoneforteachers.com

Differentiated Instruction
www.caroltomlinson.com

Learning-Styles-Based Instruction
www.learningstyles.net

Learning Styles Classrooms
www.flipthisclassroom.com

Multiple Intelligences
www.howardgardner.com

School Improvement Research Series at Education Northwest
http://educationnorthwest.org/resource/825

8

What Next? Reviewing and Evaluating Integrated, Collaborative ESL Programs

Everything that can be counted does not necessarily count; everything that counts cannot necessarily be counted.

Albert Einstein

OVERVIEW

The goal of this chapter is twofold. It is designed (1) to help create a framework for reflection on the process and outcomes of collaborative practices designed specifically to support ELLs and (2) to offer tools to conduct both formative and summative evaluations of an integrated, collaborative ESL program model. We offer guidance on introducing reflective practices to be used among teachers and share several self-assessment tools to aid reflective, collaborative practitioners in their effort to improve their instruction.

Voices From the Field

The warm air surrounded G. Walter Joseph, principal of Ruth Jewell High School, as he eagerly made his way to the library for his first give-and-take meeting with his ESL department. Mr. Joseph, a novice school administrator filled with optimistic stamina, was viewed by many in his school community as a progressive educator.

It was his second year at Ruth Jewell, a suburban public institution of approximately 2,000 predominately Caucasian pupils in the southeastern United States. Over the past decade, his high school had experienced a rise in its enrollment of English language learners from 2.2 to 7.9 percent.

Since his arrival to Ruth Jewell, Mr. Joseph already had hired two new ESL teachers, and he had encouraged them along with the veteran ESL specialists on staff to experiment with innovative ideas—ideas they had learned at the various staff development courses provided by the school district. Teachers, over the summer break and during the first school semester, participated in small-group sessions regarding differentiated instruction, collaborative practices, professional learning communities, and inclusion programs for special student populations. So now, at the end of the school year, Mr. Joseph was anxious to attend to his ESL teachers, who would report the outcomes of some innovative strategies they had piloted during the second part of the school year.

As the meeting got underway, each ESL teacher took turns describing the specific new strategy or approach that he or she instituted with ELLs. One particularly enthusiastic young teacher stood up to share her experiences concerning an inclusion ESL program she piloted with a ninth-grade social studies teacher. Ms. Rose Coser described how she and her general-education counterpart used common prep periods and lunchtime to plan lessons together for the co-taught social studies class. She recounted in great detail how the students were grouped in ways to accommodate the use of appropriate instructional strategies for ELLs, and she highlighted several projects and hands-on activities that delighted and benefited all the students.

Mr. Joseph had listened intently. He was very impressed by this first-year teacher's ardency and complemented her willingness and ability to put her resourceful plan into action. He then asked how she had evaluated the success of the program, and Ms. Coser repeated her description of the avid participation of her students and the wonderful experience she had shared with her fellow co-teacher. The principal smiled at Ms. Coser, and then he addressed the entire group of assembled teachers, "It's all well and good when students and their teachers have had an interesting learning experience, but where are the data to show that it worked?" The meeting became silent for a moment as if everyone was stunned by the question. It was just at that moment Mr. Joseph realized that although his ESL faculty had been given carte blanche to experiment with new ideas and the staff development to support their learning, they had not been given the guidance to evaluate the effectiveness of their efforts.

Vignette Reflection

In our vignette, Mr. Joseph understood the need to assess new ESL methods and approaches to learning to determine their ability to improve the quality of education for ELLs. His school district provided staff development to guide teachers on how to implement new program strategies; however, little was done to prepare these same educators to assess their innovations. Many school districts institute new programs without the necessary mechanisms in place to evaluate their significance. According to Love (2009),

> Without a systematic process for using data effectively and collaboratively, many schools, particularly those serving high-poverty students, will languish in chronic low performance in mathematics, science, and other content areas—no matter what the pressures for accountability. (p. ix)

Decisions must be made regarding what measures will be used to determine the value of new programs and their power to affect learning for ELLs.

REFLECTIVE PRACTICES

How do we know how we are doing in the day-to-day business of collaboration? Do we stop and reflect often enough to see if we are still accomplishing what we have set out to do? How do we connect our collaborative practices with student progress, and why is reflection a worthwhile process to gather valuable program data?

Reflective practice entails the periodic consideration of one's teaching methods and their effects on learning outcomes. Although sharing one's thoughts about teaching can be conducted informally with friends and colleagues over coffee, developing a structure for formal reflection can enhance decision making and help render judgments regarding classroom practices that positively affect student learning. Simple yet powerful measures can be established to guide teachers to examine and confirm their use of the best approaches with their students.

Historical Perspectives on Teacher Reflection

The importance of reflection has been documented for generations in and outside teacher education (Boyle-Baise & Sleeter, 1996; Dewey, 1933). Zeichner and Liston (1996) celebrate teachers who are aware of and question the beliefs and values they bring to teaching. Through reflective practices, they encourage all educators to examine their experiences and solve problems in a constructive manner. As Schon (1990) states, reflective practitioners engage both in *reflection in action* (while being engaged in a classroom experience with students) and *reflection on action* (through action research and lifelong learning). Airasian and Gullickson (1994) suggest that teachers develop scientific or technical knowledge in their teacher preparation programs, but experiential learning takes place once they are practicing in the classroom and are *learning by doing.* They claim that "it is the constant cycle of experience, reflection, and improvement that marks a teacher's growth and development; teachers do learn by doing, but only if they also reflect upon, critique, and base future actions on knowledge gained from past actions" (p. 195).

Tremmel (1999) explains simply yet expressively what reflection means for teachers. It is "using such abilities as feeling, seeing, or noticing to examine what it is you are doing; then learning from what you feel, see, or notice; and, finally, intelligently, even intuitively, adjusting your practice" (p. 89).

To further support the importance of reflection in the context of collaborative teaching practices, we adapted Osterman and Kottkamp's (2004) outline of reflective practice developed for professional development and applied it to collaborative instructional practices. Figure 8.1 represents the purpose and context of collaborative reflective practices, assumptions underlying such practices, and strategies used to engage in reflections. As you review Figure 8.1, consider Ms. Coser and her colleagues presented in our opening vignette.

How to Get Started With Reflection

What happens when you reflect on your teaching practices alone? You develop a deeper understanding of your own actions, a firmer grasp on the processes that take place in your classroom, and you build stronger problem-solving skills. When reflection becomes a shared experience, you gain additional insights into the teaching-learning process through a second (or third or more) set of lenses.

| Figure 8.1 | Reflective Practice for Collaborative Endeavors |

Reflective Practice

| Purpose | To understand one's own and colleagues' teaching |
| | To build own and shared competencies |

Assumptions	Learning is co-constructed.
	Learning is personally and interpersonally meaningful.
	Knowledge is a shared tool.

| Context | Job-embedded learning |
| | Experiential, classroom-based knowledge construction |

Strategies	Reflective journals or logs
	Collaborative conversations
	Collaborative inquiry
	Peer coaching and mentoring
	Collaborative action research

As Zabolio McGrath and Holden Johns (2006) suggest,

We encourage you to view the events of your school day as they unfold. In so doing, we challenge you to not only fully involve yourself in each day's events, but also to look for occurrences that call for reflection, events that challenge you to redirect your teaching strategies, and dynamics in your day that give you inspiration. (p. vi)

Tremmel (1999) refers to a similar practice of paying attention to as many details as possible as capturing a "slice of life." More specifically, we would like to invite you to reflect on both the processes and the outcomes of the various collaborative practices and co-teaching endeavors in which you are currently participating. Osterman and Kottkamp (2004) emphasize the value and focus of reflective practice as "a collaborative search for answers rather than an effort to teach a predetermined response to a problem" (p. 17). In agreement with Dieker (2002), we encourage you to not only search for answers jointly as a team but also design your own collaborative reflective framework. We like to call it *Collaborative Professional Reflections,* or the CPR of collaboration. It works by following these steps:

1. Decide on how much time you will devote to collaborative reflection (5–10 minutes per session will suffice).

2. Generate a few manageable, yet critically important, reflective questions that best fit your collaborative practices (see Table 8.1 for ideas).

3. Establish simple yet effective ground rules (one voice at a time; respect and reflect before resent and repent).

Consider the list of reflective questions in Table 8.1 to get you started on your collaborative search for answers.

Table 8.1	Key Reflective Questions

What?	**How?**
• What is my role in this collaborative situation? • What are my strengths and major contributions to this partnership? • What works in our collaborative practice? • What do we do well? • What can we improve?	• How do I contribute to the collaborative partnership? • How do I support my colleagues? • How do my colleagues support me? • How do we impact our students' language acquisition and academic, social, and affective development? • How do I make a difference? • How do we, collaboratively, make a difference?

Setting a Course for Ongoing Reflection

As you begin to consider how your reflective practices will take shape, you may wonder what types of strategies are needed to make ongoing reflection a success. You must be able to identify or devise different approaches to support your efforts with your collaborative team members and co-teaching partners in order to integrate your reflective inquiry. In addition, simplicity should be key. For reflection to be continual, its documentation needs to be easily and readily accomplished.

Dieker (2002) emphasizes the importance of creating a reflective framework for co-teachers. The use of a framework allows teaching partners to reflect on the same topics in a nonjudgmental way. Based on their research, McEntee et al. (2003) suggest that creating a protocol or guide will enable "teachers to refine the process of reflection, alone or with colleagues" (p. 34). The use of these concrete devices can reveal more specific information about teaching practices and student learning. We also affirm that a framework for thinking about a range of different types of teacher collaboration and engaging in regular, professional dialogues with colleagues benefits everyone. We educators need opportunities to share our stories of success and our challenging moments; we must express our frustrations, offer our words of wisdom, and request help or suggestions.

Strategies for Ongoing Reflection

Here are some ideas to help foster continuing reflection through self-examination of practices as well as in concert with your colleagues.

Strategy 1: Daily Deliberations

When reflecting on everyday practices, try using a simple log format that encourages you and your collaborative partners both individually and collectively to keep track of what works and what could be done better. A log may be used both in varied contexts of collaborative activities and co-teaching settings (see Tables 8.2 to 8.4).

Strategy 2: Weekly Wonders

Once a week, reflect on your successes. Select one outstanding event, activity, or moment that made you stop, pause, or even *wonder*. Take a mental snapshot of the best moments of the week and reflect on them. Another way to implement Weekly Wonders is by engaging in collaborative conversations and identifying one area for improvement. As you reflect on the week with your colleagues, try to finish the sentence stem *I wonder if we . . .* or *I wonder what would happen if . . .* You may also choose to brainstorm new questions and directions you might have or new strategies you might try that will help you achieve your goals.

Strategy 3: Monthly Milestones

Once a month, set aside time to recognize and celebrate milestones and accomplishments. During that time, identify at least one new step you took together toward building a stronger collaborative relationship or a more effective co-teaching partnership. Document these milestones and share them with colleagues, administrators, parents, and students in appropriate formats.

Vignette Revisited

Mr. Joseph in our opening vignette encourages his faculty to engage in collaborative reflection that supports teaching practices and fosters school improvement. Since his goal is to ensure increased student success, he believes that when school communities lay the groundwork for implementing reflective initiatives, the heightened level of communication among its faculty has the potential to transform the school.

Table 8.2 A Basic Collaboration Log

Date	Collaborative Activity	Successes	Challenges

Table 8.3 A Reflective Log Template for Co-Teaching

Date	What Worked for Us Today	What We Could Improve Next Time

Table 8.4 A Co-Teaching Log Template to Include Detailed Notes

Guiding Questions	Notes
What was our goal today?	
How did we approach the goal?	
What did we do well?	
What do we want to do better?	

Reflective Practice for School Improvement

In a broader context, York-Barr, Sommers, Ghere, and Montie (2006) identify four levels of reflective practice to improve schools. When transferred into the collaborative ESL context, the four levels serve as critical guides for improving interpersonal and communication skills, as well as productivity. The contents of Table 8.5 are organized around the four overarching questions for reflection (What happened? Why? So what? Now what?).

Table 8.5 Four Critical Steps for Reflective Questions

1. What happened? (Description)	2. Why? (Analysis, interpretation)
• What did I do? What did others (e.g., co-teachers, students, adults) do? • What was my effect at the time? What was their effect? • What was going on around us? Where were we? When during the day did it occur? Was there anything unusual happening?	• Why do I think things happened in this way? • How might the context have influenced the experience? • Are there other potential contributing factors? • What are my hunches about why things happened the way they did?
3. So what? (Overall meaning and application)	4. Now what? (Implications for action)
• Why did this seem like a significant event to reflect on? • What have I learned from this? How could I improve? • How might this change my future thinking, behavior, or interactions? • What questions remain?	• Who should be actively included in reflecting on this event? • The next time a situation like this presents itself, how do I want to behave? • How can I set up conditions to increase the likelihood of productive interactions and learning?

Adapted from York-Barr, J., Sommers, W. A., Ghere, G. S., & Montie, J. (2006). *Reflective practice to improve schools: An action guide for educators.* Thousand Oaks, CA: Corwin. (p. 84)

SELF-ASSESSMENT TOOLS

As a form of reflection, self-assessment focuses your attention both on your own individual and collaborative practices. Checklists, rubrics, scoring guides, and other measurement tools often help collaborating teachers to gather more systematic data about their interactions, their effectiveness during the teaching-learning process, and their impact on their students' learning. The next two tables contain a self-assessment checklist for collaboration (Table 8.6) and for co-teaching (Table 8.7), whereas Figure 8.2 offers a self-assessment template for co-teaching that requires additional descriptive or narrative input from teachers completing it.

Table 8.6	A Collaboration Self-Assessment Checklist

Yes	No	Factors Impacting Collaboration
		1. Communication: Our collaboration has open and clear communication.
		2. Goal Setting and Evaluation: Our collaboration has established goals, and we collect data to measure how we meet our goals.
		3. Climate: The school environment supports teacher collaboration through shared decision making.
		4. Resources: Our collaboration has access to needed resources.
		5. Leadership: Our school leadership facilitates and supports team building and capitalizes upon diversity and individual, group, and organizational strengths.

Adapted from Borden, L. M., & Perkins, D. F. (1999). Assessing your collaboration: A self-evaluation tool. *Journal of Extension*, 37(2). Retrieved August 18, 2009, from http://www.joe.org/joe/1999april/tt1.php

How to Use Self-Assessment Tools

The goal of using any self-assessment approach is "to share experiences and to negotiate areas where improvement could . . . be attempted. These reviews and discussions should be seen as part of an ongoing formative-assessment and self-improvement process carried out in a non-threatening manner" (Walkin, 2000, p. 250). Self-assessment checklists or other tools may also be collaboratively developed as the outcome of reflections and professional dialogues, thus making the development of a self-assessment tool a creative, collaborative activity in and of itself.

Once a self-assessment tool is selected, adapted, or developed, several approaches may be chosen to implement the tool. For example, if you decide to use one of the previously presented self-assessment checklists, you can choose any of the following approaches to apply them:

1. Complete the self-assessment checklist in cooperation with your colleagues at the beginning of the year and set it aside for a designated period of time (three months, a semester, or even an entire year), after which you will reassess. Compare the results. Identify necessary courses of action and appropriate modifications to your collaborative practices.

2. Complete the self-assessment checklist independently at the beginning of the year. Periodically reassess yourself to reveal areas in need of improvement and areas of effectiveness.

3. Complete the self-assessment checklist independently at the beginning of the year and then periodically throughout the year. Each time you meet with your teaching team members, compare your answers through collaborative conversations. Identify shared concerns, chart your joint progress, and set new, attainable goals based on the results.

Table 8.7	A Co-Teaching Self-Assessment Checklist

Yes	No	In Our Co-Teaching Partnership
		We decide which co-teaching model we are going to use in a lesson based on the benefits to the students.
		We share ideas, information, and materials.
		We identify each other's resources and talents.
		We are aware of what our co-teacher(s) is (are) doing even when we are not directly in one another's presence.
		We share responsibility for deciding what to teach.
		We agree on the curriculum standards that will be addressed in a lesson.
		We share responsibility for deciding how to teach.
		We share responsibility for deciding who teaches what in each lesson.
		We are flexible and make changes as needed during a lesson.
		We identify student strengths and needs.
		We share responsibility for differentiating instruction.
		We include other people when their expertise or experience is needed.
		We share responsibility for how student learning is assessed.
		We can show that students are learning when we co-teach.
		We agree on discipline procedures and carry them out jointly.
		We give feedback to one another on what goes on in the classroom.
		We make improvements in our lessons based on what happens in the classroom.
		We communicate our concerns freely.
		We have a process for resolving our disagreements and use it when faced with problems and conflicts.
		We have fun with the students and with each other when we co-teach.
		We have regularly scheduled times to meet and discuss our work.
		We use our meeting time productively.
		We can effectively co-teach even when we don't have enough time to plan.
		We explain the benefits of co-teaching to the students and their families.
		We model collaboration and teamwork for our students.
		We are both viewed by our students as their teachers.
		We depend on one another to follow through on tasks and responsibilities.
		We seek and enjoy additional training to make our co-teaching better.
		We can use a variety of co-teaching models.
		We communicate our need for logistical support and resources to our administrators.

Adapted from Villa, R. A., Thousand J. S., & Nevin, A. I. (2008). *A guide to co-teaching: Practical tips for facilitating student learning.* Thousand Oaks, CA: Corwin. (pp. 193–94)

Figure 8.2 Co-Teaching Self-Evaluation

School _____   Name _____

Grade/Content Area _____   Date _____

Role _____ (general educator, ESL specialist, paraprofessional, administrator, other)

Share strengths (*Shine*) and suggestions or concerns (*Refine*) for each of the following:

Planning (use of scheduled time; creative ways of finding time to cooperate and communicate; clarity and articulation of content and language goals or objectives; preparation of differentiated learning activities; collection of supplementary materials; sharing of ideas)

Shine	**Refine**

Instruction (flexible, interchangeable roles; implementation of specially designed, differentiated learning activities; appropriate use of a variety of co-teaching approaches; flexible grouping configurations; effective use of modified instructional materials)

Shine	**Refine**

(Continued)

Figure 8.2 (Continued)

Assessment (use of informal and formal assessment tools; offering informal and formal feedback; shared responsibility for student assessment and evaluation, focusing both on academic and linguistic development; grading)

Shine	Refine

Additional Factors (sharing all responsibilities; joint use of available resources; shared accountability; dispositions toward collaboration; professional growth; commitment and enjoyment)

Shine	Refine

Benefits of Self-Assessment

What are some documented benefits of teacher self-assessment? Self-assessment leads to professional growth by shaping teachers' concept of excellence in teaching and by enhancing their ability to recognize outstanding teaching-learning experiences that lead to student mastery of new content (Ross & Bruce, 2007). Self-assessment practices also help teachers define their own professional-development goals since they can better grasp the difference between desired and actual teaching practices. Finally, self-assessment tools not only facilitate communication among teachers, they may also serve as a menu of choices for future action.

ONGOING (FORMATIVE) COLLABORATIVE PROGRAM ASSESSMENT

When teachers, administrators, and other stakeholders are fully committed to a collaborative ESL service delivery model, ongoing (formative) collaborative assessment practices must be initiated. Many school district administrators and teachers are not only interested in examining the research behind particular collaborative practices, they also understand the need to evaluate initiatives that have been undertaken on a local level.

Genesee (2001) recognizes the growing interest in ongoing, formative evaluations for ESL/EFL curricula and program development. He suggests that "ideally, the development of new programmes and curriculums are modified continuously in response to ongoing assessments of their effectiveness" (p. 146). According to Genesee, in order to promote collaborative curriculum and program evaluations, classroom teachers, along with district-level personnel, researchers, or both, must participate.

The ultimate question is: How do we know that our collaborative approach to ESL service delivery is working? In order to gauge the effectiveness of your ESL service delivery model, there are several formative-assessment techniques you and your colleagues may use, including the following:

1. Engaging in professional conversations
2. Participating in peer observations
3. Monitoring student development and performance
4. Designing a collaborative inquiry framework
5. Establishing a program review-and-assessment committee that meets regularly

Quick Tips on How to Get Started With Formative-Assessment Practices

Professional Conversations

Start by regularly engaging in professional dialogues about your practices with your collaborative colleagues. Share your lesson plans and unit plans, explore your classroom dilemmas, and offer support and input to your fellow teachers.

Peer Observations

Teachers who collaborate regularly but do not have the opportunity to co-teach miss out on the opportunity to see each other in action. Visit your collaborative team members and observe each other teaching the English language learners for whom you share responsibility. Try to split your attention between (a) teacher watching (determining the best practices and successful techniques your colleagues are using with ELLs) and (b) student watching (how do ELLs respond to the instruction?).

Monitoring Student Performance

Though in Chapter 4 we discussed various protocols for collaborative assessments of student work, we are revisiting the approach here for program assessment purposes. Regularly review student work, in a collaborative fashion, to document the impact collaborative practices (including co-teaching) have on student learning. Analyze the outcomes of formal and informal learning and performance assessments. Prepare and review case studies of students whose linguistic, academic, or social-emotional learning (acculturation) is cause for concern.

Collaborative Inquiry

Among so many others, Goodlad, Mantle-Bromley, and Goodlad (2004) recommend that teachers engage in a process of inquiry that consists of four cyclical, ongoing steps of dialogue, decision making, action, and evaluation focused on a shared purpose. They claim that such collaborative inquiry is "the single-most important vehicle for school renewal" (p. 110). For formative-assessment purposes, similar to Gajda and Koliba (2008), we suggest adapting Goodlad et al.'s four-step framework to your local context:

1. *Dialogue:* Regularly engage in preplanned professional dialogues about key instructional issues and ELLs' academic and linguistic development and performance.

2. *Decision making:* Collectively decide what collaborative practices you wish to initiate, develop, continue, or discontinue.

3. *Action:* Based on the collaborative decisions, actively engage in initiating, developing, continuing, or discontinuing certain practices.

4. *Evaluation:* Regularly collect and analyze both informal and formal data about both your teaching practices and ELL student learning.

Collaborative inquiry can be a powerful approach to increasing student achievement on standardized tests as well as improving school culture through the ongoing reflection and sharing of its members (Love, 2009). One way to examine the extent to which collaborative practices are in place in your school is to conduct a survey.

Administrators may use the following survey (see Figure 8.3) to determine how teacher collaboration already is being used in their schools. In this way, principals and other building administrators can hone in on the specific needs of their faculty and devise particular initiatives to help make collaborative practices successful. Additionally, this same survey can assess to what degree collaborative initiatives have been achieved after they have been operational for a period of time.

Periodic Program Review-and-Assessment Meetings

In order to review key aspects of the collaborative ESL program, set up an assessment committee to meet periodically. Schedule meetings with a clear and concise agenda and well-defined roles. Manage the logistics of the meetings by identifying a

Figure 8.3 Evaluation Survey

Evaluation Survey
Collaboration and Co-Teaching for ELLs

Directions: Use the following statements to identify the successes and challenges of co-teaching or collaboration activities in your school. Circle a number from 1 to 5 for each statement (1 = Strongly disagree, 2 = Somewhat disagree, 3 = Neither agree nor disagree, 4 = Somewhat agree, 5 = Strongly agree).

Leadership and Collaboration

District and building administrators value teacher collaboration.	1 2 3 4 5
Building administrators encourage and support collaboration efforts between ESL instructors, general-education teachers, and other specialists.	1 2 3 4 5
Professional development is provided to train teachers in collaborative planning and decision making.	1 2 3 4 5
Teachers are provided scheduled time to collaborate with other teachers.	1 2 3 4 5
Teacher recommendations derived through collaboration are given serious consideration.	1 2 3 4 5

Teacher Collaboration

ESL and general-education teachers maintain ongoing conversations about the teaching and learning of ELLs.	1 2 3 4 5
Teams of faculty members along with others in the school community work together to identify and solve ELLs' learning difficulties.	1 2 3 4 5
ESL and general-education teachers converse across grade levels and content areas to promote understanding of ELLs and to share teaching strategies.	1 2 3 4 5
Teachers experiment with new ideas they learned through teacher collaboration in their classrooms.	1 2 3 4 5
Teachers collaborate with each other after school hours.	1 2 3 4 5

Shared Values for the Education of ELLs

The school community together has established a common vision for the education of ELLs.	1 2 3 4 5
ELL student learning is the responsibility of all teachers.	1 2 3 4 5

(Continued)

Figure 8.3 (Continued)

Formal and informal communication practices for the benefit of ELLs have been established between faculty and staff members.	1 2 3 4 5
Parents of ELLs and other community members have had formal opportunities to share their ideas and concerns about the education of ELLs.	1 2 3 4 5
Teachers have had input in the decision-making process for the education of ELLs.	1 2 3 4 5
School Support for Teacher Collaboration	
All teachers and staff members are perceived as valuable members of the school community.	1 2 3 4 5
Adequate time is provided for teachers and staff to meet and discuss ELL issues.	1 2 3 4 5
Conversation protocols have been established to make optimum use of collaborative meeting time.	1 2 3 4 5
Teachers serve on committees to select new teachers, administrators, and other staff members.	1 2 3 4 5
Extracurricular activities are planned for faculty and staff to promote camaraderie and reduce isolation.	1 2 3 4 5
Shared School Practices	
Faculty and staff both individually and collectively reflect upon their practices with ELLs.	1 2 3 4 5
Teachers are able to determine their own professional-development needs with regard to ELLs.	1 2 3 4 5
Parents of ELLs are offered workshops on a regular basis throughout the school year.	1 2 3 4 5
Administrators participate in professional-development activities along with teachers.	1 2 3 4 5
Regularly scheduled collaborative team meetings are conducted by teachers to benefit the instruction of ELLs.	1 2 3 4 5

Adapted from Roberts, S. M., & Pruitt, E. Z. (2009). *Schools as professional learning communities: Collaborative activities and strategies for professional development*. Thousand Oaks, CA: Corwin. (pp. 27–29) facilitator who will set the topic, goal, or purpose for each meeting and create an agenda with specific time slots and allotted discussion times for each item. This type of organization will help the flow of the meeting and assure that each topic is addressed. Program review-and-assessment meetings may address the agenda items in Table 8.8 throughout the year.

Table 8.8 Year at a Glance: Program Review-and-Assessment Meeting Agendas

Month	Key Agenda Item
September	Program Initiation, Goal Setting, Logistics
October	Partnerships and Implementation Needs
November	School Context
December	Strategies for Ongoing Collaboration
January	Administrative and Teacher Leadership
February	Professional-Development Practices
March	Resources
April	Teacher Evaluation/Satisfaction
May	Student Performance Data
June	Planning for Next Year

Several different formats may be used to capture the essence of each meeting. In addition to more traditional meeting minutes, we suggest you try the SNAPS template in Figure 8.4. *SNAPS* stands for the following:

- *Successes* the team has experienced related to the agenda item to start the meeting off on a positive, welcoming note
- *New approaches*, initiatives, or suggestions recommended by a committee member are discussed and recorded next
- *Appreciative comments* allow for staff recognition
- *Problems* then are discussed related to the topic
- *Solutions* are brainstormed by the team to end the meeting productively

FORMAL PROGRAM EVALUATION

Stufflebeam and Shinkfield (2007) claim that evaluations must look beyond whether a particular program met its objectives and what the outcomes were. Instead, they also need to "examine a program's goals, structure, and process" (p. 8). Sanders and Sullins (2006) remind us that "evaluation gives direction to everything that we do when changing and improving school programs" (p. 2). They enumerate several key goals for formal program evaluation. See Table 8.9, in which the left column contains the universal program evaluation goals, and the right column is left blank for your team to determine the most appropriate locally developed goals.

Figure 8.4 Meeting Minutes Template (SNAPS)

Successes:

New approaches:

Appreciative comments:

Problems:

Solutions:

| Table 8.9 | Setting Program Evaluation Goals |

Universal Program Evaluation Goals	Our Own Goals
To identify student needs	
To set priorities for addressing needs to generate program objectives or modify existing objectives	
To identify and select among different program approaches, methods of organization, staff assignments, materials and equipment, facilities, schedules, and other structuring choices in order to build a program that has a high likelihood of success	
To monitor and adjust the programs as they are implemented	
To determine whether a program is resulting in desired outcomes and why the outcomes are as they are	
To judge requests for resources to support the program	
To determine whether a program should be supported, changed, or terminated	

Adapted from Sanders, J. R., & Sullins, C. D. (2006). *Evaluating school programs: An educator's guide* (3rd ed.). Thousand Oaks, CA: Corwin. (p. 2)

Guiding Principles for Program Evaluation

The American Evaluation Association (2004) suggests that educators observe the five essential principles presented in the following textbox when they conduct program evaluations.

FIVE ESSENTIAL PRINCIPLES OF EVALUATION

1. *Systematic Inquiry:* Evaluators conduct systematic, data-based inquiries.

2. *Competence:* Evaluators provide competent performance to stakeholders.

3. *Integrity and Honesty:* Evaluators display honesty and integrity in their own behavior and attempt to ensure the honesty and integrity of the entire evaluation process.

4. *Respect for People:* Evaluators respect the security, dignity, and self-worth of respondents, program participants, clients, and other evaluation stakeholders.

5. *Responsibilities for General and Public Welfare:* Evaluators articulate and take into account the diversity of general and public interests and values that may be related to the evaluation.

Excerpts from American Evaluation Association. (2004). *Guiding principles for evaluators.* www.eval.org/Publications/GuidingPrinciplesPrintable.asp

---

Essential Questions Aligned to the Five Evaluation Principles

We developed essential questions to consider for each principle of collaborative ESL program evaluation following the inquiry stance we established earlier in this book.

1. Systematic Inquiry
   a. What steps are we going to take to perform a useful evaluation?

2. Competence
   a. What skills and resources are needed to complete the program evaluation?
   b. How are we going to ensure that evaluators demonstrate not only all the necessary knowledge and skills but cross-cultural competence as well?

3. Integrity and Honesty
   a. How are we going to ensure that the evaluation process yields valid and reliable information?

4. Respect for People
   a. Who will be affected by the evaluation process and how?

5. Responsibility for General and Public Welfare
   a. Who are the stakeholders whose interests need to be considered?
   b. Who will be informed about the outcomes of the evaluations?

We encourage our readers to devote additional time and effort to refine the guiding questions presented here.

Based on the five guiding principles set by the American Evaluation Association, Kaufman, Guerra, and Plat (2006) suggest a four-phase Evaluation Action Plan (EAP) be implemented. We adapted their four phases to better respond to the context of ESL service delivery; matched each phase with an appropriate, broad purpose; and aligned each purpose with three essential questions to guide educators in the process of planning a systematic program evaluation (see Table 8.10).

Select Tools to Use for Program Evaluation

Questionnaires and Surveys

Open-ended questionnaires allow program stakeholders to share their ideas (along with positive and negative experiences, needs, concerns, and problems) in broad terms. As a follow-up, more structured questionnaires or surveys are often developed to focus on select concerns using multiple-choice and true-or-false formats or three-to-seven-point scales to solicit various degrees of agreement or disagreement with the statements. Such structured data gathering and evaluation tools guide respondents to address a limited number of purposefully included, critical items related to the ESL program.

Table 8.10 Evaluation Plan for Collaborative ESL Services

Evaluation Plan	Alignment and Direction	Selection of Evaluation Methods	Results	Action and Adjustment
Purpose	To ask the right questions and to plan the evaluation process	To determine an approach for collecting valid and useful data	To compare what was accomplished to the program goals	To determine what to keep and what to change
Key Questions Related to Collaborative ESL Services	1. What collaborative practices have been implemented to meet our program goal? 2. What aspects and outcomes of our collaborative practices are we going to evaluate? 3. What are the desired outcomes?	1. What information are we going to collect? 2. What tools and instruments do we need to collect the data? 3. Who is going to collect what type of data? Where, when, and how?	1. Did the outcomes match our original goals and intentions? 2. What trends and patterns are observed in student achievement and teacher performance? 3. What factors contributed to the outcomes and how?	1. What steps should we take to improve our program? 2. What practices should we retain, adjust, or eliminate? 3. What are the intended and unintended outcomes of our collaborative practices?

Adapted from Kaufman, R., Guerra, I., & Plat, W. A. (2006). *Practical evaluation for educators: Finding what works and what doesn't.* Thousand Oaks, CA: Corwin. (p. 3)

Focus-Group Discussions

Focus-group discussions are also called group interviews and usually include 8–12 teachers (or other stakeholders meeting in their own groups) who explore a predetermined set of questions that focuses on their shared experiences. Focus groups offer an effective format for gathering rich, authentic data about group members' perceptions of underlying issues and concerns as well as their actual and intended action.

Interviews

Interviews are usually defined as one-on-one (face-to-face or telephone) interactions between the evaluator and the interviewee. Individual interviews with representative members or randomly selected members of each constituency group offer further insights into the data collected through questionnaires, surveys, and focus-group discussions.

Formal Observations

Observations planned for program evaluation purposes usually focus on (a) teacher activities in and outside the classroom, such as during professional-development settings or while participating in a range of collaborative practices; and (b) student activities while engaged in learning in the classroom, extracurricular programs, or other interactions.

ADMINISTRATORS' ROLE: LEADING EFFECTIVE ASSESSMENT PRACTICES

Reflection and Self-Assessment

Reflection and self-assessment tools are not only helpful for teachers but will also aid administrators in their quest for developing a method for ESL program evaluation. Based on Harvard University's Ronald F. Ferguson's (2006) work on effective staff development, we have designed the following self-assessment or reflection questions as a tool for administrators:

1. Did I introduce the concept of an integrated, collaborative ESL program in ways that foster trust (feelings of security) and interest?

2. Did I assign responsibilities to teachers and manage accountability for collaborative practices in ways to achieve a balance of leadership control and teacher autonomy?

3. Did I plan, initiate, and monitor implementation of the integrated, collaborative ESL program in ways that inspire ambitious goals and commitment?

4. Did I support ongoing implementation of the integrated, collaborative ESL program in ways that motivate sincere, continued commitment and hard work, despite setbacks and inevitable challenges?

5. Did I recognize, celebrate, and reward accomplishments in ways that sustain and strengthen positive changes?

Assessing the Level of Collaboration

Assessing the level of collaboration within a school or, more specifically, within an ESL program may be challenging. Using the assessment tool presented in Figure 8.5 will

Figure 8.5 Assessing an Integrated, Collaborative Model to Serve ELLs

Assessing an Integrated, Collaborative Model to Serve ELLs

Rate the following activities on a scale of 1 to 5, with *1* indicating that it never takes place and *5* indicating that it is a most common practice.

1 = Never   2 = Rarely   3 = Sometimes   4 = Frequently   5 = Always or almost always

1. Interdisciplinary, cross-specialization conversations
   a. to discuss students' linguistic and academic development   1 2 3 4 5
   b. to consider ELLs' changing curricular and instructional needs
      and appropriate adaptations   1 2 3 4 5
   c. to explore extracurricular opportunities for ELLs   1 2 3 4 5
   d. to examine student work   1 2 3 4 5
   e. to enhance parental involvement   1 2 3 4 5

Other:

2. Common planning opportunity
   a. to compare and align lesson objectives   1 2 3 4 5
   b. to design or modify instructional materials   1 2 3 4 5
   c. to adapt instructional strategies   1 2 3 4 5
   d. to adapt curriculum   1 2 3 4 5
   e. to align curriculum   1 2 3 4 5
   f. to engage in curriculum mapping   1 2 3 4 5

Other:

3. Shared classroom experiences
   a. classroom visits to observe each other's best practices   1 2 3 4 5
   b. classroom visits to observe ELLs' participation in various instructional settings 1 2 3 4 5
   c. classroom visits to peer coach (such as using the 2 + 2 model)   1 2 3 4 5
   d. co-teaching to deliver instruction collaboratively   1 2 3 4 5

Other:

4. Reflection and inquiry
   a. working in well-established teacher teams   1 2 3 4 5
   b. participating in collegial circles   1 2 3 4 5
   c. participating in teacher study groups   1 2 3 4 5
   d. sharing professional readings (sharing literature on collaboration and ESL topics) 1 2 3 4 5
   e. conducting collaborative action research   1 2 3 4 5
   f. engaging in lesson study   1 2 3 4 5
   g. offering internal staff development for colleagues (on collaboration and ESL topics) 1 2 3 4 5

Other:

5. Administrative support and feedback
   a. offering instructional leadership (being knowledgeable about both
      ESL and collaborative practices)   1 2 3 4 5
   b. establishing logistical support for all levels of collaboration   1 2 3 4 5
   c. securing necessary materials and resources   1 2 3 4 5
   d. offering ongoing professional-development opportunities that foster collaboration 1 2 3 4 5
   e. creating a professional learning community   1 2 3 4 5

Other:

allow administrators to gain insight into the types of collaborative activities that take place or should take place. By closely examining the following key areas, they can maximize the effectiveness of ESL programs and can more fully addresses the linguistic, academic, and cultural needs of English language learners through collaboration:

1. Interdisciplinary, cross-specialization conversations
2. Common planning opportunity
3. Shared classroom experiences
4. Reflection and inquiry
5. Administrative support and feedback

SUMMARY

An effective collaborative ESL program model must have a carefully designed assessment component. A range of formal and informal approaches to assessment are available to support reflective, collaborative practices among ESL specialists and their general-education colleagues. The ultimate goals of assessment are to enhance the effectiveness of all teachers' classroom instruction and to ensure improved student achievement.

DISCUSSION QUESTIONS

1. Select one or more reflection, assessment, or evaluation tools presented in the chapter and try to implement them for a set period of time. Discuss the tools' effectiveness in your context and make adjustments if needed to match your existing framework, your school's mission, your own philosophy of education, or, in short, your needs!

2. Gajda and Koliba (2008) offer systematic recommendations to administrators on improving teacher collaboration at the secondary level. Without any specific reference to English language learners, they assert the importance of ensuring that teachers work in teams. Specifically, they describe high- and low-functioning teams this way:

   > Teachers in high-functioning teams will systematically collect and analyze both quantitative information (such as summative test scores or tallies from observational checklists) and qualitative information (such as notes taken during a classroom observation of a colleague and student written work), whereas low-functioning teacher teams tend to rely on anecdotes, hearsay, and general recollections to inform their dialogue and decision-making. (p. 146)

   Reflect on this quote and generate a list of quantitative and qualitative data sources—relevant to your teaching situation—that would be useful to inform your decision making about a collaborative ESL program.

3. Consider the following three levels of assessment. How would you collect relevant data for each of them to inform all stakeholders about the effectiveness of your collaborative ESL program model?

- Teacher perception: What do teachers really think of collaborative practices? Do they value them? What do they gain from them?
- Instructional practices: As a result of collaboration, do teachers enhance or change their teaching practices? Are their instructional strategies appropriate for ELLs? Observations by the principal, peers, or interviews may be used to collect data.
- Student learning: Does collaboration have an impact on ELLs' language development and overall academic learning?

KEY ONLINE RESOURCES

American Evaluation Association (AEA home page with links to evaluation organizations, training programs, and Internet resources)
     www.eval.org

Center for Social Research Methods
     www.socialresearchmethods.net

Joint Committee on Standards for Educational Evaluation
     www.jcsee.org

National School Reform Faculty: Protocols
     www.nsrfharmony.org/protocols.html

Northeast and the Islands Regional Technology in Education Consortium (Collaborative Evaluation)
     www.neirtec.org/evaluation

NSF User-Friendly Handbook for Project Evaluation
     www.nsf.gov/pubs/2002/nsf02057/start.htm

Program and Process Evaluation (The Education Alliance at Brown University)
     www.alliance.brown.edu/ae_progeval.php

Self-Assessment Checklists From Scholastic
     http://teacher.scholastic.com/professional/selfassessment/checklist/index.htm

Portraits of Collaboration

Written in collaboration with all the teachers featured in this chapter
and Kelley Cordeiro, Research Assistant

I hate quotations. Tell me what you know.

Ralph Waldo Emerson

OVERVIEW

In this chapter, we'll tell you what we know. We visited or interviewed numerous teachers who are engaged in collaborative teaching practices to benefit ELLs on a daily basis. We selected six exemplary ESL specialists and their collaborative teachers working at the elementary, middle, and high school levels to be showcased in the following case studies. Each case study starts with a snapshot describing *who* the teachers are, *what* they teach, *where* they work, *when* they collaborate, and *why* they believe in collaborative practices. The case studies will reveal the featured teachers' unique collaborative contexts, common and uncommon collaborative practices, challenges and successes, and words of wisdom they are willing to share. Finally, each case study is supplemented by lesson plan examples or other collaboratively developed resources or materials that further illustrate the teachers' experiences with collaboration. All names and locations are real.

ELEMENTARY SCHOOL CASE STUDY #1

Who: Barbara Suter (ESL) and Vera Zinnel (second-grade teacher)

What: ESL in the general-education classroom

Where: Bowling Green Elementary, East Meadow, New York

When: Before and during school and lunch periods

Why: Barbara on her experience with collaborative teaching: "I always felt as an ESL teacher I was not as well informed as I'd like to be about how my students compared with their peers in their classrooms. Now that I'm co-teaching in mainstream classrooms, I see that the ELLs are just like their monolingual counterparts. Some have strong literacy skills in English, some are emergent bilinguals, and some have learning difficulties."

Vera on her collaborative relationship with Barbara: "We both trust each other. We have released responsibility and know that what happens in each other's rooms is equally important."

Context of Collaboration

Bowling Green Elementary is a K–5 school in Nassau County, with approximately 900 students. The school has a diversified ESL population of about 80 students, including children from Asia, Central and South America, and parts of Europe. Most ELLs speak English in school with occasional code switching, but they are still able to communicate effectively. At home, their native language is usually spoken with parents, grandparents, and siblings.

ESL students in all grades, except Grade 2, are divided up among the grade-level teachers. In the past three years, the principal has helped to cluster a group of six to eight ESL students in one second-grade classroom so that the ESL teacher (Barbara) and the second-grade classroom teacher (Vera) can collaborate daily on successful instruction and outcomes for these students. There are other teachers with ELLs in their classes who are willing to collaborate on special projects.

In the last few years, both the school and the district have supported ESL teachers in aligning curriculum for ELLs to that of the general-education classrooms. There have been and will continue to be opportunities for general-education teachers to learn about the practices and strategies incorporated by ESL teachers through inservice courses, professional development, and mentoring opportunities.

Vera and Barbara have a shared educational philosophy. They both participate in the district's AUSSIE (Australian United States Services in Education, www.aussiepd.com) joint professional-development program. For the past three years, Bowling Green has been fortunate to have an ongoing, on-site staff development opportunity. Their principal supported both Barbara and Vera in their quest to expand their knowledge base by becoming part of the AUSSIE program. Because the AUSSIE program is on-site and individualized to each teacher's and classroom's needs, Barbara and Vera were able to tailor this wonderful program to their specific classes. AUSSIE also helped to further their collaboration by suggesting strategies such as using mentor texts for writing.

Barbara and Vera chat in their classrooms before the school day begins about what they plan to do that day. They also meet during lunch periods to collaborate on planning. They confer about particular ELLs together to plan for building intervention and CSE (Committee on Special Education) meetings if necessary.

Collaborative Practices

Each day after a mini-lesson, Vera, the classroom teacher, assigns a certain amount of independent work for students to complete as a part of their morning learning centers. When Barbara joins the class, she checks with the teacher to see if there are specific activities or concepts to be addressed or reviewed with ELLs. Depending on the nature of the activities, she may either stay in the general-education classroom to help them (push-in) or bring them to her ESL classroom to do other relevant work (pull-out).

The nature of Barbara and Vera's collaboration is very flexible. Occasionally, Barbara will independently design an activity for the entire class related to what they are studying. She will choose books or projects that extend whatever topic Vera is working on, or she will help develop background information and vocabulary for all the students in the classroom. At other times, the two teachers will plan a whole class unit together, jointly deciding on activities, topics, materials, and schedules, and co-teach the unit.

More specifically, the collaborative practice usually follows the following format:

> Co-teachers teach together at the same time each day, for approximately 70 minutes, allowing the ESL teacher to give the full amount of time allotted to ESL beginners. Sometimes this is push-in time, sometimes it is pull-out time, and sometimes it is a shared lesson, depending on the needs of the ESL students and the work going on in the general-education classroom.

As word of their collaborative successes has permeated the school, other general-education teachers have approached Barbara requesting to work with her as well, whether on one class or an entire unit. Whatever the case, Barbara strives to model and apply her ESL strategies to the content and skills the teacher is working on. Most of the time she is modeling the simplified language for the classroom teacher, streamlining a concept to make it more comprehensible, or helping the classroom teacher adjust lessons in a way that makes them more accessible for ELLs, such as providing media or pictures for the topic being addressed. At times she does initiate and co-teach the lesson with the general-education teacher.

Challenges and Successes

The greatest challenge? Time! It can be difficult to find common time for planning and collaborating. For collaboration to work smoothly, the schedules of collaborative teachers must be compatible, which requires the support of administrators. Even though Bowling Green is a large school, which can make scheduling complicated, the principal has succeeded in making it possible for them to collaborate. Another identified deterrent to collaborative teaching is the New York State testing schedule, which often pulls ESL teachers away from the classroom for several weeks a year to administer state tests to ESL students, making consistency in co-teaching not always possible. Many teachers whose classroom populations are changing are becoming more attuned to the need for differentiation of instruction to the extent required by ELLs, and they are seeking out the ESL teacher for support. An opportunity exists to turn these sessions into a mentoring experience.

What would success look like in a collaborative context? In part, success would mean having ESL teachers continue to participate in schoolwide planning and professional meetings across the district for input concerning instructional practices that will benefit ELLs and other struggling students in the classroom.

Words of Wisdom

Barbara and Vera offer the following advice to teachers engaging in co-teaching or other forms of collaboration:

1. First, find someone in your school you have enjoyed working with already and build on that. Suggest that you attempt to do a project or two collaboratively and see how it works out. Sometimes the best friendships do not result in the best collaborations; sometimes unlikely people turn out to be great co-teachers! If things go well, at that point you might want to consider presenting the idea of a possible ongoing collaboration to your "significant other."

2. Start out very slowly. Take the time to sit in on each other's lessons and really listen to what the other teacher is trying to accomplish. You and your ESL teacher will each have a different focus and perspective, but they can and should reinforce each other for the benefit of the students. Don't attempt to collaborate right away; get to know each other and each other's students. Allow the students time to get to know you, too.

3. It helps to put time limits on your early collaborations, so everyone understands what will take place. For example, you may plan to collaborate on a lesson twice a week for 30 minutes per session. When that becomes comfortable for both of you and you are getting good results, you may both want to consider extending the collaboration. It is very important to have some boundaries, however, so no one feels put upon.

4. Be extremely flexible. All kinds of things come up unexpectedly in the general-education classroom, so both teachers must realize that schedules are constantly in flux, and planned sessions may have to be delayed or postponed for a while. This is not ideal for collaborative teaching, but it must be acknowledged or frustration will mount quickly.

5. Above all, keep the academic success of the children in mind. The road is bumpy, but the rewards are many. It is wonderful for ELLs to be able to experience the ESL teacher in their general-education classroom, and it is an equally important experience for non-ELLs to get to know the ESL teacher better and to see that ELLs can participate actively in a lesson, too, if given the right support. The reinforcement of ideas by both teachers and the richness of the language experience will benefit all the children in the classroom so much that you will want to collaborate more, not less. Good luck!

Sample Materials: Horseshoe Crabs (A Short Study Unit by Barbara Suter and Vera Zinnel)

Purpose: The purpose of the unit is threefold: to immerse students in learning and researching information about a particular species, horseshoe crabs, that is in danger of becoming extinct; to model for all students how to ask questions in order to learn about a topic; and to model for ELLs how to correctly formulate questions and answers.

Target Audience: The target audience for this unit is a second-grade classroom that includes a cluster of six ESL students.

Method: The general-education and ESL teachers collaborated on both creating and presenting the lessons. Throughout the year, whenever possible, they have used a "shared time" on Friday mornings for approximately 60 to 90 minutes for presenting collaborative lessons.

1. KWL Chart

First, we asked the students what they know about horseshoe crabs; then we asked them what questions they might have about them. This list of questions was the basis for the writing that followed. We charted their answers in two columns. A third column entitled "What Did You Learn About Horseshoe Crabs?" was completed later in the unit.

2. Use of Realia

One of the teachers brought in two fairly intact horseshoe skeletons she had found on the beach. The children were invited to touch, observe, and comment on the features of the specimens. Their observations were recorded on a chart entitled "Observations About Horseshoe Crabs."

3. Reading a Nonfiction Book for Information

To reinforce what they had already learned, and to further expand their knowledge and understanding of horseshoe crabs, one of the teachers read a nonfiction book to them entitled *Horseshoe Crabs* by Lola M. Schaefer (Heinemann Library, c. 2002). Vivid photos and a clear and well-written text encouraged further lively discussions and insights. New concepts and vocabulary were added to the existing charts.

4. Reading Strategy: Questioning
Language Strategy: Asking and Answering Questions

In order to encourage participation in the inquiry process and in the very important strategy of asking questions while reading (*Strategies That Work* by Harvey and Goudvis, 2007), students were invited to write a significant question of their choice as well as what they had learned in order to answer their question on a black-and-white worksheet that was provided. In addition, at the bottom of the worksheet they were given space to illustrate their question and answer.

Since beginning and intermediate ELLs sometimes have difficulty formulating questions using correct syntax and vocabulary, the ESL teacher felt it was important to focus this component of the unit on the strategy of formulating specific questions and answers so that ELLs as well as general-education students in the class could practice these skills.

5. Writing Process

Upon completing their sloppy copies, each student had a mini-conference with one of the two teachers to confer on spelling, grammar, and other issues.

Students were then asked to complete "their best effort" on the colorful worksheet provided that would become a page in a book entitled *Questions and Answers About Horseshoe Crabs.*

Students were told their final pages would be incorporated into this book and placed in the library next year for other students in the school to read. Each student was given a black-and-white copy of the book.

	ELEMENTARY SCHOOL CASE STUDY #2
Who:	Caryn Bachar (ESL lead teacher/coordinator) and fellow general-education teachers
What:	Elementary ESL support
Where:	Ogden Elementary School, North Woodmere and Hewlett Elementary School, Hewlett, New York (Hewlett-Woodmere school district)
When:	Before, during, and after school
Why:	Caryn explains, "If the school is a community, you have to make each child part of that community; it behooves you to be part of the community. You have to foster that kind of acceptance, and it starts with you and your co-workers."

Context of Collaboration

The Hewlett-Woodmere school district in New York has an ELL population comprised of students from Latin America, Asia, Africa, and Europe. While the majority is made up of Spanish speakers, Hebrew and Russian speakers are of almost equal numbers. In this district, the majority of ELLs, who are mostly American born or who immigrated to this country at an early age, are found in grades K–2. However, the number of ELLs in upper grades has evidenced an upward trend that has been primarily attributed to an increasing number of ELLs being designated with special needs. These students, who may have become English dominant, have difficulty exiting the program, as their disabilities often hinder their achievement on the New York State English as a Second Language Achievement Tests.

Collaboration in this district occurs among general-education, reading, special education, and ESL teachers. It is widely supported by administrators and staff, who regard collaboration as an integral element of the school culture. It is also supported by support staff, including school psychologists, the guidance department, and social workers, as well as the PTA, all of whom look to include ELLs and their families in their efforts as much as possible. ESL teachers are afforded a wealth of materials, training, and professional-development opportunities, as well as formal prep time to collaborate. These teachers share students and maintain an ongoing dialogue about the content, amount, and level of instruction. Departmental meetings, at which collaborative planning and issues are discussed, are attended by district-level administration as well as building principals.

As part of their collaborative efforts, Hewlett-Woodmere schools have instituted *articulation* on a districtwide level, which translates into communication on a broad scope between grade levels, during which current grade teachers discuss students with their future grade teachers. This successful practice includes general-education and support personnel (ESL, special education, and speech language teachers, as well as social workers and psychologists). Articulation occurs within each school and also between schools when students are graduating from one school level to the next, such as from early childhood to elementary, elementary to middle school, and so on.

Another successful collaborative effort results in forming Instructional Support Teams (IST). In ongoing ISTs, teachers work together to support ELLs who are experiencing non-language-related difficulties, such as emotional, academic, or social issues.

Caryn teaches at two schools within this district, both of which have established collaborative classrooms for ESL and special education students being taught in an inclusive setting. In these classrooms, two teachers, one general education and one special education, work together the entire school day. Beyond these classrooms, collaboration spans across the entire curriculum and student body. Each of these schools has carved out specific time within the daily schedules for collaboration among general-education and support personnel. Additionally, teachers who teach in the designated collaborative classes are allotted extra time for co-planning. Caryn also appreciates that support for collaboration is so strong within these schools that administrators will almost always accommodate teacher requests for additional meeting time.

Collaborative Practices

Dividing her time between two schools requires that Caryn maximize her free time to effectively collaborate with her co-teachers in each setting. Her schedule in one school allows time for meeting with teachers in the morning before classes begin. At the second school, she meets with colleagues for quick exchanges during prep time and lunch periods and at weekly faculty meetings. But their dialogue does not end there; communication is ongoing and is supplemented via frequent e-mails. Additionally, some instances require greater discussion and meeting time with appropriate personnel, such as issues concerning students with severe disabilities or special circumstances affecting ELLs. These meetings will either occur informally or by requesting that the principal provide class coverage and additional release time for teachers if the situation requires that they meet formally at a specified time.

Caryn's collaborative routines take a variety of forms. On the second-grade level, she works as both a push-in and a pull-out teacher, alternating with the general-education teacher to either lead the class or to work with a smaller group of ELLs or other students needing support. Many students have double periods with Caryn, which are designed to give them individual instruction in specific skills or content in a pull-out format, followed immediately by a push-in class in which Caryn can support the students during the general-education classroom lesson. While lesson content is primarily driven by the general-education teacher's weekly lesson plans, the roles each teacher plays in the delivery of a lesson are decided during their weekly meetings. Although communication is often informal, the results are structured so ELL language support and instruction are aligned to the general-education curriculum.

On the third-grade level, Caryn collaborates with a teacher who provides her with her lesson plans for the week. Caryn modifies the lesson to the needs of those students who require special education services, ESL services, or both, including tailoring textbook chapters, creating adapted worksheets, offering explanations and unit reviews, and providing copies of ESL resources to the general-education teacher. They also often create the differentiated instructional materials together. Through this process, they have created a substantial library of resources to use with future students.

Challenges and Successes

One of Caryn's greatest challenges is collaborating with teachers who are uncomfortable with co-teaching, or in finding the balance in personalities, abilities, and experience. Her greatest satisfaction comes from the districtwide recognition of the collaborative efforts spanning grades K–12, which permeates through each building and at every level, including administration. Her contributions to these efforts are acknowledged and genuinely valued, which is a great sign of success.

Words of Wisdom

What is Caryn's advice to those embarking on collaborative efforts? "Find a teacher who is willing to try—there will be successes and failures along the way. Just as the students learn, sometimes you learn the most from your failures and mistakes."

Sample Materials: A Social Studies DBQ (Document-Based Question) Framework

Here is an example of how Caryn supports content-based instruction in the fifth-grade social studies class.

Mrs. Bachar   Name: _____

ESL   Date: _____

SOCIAL STUDIES—DBQs
What is a DBQ (document-based question)?

A ***document-based question*** is a question that asks you about information you have read. You get this information from documents.

What is a document?

A ***document*** is anything that is printed and gives information.
Examples of documents are the following:

- maps
- letters
- articles
- photographs
- illustrations (drawings, cartoons, etc.)
- graphs
- journals
- laws

What is a primary source?

There are two kinds of documents—***primary source*** and ***secondary source***. A primary source is an original document from a specific time; a secondary source is a document that someone else wrote. For example, a biography is a secondary source, but an autobiography is a primary source.

Examples of primary-source documents are the following:

- letters
- journals
- posters

- illustrations
- photographs
- government papers

Examples of secondary-source documents are the following:

- chapter of a history book
- graphs

When you look at a document, look at *everything*. Read the **captions** (words below a picture, illustration, etc.) and **titles** (the name of a book, article, story, etc).

Ask yourself the following questions:

- Who is in the document?
- Who wrote or made the document?
- Who is the audience of the document?
- What is the document about?
- What kind of document is it?
- What is the purpose of the document?
- When was the document written or made?
- Where was it written?
- Why was the document written or made?
- What does it show?
- How is the time of the document different from today?

MIDDLE SCHOOL CASE STUDY #1

Who:	Nancy Berg (special education and ESL) and Matt Fliegel (general education)
What:	Seventh- and eighth-grade ESL
Where:	Dodd Middle School, Freeport, New York
When:	Before, during, and after school
Why:	Matt Fliegel, on how he approached co-teaching, "It kind of approached me..." Nancy Berg, on her experience, "I have had the most positive experience since the onset of collaborative teaching."

Context of Collaboration

Nancy and Matt co-teach four out of five of their heterogeneous English class periods each day at Dodd Middle School in Freeport, New York. Dodd is the academic home to a diverse community of learners, with administrators who have established and offer ongoing support to a growing collaborative and co-teaching effort. Students are taught using a team approach that includes all four core subject teachers, special education teachers, and reading teachers. Each team of teachers teaches the same students each day and meets formally every other day to share notes, discuss students, and collaborate on instructional planning. Additionally, weekly and monthly meetings are held within each core subject department to discuss curriculum development. Special education and ESL teachers are included in all of these meetings, as well as in all collaborative efforts.

Nancy and Matt's classes are comprised of seventh- and eighth-grade general-education, special education, and ELL students. The ELL population they teach can be further broken down into the designations of limited English proficient (LEP), formerly limited English proficient (FLEP), and bilingual students. These students range from intermediate to advanced levels of English proficiency. The ELL students with disabilities (ELL/SWD) are all at an intermediate proficiency level. Their students are distributed among the four class periods, with the largest number attending the first-period class, in which Nancy and Matt say every seat in the class is filled. Nancy and Matt also instruct classes at Dodd's Saturday Academy, which was established primarily to prepare students for the ELA exam but also provides an opportunity for reinforcement instruction in other core subject areas.

Nancy, a veteran teacher with 20 years of experience at Dodd, also serves as a mentor to Matt, a first-year teacher. They each approach co-teaching with equal levels of enthusiasm and pliability.

Collaborative Practices

Although formal collaboration is conducted during team meetings, Nancy and Matt accomplish most of their collaborative efforts informally, whether via countless text messages, e-mails, and phone calls or during daily conversations and idea exchanges transpiring before, during, and after the school day, as well as during their lunch periods, which are almost always spent together. Both Nancy and Matt stressed that the key to their collaborative success lies in constant communication, flexibility, and open-mindedness. The strength of their professional relationship, which has been likened to a marriage of sorts, translates into a seamless co-teaching performance in which they complete each other's thoughts with such transparency that students are unable to distinguish between the special education/ESL and general-education teachers.

Nancy has shared with Matt her training in the Sheltered Instruction Observation Protocol (SIOP) model of teaching, and they try as often as possible to incorporate elements of this model into their daily lesson planning. The majority of their lessons are created collaboratively, with each lesson including differentiations and modifications for their ELL/SWD students. Fine-tuning lessons and activities is an ongoing process, with adjustments often being improvised midlesson in response to students' receptivity and level of engagement.

They practice frequent "quick" self-assessments to reflect upon the strengths and weaknesses of their lesson delivery, as well as to provide honest feedback to each other about what did or did not work with a group of students. This may be as simple as each writing a positive and negative comment on a small sticky note, exchanging it with each other, and discussing it over lunch or at their next informal meeting. Favorite strategies and activities include "Think, Pair, Share," question mark envelopes, and debates. They alternate primarily between team teaching and station teaching but incorporate other co-teaching models as well.

Challenges and Successes

The greatest difficulty faced by Nancy and Matt can be summed up simply: not enough time! Among their challenges are planning collaboration without common prep time and finding time to address disciplinary or behavioral issues with the students with special needs who are also in their classes. They agree that when disruptive student behavior interferes with their instructional practices, they need to be able to seek the principal's or assistant principal's attention and support. Additionally, their lack of greater input in student scheduling in the past often prevented them from having students placed in a way that would be most conducive to increased learning and achievement opportunities.

One of their proudest successes has been helping students to achieve record-breaking, increased performance levels on the New York State ELA Exam. Preliminary results from 2009 show 70 percent of the classified students in their classes passing the exam. This groundbreaking success was achieved through their efforts during regular class time, as well as supplemental efforts during the Saturday Academy.

Words of Wisdom

In closure, Nancy's advice to someone new to collaborative teaching is to "give everything a try and don't shut something down or shoot something down before you try it . . . . Be open."

Sample Materials: A Collaboratively Developed English Language Arts Lesson Plan

Mr. Fliegel and Ms. Berg

Aim: Students will understand the rules of capitalization and sequence.

Objectives:

1. Students will be able to use sequence words to sequence the beginning, middle, and end of a reading passage.

2. Students will be able to correctly capitalize proper nouns.

New York State ELA Standards:

ELA 1: Students will read, write, listen, and speak for information and understanding.

ELA 2: Students will read, write, listen, and speak for literary response and expression.

ELA 3: Students will read, write, listen, and speak for critical analysis and evaluation.

ELA 4: Students will read, write, listen, and speak for social interaction.

Materials: Students will use definition worksheets, PBJ worksheets, capitalization worksheets, and comic strips.

Motivation/Do Now: Each student will receive a comic strip cut into three or four segments. These directions are given to students: Put your comic strip in order so it makes sense. Did your comic make sense out of sequence? Explain the importance of understanding the order of a story.

Key Questions:

1. Why is sequencing important to us as writers?

2. Explain the difficulties readers might experience if writers didn't use sequencing.

3. Outside of this class, where else do we use sequencing?

Procedure:

1. Students will receive a copy of the sequence definition handout. Students will read the worksheet aloud. Emphasis will be placed on the sequence words. (Modification: sequence words will be highlighted.)

2. Students will receive a peanut-butter-and-jelly handout. Each student will write a sequential paragraph (using at least five sequencing words) on how to make a peanut-butter-and-jelly sandwich. When all students are finished, they will share their responses with one another and respond to each other's work. (Modification: students will work in pairs.)

3. On the back of the worksheet, the students will volunteer all the sequence words they can think of for each column (beginning, middle, and end).

4. Students will receive capitalization worksheets. The rule at the top will be read. Students will be asked to explain it in their own words. Several incorrect examples will be on the board. Students will be asked to correct the mistakes in a relay race fashion.

5. If time remains, students will complete capitalization worksheets independently.

Assessment:

1. Homework will be collected the following day to assess students' comprehension of capitalization rules.

2. There will be a capitalization quiz on Friday.

3. Teachers will circulate the room during the peanut-butter-and-jelly activity to assess students' understanding of sequencing and using sequence words. Additionally, teachers will have students volunteer completed work.

Homework:

1. Students will complete the capitalization handout.

MIDDLE SCHOOL CASE STUDY #2

Who:	Linda Rauch, ESL teacher
What:	Sixth- through eighth-grade ESL
Where:	Bay Shore Middle School, Bay Shore, New York
When:	Before, during, and after school
Why:	"Often times you get teachers that are not as comfortable working with ESL students as others, and they will come to you perhaps a little frustrated, and I gear a success on whether or not we both walk away feeling good about what we've decided for each individual child."

Context of Collaboration

Linda is an ESL teacher at Bay Shore Middle School, in Bay Shore, New York. This school has approximately 60 ELLs, the majority of whom are Hispanic students. The ELL population also includes two students from Haiti, two from Pakistan, and one from India. About one-third of the ELLs are at the beginner level of English proficiency.

The middle school administration is very sensitive to incorporating ELLs into all programs and activities at the school and sets the tone for the building as they cultivate an atmosphere of communication and collaboration, which permeates throughout the school. The school uses a team approach to teaching, with each team comprised of teachers from each content area: the math, science, social studies, and English teachers on each team have a common planning period daily, and each grade level also meets monthly. The ESL teachers each work with a full-day paraprofessional, allowing them the coverage they need to attend most team and grade-level meetings. This also provides them with flexibility to communicate with content-area teachers.

In addition to the teams used during the regular school day, another collaborative program found at Bay Shore is the Triple A (AAA) Academy, with sections focusing on state test preparation for mathematics, social studies, ELA, and NYSESLAT. While this program is open to all students, a special section is designated for ELLs, all of whom are enrolled. The AAA mathematics classes are team taught three days a week from October through March.

The success of Bay Shore's collaborative efforts can be largely attributed to an experienced ESL staff working side by side with teams of other highly dedicated teachers who want to work with ELLs, as well as an administration that understands the necessity of ELLs accessing information in all classes.

Collaborative Practices

Linda's daily schedule entails an early arrival and a late departure, providing her with opportunities to make the time for informal collaboration with content-area teachers on an ongoing basis. In her experience, she has found that the people who are very willing to work with ELLs, who may be on informally designated teams, will make that time as well, whether before or after school, during their regular prep time or lunchtime, or perhaps in having a paraprofessional run down and deliver work to another teacher or bring something back. They visit each other's classrooms to observe one another's teaching strategies and maintain a continuous dialogue through school mailboxes and e-mail to communicate about issues such as assignments, tests, and projects. Formal opportunities for collaboration occur primarily during team and grade-level meetings, which she attends on a weekly and monthly basis.

In Linda's definition, collaboration can be anything, from providing a child the support necessary to finish a test, to assisting a content-area teacher to design an alternate assignment that is more appropriate for a student's specific proficiency level.

In math classes, collaboration usually means predetermining the work and preteaching the concepts that will be introduced in a particular week for each grade level. Using the content-area teacher's lesson plans, Linda outlines the key vocabulary and provides ELLs with support in comprehending the language aspect of the lesson while the math concepts are being taught by the general-education teacher. A variety of co-teaching models are incorporated into her teaching, which often includes small-group instruction, monitoring, reteaching concepts, and teaching on purpose for students indicating difficulty in grasping specific concepts.

In other areas, such as social studies, in addition to regular class support, school trips provide an opportunity for the collaborative ESL teacher to preteach background information through mini-units aligned to the content-area teacher's lesson as well as to state curriculum standards. Overall, these collaborative efforts often rely on intuition as well as an awareness by the ESL teacher as to where the content-area teacher is and where they are going within their lessons.

Challenges and Successes

While Linda considers administrators in her school to be very supportive and accommodating with regard to collaborative planning and practices, she still finds that one of her greatest challenges stems from scheduling that does not allow for more common prep time for lesson development. As far as success is concerned, Linda uses her ELLs as a barometer to gauge the effectiveness of her collaboration with her colleagues; monitoring the rises and falls in frustration levels among her ELLs serves as an indicator of how well she is doing, what works, and where fine-tuning may be required.

Words of Wisdom

Linda believes that "ESL teaching practices are sound teaching practices that should be occurring in every classroom. Besides teaching our ELLs English, we need to help them access information throughout their school day. We can't afford to teach in isolation. ESL teachers must make every effort to find out what is going on in other classrooms by sharing, collaborating, and teaming up with other professionals."

Sample Material: A Collaborative Science Lesson

Below is a lesson example that Linda developed as a result of collaborative planning with her science teachers.

Linda Rauch   Beginner Language (Grades 6, 7)

Class Description: This is a group of beginner-level English language learners. There are six sixth graders and one seventh grader. One sixth grader was retained this year. The seventh grader barely passed. Three of the five have very limited skills.

Previous Lesson: This is a two-week interdisciplinary unit on Christopher Columbus. We have done map work and are presently working on a step-into-reading book on Christopher Columbus. We have covered a great deal of vocabulary good for both BICS and CALP. The students have been working on the scientific method in both their sixth- and seventh-grade science classes. They have had great difficulty following their lab experiments because of the science-specific vocabulary. The science teachers have asked me to review the scientific method with the students. We will do an experiment that will tie into our study of Columbus and exploration.

Aim:

1. The students will review their knowledge and the vocabulary of Columbus's exploration.

2. The students will discuss spices and food preservation.

3. The students will learn to navigate the scientific method by actually doing an experiment with spices. They will observe which spice will preserve a piece of potato best. This will be over the course of several days.

4. In groups, and via the overhead projector, the students will do a lab write-up (Bloom's application).

5. Students will play a game to guess the parts of the scientific method.

NYS ESL Learning Standards Addressed:

NYS ESL Standard 1: Students will listen, speak, read, and write in English for information and understanding.

NYS ESL Standard 2: Students will listen, speak, read, and write in English for literary response, enjoyment, and expression.

NYS ESL Standard 4: Students will listen, speak, read, and write in English for classroom and social interaction.

Procedures: The students will practice their routines of a "Do Now" and reading the morning announcements. They will review orally the concepts and the vocabulary from their reading. They will also discuss the scientific method. The students will then do the experiment with Mrs. Rauch. The students will work in pairs to try to come up with the parts of the lab write-up: the problem, the hypothesis, and the materials. We will go over this on the overhead projector and will continue to do the procedure. We will discuss our plans for the observations, results, and conclusion.

Assessment: The students will be informally assessed during our discussion. Their ability to do the lab write-up will also be assessed formally. The game will also assess how well they have learned the scientific method.

Follow-Up Activities: The students will complete the experiment over the next few days. The students will complete a cartoon on the king and queen of Spain. The cartoon will be about the king and queen's discussion of spices and preservation of food.

HIGH SCHOOL CASE STUDY #1

Who:	Susan Dorkings, Study Skills/ESL Department Chairperson
What:	ESL three-part program, including ESL classes, Study Center, and content-area ESL classes
Where:	William A. Shine Great Neck South High School, Great Neck, New York
When:	During the school year, collaboration is an ongoing process that takes place throughout the school day as well as before and after scheduled classes. In addition, summer workshops provide further opportunities for colleagues to work together.
Why:	"When ESL students arrive at Great Neck South High School, they have to attain proficient English skills while taking challenging academic classes. Many students come with the expectation of graduating in four years and then going to college. Administrators and teachers developed a program aimed at providing extensive support for ESL students throughout the day. This program includes ESL classes, participation in Study Center, and many content-area ESL classes. Collaboration is a key component of the program and one that is embraced by all members of the Study Skills/ESL Department."

Context of Collaboration

Great Neck South High School has approximately 60 ELLs. The majority of this diverse population is Korean, followed closely by Chinese students. There are also a few Hispanic, Japanese, Indian, and Pakistani students. This is a shift from a little over a decade ago when the ELL population of the school was predominately Spanish speaking. Within the diverse cultural backgrounds, ELLs also come to this school from a wide variety of academic backgrounds. Some students bring with them a solid history of formal education, while others have a background marked by frequent interruptions or, perhaps, no formal education at all. Also, a number of ESL students have learning disabilities that parallel those of the general-education population. These factors, combined with individual learning styles, family background, and acclimation to American culture, influence the structure of the program.

Under the leadership of the former and current principals, the ESL program has flourished. Presently, this program has three main components: ESL classes, Study Center (see Chapter 7), and content-area ESL classes. All teachers involved in this multifaceted program collaborate in order to provide the most effective instruction.

Collaborative Practices

Although it is difficult to find common planning time for all teachers involved in the program, there are various ways in which they communicate to best facilitate the needs of the students. Formally, Study Center teachers meet with ESL teachers one period per week to discuss the needs of individual students as well as their progress. Along with academic issues, various social and psychological issues that interfere with learning are also discussed so that appropriate action can be taken. Many times, collaboration occurs in informal ways before, during, and after school. Often, a spontaneous conversation between teachers regarding the needs of a particular student can result in specific instruction. For instance, Study Center is staffed by two English teachers whose schedules rotate so that English instruction is offered throughout the day. While one of these teachers may brainstorm a research topic with a student, later in the day the other teacher may help the same student find reliable reference sources online. This is a process that continues through the completion of the research paper. The seamless effort demonstrates the effectiveness of informal collaboration between two members of the department.

Many ELLs are enrolled in content-area ESL classes that follow the SIOP (Sheltered Instruction) model. These classes, taught by content-area teachers, develop academic and language proficiency. Similar to the joint efforts of study skills and ESL teachers, content-area teachers collaborate with members of the Study Skills/ESL Department. Sometimes it is difficult to find time to meet due to conflicting schedules, so other forms of communication, including e-mail and phone calls, are used. When this is not sufficient, administrators will facilitate common meeting times. It is important that the study skills/ESL chairperson meet periodically with the department chairpersons of the content areas to discuss curriculum, find appropriate materials, and evaluate the success of the content-area ESL program.

An important aspect of the TESL and content-area ESL classes is the inclusion of bilingual staff in the classroom. Great Neck South High is fortunate to have team members who speak Korean, Chinese, Hebrew, Farsi, Spanish, and Greek. Over the years, these teachers and teaching assistants have been able to support students in important ways. For example, one teaching assistant, who works in the Study Center, also assists students in the math ESL, biology ESL, and TESL 1 classrooms. This gives her a unique perspective on these students' overall performance in school, which, in turn, she shares with all instructors. She also works in the Study Center, where she provides additional support to the students enrolled in these classes. Due to her presence in the content-area classes, she can effectively provide follow-up instruction in the Study Center and help these students even when they start to feel overwhelmed by the demands of homework and tests. Her ability to speak Chinese allows her to communicate on a deeper level, and sometimes students will share important information with her that they would not be able to articulate in English. Her second language skills are also an asset to the school because she can communicate with parents. In this way she serves as a liaison among administrators, teachers, guidance counselors, and families.

Collaboration also exists in the form of mentoring. When new members join the department, strong working relationships form. The success of this form of collaboration is marked by a natural and easy exchange of ideas. As Susan noted, "When new teaching assistants join our department, everyone is eager to help them understand the mission of our Center and model teaching strategies that meet the diverse needs of our students. The culture of the study skills/ESL program is shaped by a spirit of teamwork that is embraced by all its members."

Challenges and Successes

A unique challenge that faces ESL teachers and faculty that support the high school population is the lack of time. When elementary or middle school students arrive in the United States, they have more time to strengthen their language skills before they are faced with high school graduation requirements. Over the past five years, more students are arriving in the United States during the ninth grade or later. Some students are in their middle-to-late teens and are just starting out in TESL 1 classes. These students, who have very limited English language skills, must pass rigorous Regents exams, including a four-essay English Regents, in order to graduate. Besides providing language and academic support, teachers must also balance the message they send students. As Susan emphasized,

"Yes, we want them to work hard, but we want to make sure that they are not over-whelmed by anxiety." Another challenge some students face is that they have to work after school or care for younger siblings. Teachers respond to these time constraints in a number of ways, including offering students an extra year of high school or encouraging them to attend summer school classes. Great Neck South High has recently expanded the summer school ESL program and added a course that targets all language skills, including writing skills, which many students find most difficult.

All ESL students are assigned to one of two guidance counselors who have developed an expertise in all issues facing ELLs. They are an important part of the team that plans the best course of study for students, and they are experts on graduation requirements. When new students arrive in school, counselors play an important role in assessing their needs. Working closely with the counselors, the Study Skills/ESL Department can place students in appropriate classes. This collaborative effort is another key component of the program.

Due to scheduling constraints during the school year, Susan finds that summer work-shops provide an opportunity for everyone involved in the team to meet. The school district encourages teachers to participate and provides funding for these summertime sessions. The ESL program has been approved for many workshops including Sheltered Instruction, ESL and Technology (the use of laptops, iPods, and SMART Boards), and Best Practices. Workshops provide an opportunity for teachers, guidance counselors, and specialists to learn new skills, review current practices, and plan for the future. Frequently, an outside expert is invited to facilitate the workshop and present the latest research. During work-shops, there is always time for every participant to share ideas; this exchange of information is so important. Other times, workshops are lead by members of the school community. Summertime is ideal because the relaxed atmosphere gives colleagues a chance to reflect on the challenges they faced during the school year and share their strategies for success.

Words of Wisdom

As Susan concludes, "In spite of all the challenges facing our ESL students, they meet with great success in our school due in large part to their hard work and perseverance. As we continue to look for ways to provide the best instruction for them, our teachers agree that collaboration helps us design and implement a strong, comprehensive ESL program."

Sample Materials: Scaffolded Biology Activities

The biology teacher, ESL teacher, reading teacher, and bilingual teaching assistant col-laboratively developed several differentiated and scaffolded biology activities. The resources they created included the following:

1. Sample lab report with or without guiding questions and scaffolds

2. Practice test question (with or without modifications)

3. Practice question in the students' native language, used as a reference

Some students in the class were able to complete a lab report by following an outline. For others, however, the outline was modified with questions that aid comprehension (see below). Later, students were given a practice test question to familiarize them with a typical New York State Regents question. Some students were provided with a modified version of the same task; the task was simplified to aid comprehension. In addition to a modified test version, ESL beginners were provided with a translated (Chinese) version of the test question.

Bio Lab Report Outline (With Guiding Questions)

Title:

Hypothesis: Educated guess: What do you think will happen?

Methods (What did you do?) **and Materials:** (What materials or things did you use?)

Experimental Group

Control Group

Data Collected:

Make a chart (independent, dependent variables)

Record (write) your results

Discussions and Conclusions:

Write a paragraph discussing your results. What do the data show?

Suggestions for Improvement:

How can you improve this experiment?

Suggestions for Further Research:

What other types of experiments could you perform?

HIGH SCHOOL CASE STUDY #2

Who: Christine Rowland, UFT (United Federation of Teachers) Teacher Center staff and fellow high school teachers

What: High school ESL classes and professional development

Where: Christopher Columbus High School, Bronx, New York

When: During ESL content-area classes, professional-development sessions, and other meeting times

Why: Christine relates, "Collaborating in the classroom seems to be a far more powerful way to share strategies and concepts than explanation and discussion. Experiencing a technique alongside a colleague, and watching them problem-solve, can be tremendously helpful. These are just some of the reasons why the UFT Teacher Center strongly promotes classroom collaborations, with Center staff engaging in collaborative teaching relationships where possible and also by providing central professional development in co-teaching models."

Context of Collaboration

Christopher Columbus High School, located in the Bronx, is a comprehensive high school with approximately 1,400 students. It has four nonthematic smaller learning communities, with a total of about 260 ELLs distributed throughout. About 60 percent are Hispanic, 15 percent are Albanian, and the rest of the students come from a wide range of nations in Africa, the Middle East, and Southeast Asia. They also come with all ranges of academic background. There are students who arrive with strong skills in their native language and those who had interrupted or limited formal education.

Collaborative Practices

The school has tried to create opportunities for the content-area teachers of ELLs to meet during regularly scheduled professional periods twice a week. One team Christine works with closely includes two math teachers, one social studies teacher, one ELA teacher, and two science teachers. In this unique format, Christine facilitates professional-development sessions as well as weekly "case conferencing" meetings, where the team has an opportunity to discuss the academic and social progress of individual students.

She meets with the teachers in the UFT Teacher Center (housed within the school library), where coffee and cookies are always available. The professional-development program she offers each semester always follows a theme. Past themes have included sheltered instruction (including lesson and unit planning), while a recent semester focus on differentiated instruction included a modified lesson study format. (Each participant develops a differentiated lesson, which is shared with peers. Team members use this opportunity to receive and offer feedback to each other. Next, teachers visit one another's lessons. They then share observations and analyze resultant student work to consider the effectiveness of the differentiation strategies in helping students to meet the lesson objectives.)

Case conferencing at the beginning of the year focuses on students with similar needs on the same grade level. As the year progresses, more emphasis is given to individuals and groups that emerge as having special needs. This past year, newly admitted students, those who spoke no English, or those who were hardest to reach were most often mentioned for inclusion in the case conferences. As the semester went on, teachers started to look at student work and discuss how they could produce increasingly sophisticated responses if the types of activities teachers give them are scaffolded.

The recurring theme of these meetings has been analyzing what ELLs were doing successfully, what they have been struggling with, and what teachers could do to support ELLs' learning in the classroom. A side benefit of this practice was that students learned that their teachers were talking about them, that everyone was on the same page. Students were told, "You've been doing your homework" or, "I heard that you're doing really well in math. That's great—congratulations!" They felt a greater bond with their teachers and a sense of identity as a group—almost an informal smaller learning community.

As a former full-time ESL teacher, and then as a professional developer for the New York City Department of Education's Office of English Language Learners, Christine has extensive experience and comprehensive teaching and coaching skills to fulfill her current position as a UFT Teacher Center staff member. Her responsibilities are manifold, including coaching and mentoring, offering ongoing professional development and support to both content-area and ESL teachers, and teaching her own class at CCHS. While not in a traditional teaching position, Christine had the opportunity to take on a co-teaching assignment with Seth Mactas, a general-education social studies teacher, in his third year of teaching when they began working together on this project. Seth used this opportunity to learn about the sheltered-instruction approach and other ESL methodologies through the co-teaching experience with Christine.

Initially, Seth and Christine worked together daily for a period planning their classes. They generally co-taught one period of global history and geography a day, but as Seth became more comfortable with the various sheltered strategies that were effective with the students, they distributed the work by Seth taking on the bulk of planning, while Christine prepared the ongoing, formative assessments, and they shared grading responsibilities. One of the most valuable aspects of their collaboration became a move away from the traditional lesson of copying extensive board notes and Regents-style exams (essays and multiple-choice questions). The sheltered lesson planning they collaborated on included a more interactive mini-lesson focused on the core objectives for the day, including plenty of comprehension checks where students were asked to articulate their understanding in their own words. This was generally followed with a text-based pair-work or small-group activity, giving students the opportunity to both read (using a fourth-grade-reading-level text designed to meet the content of the curriculum) and write, often using customized graphic organizers to enhance their understanding of concepts. These activities were generally differentiated based on student readiness. Developing students' content literacy along with their English language development was followed through with teacher-created, content-based student assessments that did not merely simulate the Regents experience but assessed their content and language development more accurately and validly. Multiple-choice test items were eliminated from individual tests, since students found it too easy to "share" their answers.

The collaborative experience between a content specialist and an ESL teacher gave the students an optimal opportunity to learn. At the end of the year, students were able to show that they had learned and progressed greatly, regardless of how much English they understood at the outset, while those who came with stronger skills were able to succeed on the Regents examination.

Challenges and Successes

Lisa Fuentes, principal of CCHS, initiated the focus on ELLs in the spring of 2006 as a result of a failure to make Adequate Yearly Progress in the school's graduation rate. She has always done her best to support the program. Her commitment to addressing the needs of ELLs systemically and willingness to listen to teachers' concerns and requests made a tremendous impact. Christine strives to make the entire school leadership aware of the issues and also to share student work, showing how students make progress over time.

In Christine's experience, the most prominent obstacles to collaboration are scheduling of teachers and competing priorities. It is rather challenging to secure common planning time, so not all teachers have been able to participate in every meeting that she plans. During most semesters she has conducted a rolling meeting—most teachers coming during one period and the remainder during another.

The most rewarding experience for her was "team teaching with Seth, in that it is rare to find a teacher so willing to work collaboratively. Not only did we work together with the second year of the global history curriculum, but the following spring we worked together again for about three months with a U.S. history class."

Words of Wisdom

As Christine sums up,

Working together in the classroom can be a real pleasure. Sharing responsibility reduces stress and pressure on both teachers and provides added interest and support for students. Two heads can really be better than one when it comes to thinking up interesting and creative assignments and developing new approaches to instructional challenges. Two things seem to be essential—mutual respect and common planning time. It is vital that each teacher knows that he or she has a valuable role to play and that colleagues understand and respect this. The planning time is particularly important in the early stages of a partnership, while you begin to negotiate each element that such a relationship entails, taking time to talk through issues as they arise. With time the patterns become established, and the process thus becomes less time consuming.

Sample Materials: A Sample Agenda for a Professional-Development Session Led by Christine Rowland

SHARED STUDY OF STUDENT WORK: TEACHER-GENERATED TESTS

AGENDA

What can we learn from student tests?

How can students' performance on tests inform our instruction?

What is the objective of our tests?

How can we use what we learn to help students become more successful?

Facilitated by Christine Rowland, UFT Teacher Center staff

A Sample Social Studies Test Co-Developed by Seth Mactas and Christine Rowland

Christopher Columbus HS

Ms. Fuentes, Principal

Name: _____

Global History 3—ESL

Mr. Mactas & Ms. Rowland

TEST—WORLD WAR I

Section I: The Causes of World War I

1. How was **imperialism** a cause of WWI? (3%) _____

_____

_____

2. How was **militarism** a cause of WWI? (3%) _____

_____

_____

3. How were **alliances** a cause of WWI? (3%) _____

_____

_____

4. How was **nationalism** a cause of WWI? (3%) _____

_____

_____

5. Look at the map of Europe in 1914. Identify the following nations or areas on the map: Great Britain, France, Germany, the Ottoman Empire, Russia, Austria-Hungary, and Italy. (14%)

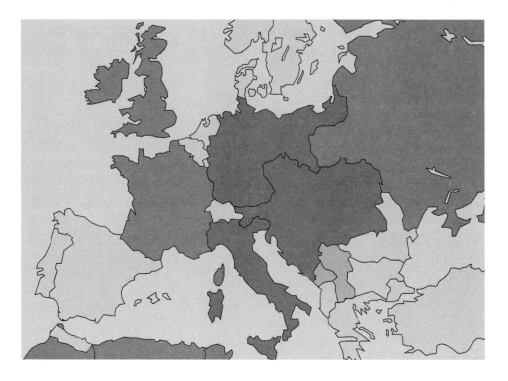

a. _____ b. _____ c. _____

d. _____ e. _____ f. _____ g. _____

6. Which countries were members of the Triple Alliance (Central Powers)? (6%)

a. _____ b. _____ c. _____

7. Which countries were members of the Triple Entente (Allied Powers)? (6%)

a. _____ b. _____ c. _____

8. The following events led to World War I. Put them in the correct order. The first has been done for you—event #1 is *e*. (12%)

  ____ a. Germany invaded Belgium to get to France.

  ____ b. Austria-Hungary blamed Serbia for the assassinations and declared war on Serbia on July 28.

  ____ c. Britain declared war on Germany.

  ____ d. Germany then declared war on France, because France was an ally of Russia.

  _1_ e. Gavrilo Princip, a Serbian nationalist, assassinated the Archduke Ferdinand and his wife.

  ____ f. Germany, an ally of Austria Hungary, declared war on Russia.

  ____ g. Russia, a friend of Serbia, mobilized its army.

Section II: The War

9. Trench warfare was very important in World War I. What was a trench? Draw a picture of a trench in the space below. Why and how were trenches used? (8%)

a)

b. Why were trenches used?

  _____

  _____

c. How were trenches used?

  _____

  _____

10. How did the war change when the United States joined the Allies? (6%)

11. What was the name of the agreement on November 11, 1918, to stop the fighting? (2%)

Section III: The Results of World War I

12. Identify three points in the Treaty of Versailles. (6%)

  a. _____

  b. _____

  c. _____

13. What was the League of Nations? (2%)

_____

_____

14. Explain four things that happened after the collapse of the Austro-Hungarian and Ottoman Empires. (8%)
    a. _____
    b. _____
    c. _____
    d. _____

15. Some nations were very unhappy after World War I. Identify three unhappy nations and the reasons for their unhappiness. (21%)

Nations	a.	b.	c.
Reason they were unhappy			

For Extra Credit (Pick only _one_ of the topics below and write a paragraph.)

Either: Describe some of the new technologies used during the war.

Or: Explain what lessons you think the world should have learned from World War I.

_____

_____

_____

_____

_____

_____

SUMMARY

Though the six ESL specialists and their colleagues we introduced in this chapter represent a range of collaborative practices, they demonstrate a shared commitment and passion for working with others to create more effective and equitable learning opportunities for ELLs. Despite the fact that all six case studies originated in the larger New York metropolitan area, the experiences and contexts in which the teachers' daily instructional and collaborative practices take place vary greatly. Each story is unique, yet many of the challenges are similar. We hope the words of wisdom they offered help everyone who reads them.

DISCUSSION QUESTIONS

1. Compare the context of collaboration in select case studies to your own context. Which of the six situations was most like your own?

2. Select one of the six case studies for closer analysis. What are two examples of collaboration that most impressed you? What are at least two possible ways the collaborative practices could be further enhanced?

3. Examine the case studies from an administrative point of view. What role did the school administrator play to make the collaboration work? What could the administrator plan as viable next steps to further enhance collaboration?

4. Develop a case study of your own by interviewing a colleague. Turn the four case study headings—context of collaboration, collaborative practices, challenges and successes, and words of wisdom—into interview questions.

Research Appendix

10 Key Research Areas to Support Teacher Collaboration and Co-Teaching for the Sake of ELLs

Ten broad topics of research or related areas of best practice are presented in this appendix to further support claims we made in Chapter 2, "Why Is Collaboration Needed?"

1. WHAT DO RESEARCH AND BEST PRACTICE REVEAL ABOUT SECOND LANGUAGE ACQUISITION AND ENGLISH LANGUAGE DEVELOPMENT?

One of Cummins's (1984) most noted contributions to the field of ESOL is the distinction between what he originally labeled as Basic Interpersonal Communicative Skills (BICS) and Cognitive/Academic Language Proficiency (CALP). BICS describes the ability to use language in social contexts, whereas CALP refers to the type of language necessary to develop conceptual understanding of cognitively and academically challenging school subjects. More recently, Cummins and Man (2007) distinguish among the following three types of language skills:

1. Conversational fluency ("the ability to carry on a conversation in familiar face-to-face situations," p. 799)

2. Discrete language skills ("the learning of rule-governed aspects of language," p. 800)

3. Academic language proficiency ("the extent to which an individual has access to and command of the oral and written academic registers of schooling," p. 800)

The most important implication of this distinction is that these three language skills often have three distinctive developmental trajectories both for first and second language learners. Cummins and Man (2007) also caution that there is minimal transfer between the development of the first two skills (conversational competence and distinct language skills) and that of academic language proficiency. Thus, all three types of language skills will need to be developed using appropriate methodologies.

Among many others, Collier and Thomas's (1999) research suggests that it takes most ELLs five to seven years to develop native-like academic language proficiency and literacy. However, they documented that students with interrupted formal education (SIFE) or those whose native-language literacy was below grade level took seven to ten years to develop grade-level proficiency and literacy skills in English. Hakuta (2000) concurs that ELLs need a minimum of three to five years to develop oral proficiency (communicative skills), whereas academic English proficiency can take even longer, at least four to seven years.

While focusing on the effectiveness of dual-language programs, Collier and Thomas (2004) also discuss the importance of keeping ELLs connected to the general-education curriculum and recognizing the challenge they face to catch up to their English-speaking peers. Collier and Thomas conclude that

> if students are isolated from the curricular mainstream for many years, they are likely to lose ground to those in the instructional mainstream, who are constantly pushing ahead. To catch up to their peers, students below grade level must make more than one year's progress every year to eventually close the gap. (p. 2)

Cummins (1987, 1991) claims that the linguistic and cognitive interdependence between bilingual children's first and second languages facilitates rather than impedes their language acquisition and attainment of academic English. Since then, second language researchers have repeatedly emphasized the importance of acknowledging, valuing, and incorporating ELLs' native languages and prior knowledge into instruction of grade-level subject matter in English (August, Carol, Dressler, & Snow, 2005; Rubinstein-Avila, 2006).

2. WHAT DO RESEARCH AND BEST PRACTICE REVEAL ABOUT ACCULTURATION AND CULTURALLY RESPONSIVE TEACHING?

Many researchers have explored the challenges of implementing culturally responsive teaching practices and the positive impacts thereof. Ladson-Billings (2000) defines *culturally relevant teaching* as "the kind of teaching that is designed not merely to fit the school culture to the students' culture but also to use student culture as the basis for helping students understand themselves and others, structure social interactions, and conceptualize knowledge" (p. 142). Similarly, Geneva Gay's (2000) extensive research on *culturally responsive education*—defined as "using the cultural knowledge, prior experiences, frames of reference, and performance styles of ethnically diverse students to make learning encounters more relevant and effective for them. It teaches *to and through* the strengths of these students. It is culturally *validating and affirming*" (p. 29)—suggests that such education helps ELLs become more connected with schools and more successful in their academic and linguistic development.

Thus, Gay (2002) urges educators to develop a type of cross-cultural understanding and cultural competence that considers the cultural characteristics, experiences, and perspectives of linguistically and culturally diverse students as catalysts for reaching them more success-fully. She explains that *cultural scaffolding* is necessary for ELLs so they better understand the cultural norms of the classroom, the acceptable set of behaviors along with common partic-ipation structures. Teachers also need to take the time and every opportunity to recognize and successfully build on their ELLs' prior learning experiences. Téllez and Waxman (2005) poignantly remind us that "we can no longer believe that ELD (English Language Development) teaching is merely language instruction. Teachers must understand how cul-ture and language interact in the development of youth as active participants in a democ-racy, as well as in the learning of English" (p. 34). Since teaching ELLs most often means teaching immigrant children or the children of immigrants, it is indispensable to have spe-cialized knowledge of and sensitivity to students' home cultures, the twenty-first-century immigrant experience, as well as a solid understanding of how out-of-school and in-school cultural experiences interact with each other.

Based on extensive research on understanding and responding to the needs of twenty-first-century immigrant youths, Rong and Preissle (2009) make these five overall recommendations[1]:

1. Acknowledge the demographic trends and changes and their implications in your school: Immigration has led to the emergence of new, diverse communities that con-tinue to transform schools. Educators must respect and capitalize on the diversity children and their families bring to the school and leave the deficit model behind.

2. Adapt curriculum and instruction to be more responsive to students' background knowledge, prior experiences, home culture, and academic/linguistic needs.

3. Create a more culturally sensitive and responsive schooling experience and learn-ing environment for immigrant students. From learning how to pronounce their names correctly to training all school personnel to be able to maintain a culturally supportive environment, schools should make an ongoing effort to improve the learning experience for all.

4. Build partnerships and strengthen existing networks with families and communities. Understand the strengths and resources that families bring to the community, while at the same time recognizing their needs and helping them establish local connections.

5. Prepare and continue to educate all school staff on how to work with immigrant families both through teacher preparation programs and through professional-development programs.

Rong and Preissle (2009) also note that "by understanding the complexity of the immigrant experience, educators will gain an increased sensitivity to the circumstances of immigrant students in their schools and classrooms" (p. 122). We must understand that this complexity is further complicated by the fact that many more ELLs are first- or even second-generation, U.S.-born children whose English language proficiency is lacking native-like fluency.

---

1. Adapted from Rong, X. L., & Preissle, J. (2009). *Educating immigrant students in the 21st century: What educa-tors need to know.* Thousand Oaks, CA: Corwin.

3. WHAT DO RESEARCH AND BEST PRACTICE REVEAL ABOUT BILINGUALISM AND NATIVE-LANGUAGE USE?

Regarding ELLs' home language, Cummins (2001) claims that "to reject a child's language in the school is to reject the child" (p. 19). Therefore, schools and all teachers working with ELLs must make a conscious effort to embrace all dimensions of their language learners' identities, especially their linguistic heritage and home language use. One suggested practice is to create a supportive school setting for all students by valuing plurilingualism and making all students' languages visible and valued (Agirdag, 2009). When students' home languages are used and affirmed in school, their identities are also affirmed, and their families feel more inclined to join the school community.

Christensen (2008) also cautions that "by bringing students' languages from their homes into the classroom, we validate their culture and their history as topics worthy of study" (p. 59). In a culturally inclusive community, written and unwritten policies and practices in schools and classrooms will ensure that all students are welcome. ELLs must feel that they belong and can learn regardless of their home languages. Their home culture is affirmed when they see aspects of their out-of-school cultural and linguistic experiences reflected in the school environment and activities (signs welcoming school community members and visitors, multilingual student work displayed on bulletin boards, culturally and linguistically diverse guest speakers at assemblies, books and nonprint media in the library, music played by the school band, or sports played at recess). Christensen also notes that "approaching students' home languages with respect is one of the most important curricular choices teachers can make" (p. 62).

4. WHAT DO RESEARCH AND BEST PRACTICE REVEAL ABOUT ELLS' LITERACY DEVELOPMENT?

An increasing body of research is concerned with exploring effective instructional strategies that support the literacy development of culturally and linguistically diverse students. August and Shanahan (2006) led a panel of experts and edited an extensive research review on ELLs and their literacy development. They found a vast amount of publications on the topic; however, only a limited number of empirical studies had definitive results. Nonetheless, they were able to make the following conclusions and recommendations:

1. ELLs may also benefit from literacy instruction that focuses on the key components of reading—as identified by the National Reading Panel (NICHD, 2000): phonemic awareness, phonics, fluency, vocabulary, and text comprehension. However, they cautioned that adjustments are necessary for enhanced outcomes among ELLs.

2. Word-level skills can be attained more successfully when instruction in the five components of reading is successful. Yet, text-level skills—such as comprehension

and writing skills—are closely aligned to oral-language development. Thus August and Shanahan suggest the development of oral proficiency in English as well.

3. ELLs' first-language oral proficiency and literacy skills can be used to assist literacy development in English.

August and Shanahan (2006) conclude that there was "surprisingly little evidence for the impact of sociocultural variables on literacy achievement or development. However, home language experiences can have a positive impact on literacy achievement" (p. 7).

Gersten et al. (2007) also conducted a comprehensive review of research on effective literacy and English language instruction for ELLs focusing on the elementary grades. Their recommendations are as follows:

1. Conduct formative assessments with ELLs to assess their progress with phonological processing, letter knowledge, word reading, and text comprehension. Based on the data, design additional instructional support and monitor ELLs' reading progress.

2. Offer intensive, small-group literacy intervention for ELLs. Among other skills, focus on the five core reading elements (phonological awareness, phonics, reading fluency, vocabulary, and comprehension).

3. Focus on systematic, high-quality vocabulary instruction that helps ELLs understand both difficult academic content and conversational English.

4. Develop ELLs' academic language proficiency necessary to function in general-education classes.

5. Design instructional activities for pairs of students at different levels of language proficiency so they may work collaboratively on academic tasks in a structured fashion.

A major theme that emerges in these recommendations is "the importance of intensive, interactive English language development instruction for all English learners. This instruction needs to focus on developing academic language (the decontextualized language of the schools, the language of academic discourse, of texts, and of formal argument)" (p. 2). Since this is the type of language needed to be successful in the general-education classroom, with grade- and age-appropriate content materials and on standardized tests, teacher collaboration to support such language development is critical.

Panofsky et al. (2005) note a significant absence of research on writing instruction for adolescent ELLs in U.S. schools. Nonetheless, their report concludes the following:

1. Effective teacher feedback should be specific: it should (a) use examples from ELLs' own writing, (b) rely on specific information from the students' personal experiences or shared texts, and (c) offer indirect error correction, which requires students to correct their error identified by the teacher.

2. If peer editing is used, it should be explicitly taught by modeling and be monitored to be effective.

3. ELLs need more direct writing instruction, which should be supported by instruction in oral-language development and structural, skills-based instruction in their general-education classes.

In addition, there are several other promising findings and practices related to ELLs' literacy development. Mindful of the complexities of second language development, Williams (2001) suggests that teachers of ELLs "encourage students to read at their reading level—not at their oral proficiency level" (p. 751).

5. WHAT DO RESEARCH AND BEST PRACTICE REVEAL ABOUT DEVELOPING ELLS' ACADEMIC LANGUAGE PROFICIENCY?

Ma (2002) notes that English-as-a-second-language (ESL) instruction is often assumed to consist of programs "in which students receive specific periods of instruction aimed at the development of English language skills, focusing on grammar, vocabulary, and communication rather than on academic subjects" (p. 4). However, many practitioners and researchers also reported that ESL programs have evolved or are being augmented to address age- and grade-appropriate, general-education content-area standards. As early as 1988, Freeman and Freeman reported that since the beginning of the 1980s, the focus of ESL instruction has shifted from merely building linguistic competence to also addressing academic language and math, science, and social studies curricula. Content-based ESL, Sheltered Instruction, followed by several other models and approaches emerged in response to this shift in focus.

Sheltered Instruction and the SIOP Model

Various interpretations of *sheltering* have been developed to enable ELLs to study grade-appropriate content that their monolingual English counterparts are exposed to. A common characteristic of all sheltered classes is that ELLs receive special assistance to help them understand general-education course content while also developing a broad range of language skills. In the 1990s, Echevarria, Vogt, and Short along with a large team of ESL and general-education practitioners developed a comprehensive model known today as the *Sheltered Instruction Observation Protocol* or SIOP (2008).

The SIOP Model consists of eight major components (Preparation, Building Background, Comprehensible Input, Strategies, Interaction, Practice/Application, Lesson Delivery, and Review/Evaluation) and 30 subcomponents or instructional strategies centering on the concept that each lesson teachers deliver must be built on matching language and content objectives to allow ELLs to acquire both necessary linguistic skills and academic content knowledge.

The features that most set SIOP apart from high-quality instruction for native English speakers include (a) extended wait time, (b) teaching key vocabulary, (c) adapting content to ELLs' background knowledge and language proficiency levels, (d) language objectives, (e) clarification in the students' native language, (f) modifying one's speech to be appropriate for ELLs' proficiency levels, (g) using a range of supplementary materials, and (h) explicitly connecting new learning to student background experiences.

Cognitive Academic Language Learning Approach

The Cognitive Academic Language Learning Approach, or CALLA (Chamot & O'Malley, 1987, 1994), is a model that integrates content instruction, academic language development, and explicit learning strategy instruction. CALLA is supported by cognitive learning theory and incorporates 18 distinct learning strategies: Chamot and O'Malley suggested that teachers systematically incorporate a choice of five metacognitive strategies (Advance Organization, Selective Attention, Organizational Planning, Self-Monitoring, and Self-Evaluation), 10 cognitive strategies (Resourcing, Grouping, Note Taking, Summarizing, Deduction, Imagery, Auditory Representation, Elaboration, Transfer, and Inferencing), and three social and affective strategies (Questioning for Clarification, Cooperation, and Self-Talk) in each lesson.

Chamot and O'Malley (1994) also created a framework for explicitly teaching language learning strategies by offering a five-step sequence for introducing, presenting, practicing, evaluating, and expanding and applying learning strategies to new contexts in other classes. By adding purposeful strategy instruction to language and content goals, ELLs become more self-directed learners and become actively participating learners (Chamot, 1995). CALLA may be used in ESL and general-education classrooms. Instructional activities encourage student participation, cooperative learning, and higher-order thinking.

ExC-ELL

Calderón (2007) conducted extensive research on effective content-based literacy instructional practices for adolescent ELLs and designed what she named Expediting Comprehension for English Language Learners (ExC-ELL). ExC-ELL is a lesson planning and delivery system consisting of the following 10 key components (pp. 14–15)[2]:

1. Content standards, objectives, indicators, purpose, outcomes, and targets

2. Parsing of text by teachers

3. Summarization/overview of unit, lesson, chapter

4. Background building of concepts

5. Review previous lesson/concepts/content

6. Systematic vocabulary instruction

7. Formulate questions for drawing background knowledge

8. Engagement with text

9. Consolidation of content and skills

10. Assessments

---

2. Adapted from Calderón, M. E. (2007). *Teaching reading to English language learners, Grades 6–12: A framework for improving achievement in the content areas.* Thousand Oaks, CA: Corwin.

Most recently, Dong (2009) highlighted ways in which content-based instruction lends itself to teacher collaboration:

Sometimes two teachers collaborate to give content-based instruction (CBI). One of the teachers is a content specialist and the other an ESL specialist. They may teach the class together or the class time may be divided between the two of them. For example, the content specialist will give a short lecture and then the English teacher will check that the students have understood the important words by reviewing them later. This kind of team teaching requires teachers to work closely together to plan and evaluate classes. (p. 30)

6. WHAT DO RESEARCH AND BEST PRACTICE REVEAL ABOUT EFFECTIVE INSTRUCTIONAL STRATEGIES?

According to Marzano, Pickering, and Pollock (2001), the following nine instructional strategies are most likely to lead to improved student achievement:

1. Identifying similarities and differences

2. Summarizing and note taking

3. Reinforcing effort and providing recognition

4. Assigning homework and ensuring opportunities for practice

5. Using nonlinguistic representations

6. Implementing cooperative learning

7. Setting objectives and providing feedback

8. Generating and testing hypotheses

9. Using cues, questions, and advance organizers

Jane Hill and Kathleen Flynn (2006) adapted Marzano et al.'s (2001) *Classroom Instruction That Works* to guide teachers of English language learners on how to use best practice in their classes. Based on an extensive meta-analysis conducted by the McREL researchers, Hill and Flynn suggest that the same nine instructional strategies may be used for ELLs when carefully scaffolded and differentiated based on ELLs' stages of language acquisition. The strategies revised for ELLs are as follows:

- Identifying similarities and differences between and among concepts
- Helping students learn to synthesize and organize information through summarizing and note-taking techniques
- Reinforcing students' efforts and providing recognition of linguistic development and academic achievements

- Offering meaningful opportunities to review new information and apply new knowledge through adapted homework and scaffolded practice
- Encouraging the use of nonlinguistic representations, thus using visual, tactile, and kinesthetic modalities
- Using cooperative learning to enhance student interactions
- Setting clear objectives and providing meaningful feedback
- Generating and testing hypotheses
- Activating students' prior knowledge and helping them process new information through cues, questions, and advance organizers

Hill and Flynn's approach supports the belief that when the same strategies are used by general-education and ESL teachers collaboratively, consistency of instruction enhances student learning. We also support the notion that careful adaptations of each of these strategies are necessary for optimal results.

7. WHAT DO RESEARCH AND BEST PRACTICE REVEAL ABOUT CURRICULUM ALIGNMENT AND MAPPING?

Udelhofen (2005) identifies curriculum mapping as a process "that is respectful of the knowledge of every teacher, encourages collaboration and reflection, and is sensitive to the complexities of student learning and the teaching profession" (p. 3). The most prevalent feature of curriculum mapping lies in its flexibility, since the process allows for addressing the changing curriculum needs of school districts. In addition, it invites active participation from all teachers and depends on their expertise and collaboration. Throughout the curriculum-mapping process, teachers engage in both reflecting on the taught curriculum and planning for the future. Both backward (journal) mapping and forward (projection) mapping invite teachers to create current, reality-based, and standards-aligned curricula.

Glatthorn, Boschee, and Whitehead (2006) caution that high-quality instruction requires clear, explicit learning goals. In too many schools, they observed a disconnect among key components of effective schooling: State standards, district curriculum guides or frameworks, the teachers' instructional plans and their actual lesson delivery, and the assessment measures used are often disjointed. "Curriculum alignment is a process of ensuring that the written, the taught, and the tested curricula are closely congruent," Glatthorn et al. argue (p. 278). It is also suggested that aligning curriculum vertically and horizontally will be closely tied to teacher professional-development activities that allow teachers to examine their own practices and collaboratively improve instruction for their students.

Though neither Udelhofen (2005) nor Glatthorn et al. (2006) focus specifically on the purpose and outcome of curriculum mapping or alignment for the sake of ELLs, such curriculum development practices are expected to result in enhanced understanding of the general-education curricula by ESL teachers and the ESL curriculum by general-education educators, thus resulting in a more enhanced, shared responsibility for ELLs.

8. WHAT DO RESEARCH AND BEST PRACTICE REVEAL ABOUT TEACHER TEAMING AND CO-TEACHING?

Teacher teaming and co-teaching have been researched for several decades. In a recent synthesis of research findings, Spraker (2003) notes that certain factors have been found to affect the quality of teaming and its impact on student learning. These include (a) administrative support, (b) training for participating on teacher teams, (c) clarity in team organization, (d) longevity of teams and their membership, (e) time for planning and ongoing discussions, (f) and integrating content and instructional practices.

Numerous research publications have addressed collaboration among general- and special education teachers (see, for example, Scruggs, Mastropieri, & McDuffie, 2007); similar attention to ESL collaboration is just emerging. As early as 1992, Fradd discussed the potential outcomes of teacher collaboration implemented to serve all kids with special needs, including ELLs. Among others, Davison (2006) extensively researched collaboration among ESL and content-area teachers with a special emphasis on the nature and challenges of developing collaborative and co-teaching relationships. She used the term *partnership teaching* (also commonly used in research and publications originating in the UK; see, for example, Creese, 2002, 2004, 2005) and emphasized that

> Partnership Teaching is not just another term for "co-operative teaching." Co-operative teaching is where a language support teacher and class or subject teacher plan together a curriculum and teaching strategies which will take into account the learning needs of all pupils, trying to adjust the learning situation to fit the pupils. Partnership Teaching is more than that. It builds on the concept of co-operative teaching by linking the work of two teachers, or indeed a whole department/year team or other partners, with plans for curriculum development and staff development across the school. (pp. 454–455)

The most important question on teachers' and administrators' minds might be, "Does it yield increased student achievement?" An emerging line of research is documenting the impact of teacher collaboration and co-teaching on student learning. Pardini (2006) describes the results of an ongoing, multiyear initiative in the St. Paul Public Schools in Minnesota, where traditional ESL programs have been completely replaced by a collaborative program model. ESL and general-education teachers on all grade levels team teach. Pardini notes that

> between 2003 and 2005, the gap in reading achievement between the district's ELL and non-ELL students fell from 13 to 6 percentage points, as measured by the percent of students showing proficiency on the Minnesota Comprehensive Assessment. In math, the gap fell from 6.7 to 2.7 percentage points. The district's ELL students also did well when compared with their peers statewide, outscoring them in each of the last three years in reading and math as measured by the Test of Emerging Academic English. (p. 21)

In fact, ELLs in Saint Paul Public Schools have made steady gains on all standardized tests administered in the state in closing the achievement gap between ELL and non-ELL students.

In 2007, York-Barr, Ghere, and Sommerness investigated the process and outcomes of a three-year implementation of a collaborative inclusive ELL program model. They not only noted that teachers shared "a strong and nearly unanimous sense that students were highly advantaged by the inclusive and collaborative instructional models—academically, socially, and in terms of classroom participation" (p. 321), but also reported positive achievement gains due to the collaborative practices. Most recently, Causton-Theoharis and Theoharis (2008) also noted significantly increased reading achievement scores over a three-year period in a Madison, Wisconsin, school that moved to a full inclusion model eliminating all pull-out services both for special education students and ELLs. Through an extensive restructuring of the school that used already existing human resources and required no extra cost, collaboration and co-teaching practices became the dominant service delivery format yielding impressive achievement results.

9. WHAT DO RESEARCH AND BEST PRACTICE REVEAL ABOUT TEACHER LEARNING?

Hammerness, Darling-Hammond, and Bransford (2005) systematically reviewed research as well as classic and current theoretical frameworks on how teachers learn and develop in their profession. After applying the three broad principals of *How People Learn* (National Research Council, 2000) to teacher learning, they suggest the following:

1. Prospective teachers should enter the classroom with preconceived notions about how teaching works, which inevitably affects their future practice. This initial understanding conditions what and how they will learn as they enter the profession of teaching.

2. To be able to apply what teachers know, they must have
   a. a strong theoretical foundation and factual knowledge base,
   b. a solid understanding of facts and ideas within the context of a conceptual framework, and
   c. an organizational framework and mechanism to retrieve and respond to new knowledge.

3. To take charge of their own learning and be able to understand and manage new situations as they arise in the classroom, teachers need to develop a metacognitive approach to their own learning.

Based on Joyce and Showers' (1980, 1988) and others' earlier work on professional learning, DuFour and Berkey (1995) conclude that when teachers participate in training, they learn best if they have an opportunity to experience the following: Teachers must have an understanding of the theory and research that supports the innovation. The trainer must offer a hands-on demonstration, while teachers need initial practice in the innovation. To ensure successful implementation, teachers need constructive feedback on their efforts followed by on-going coaching until the innovation becomes an integral part of their repertoire.

In addition, McLaughlin and Talbert (2006) also suggest that teachers learn best as members of communities of practice. New knowledge and skill development is especially effective when teacher learning is facilitated in a supportive environment with the following four approaches intertwined (we added key questions that may guide teachers as they engage in collaborative learning practices):

- Knowledge-centered
  - What are the key problems and issues?
  - What practices have been used?
  - What essential knowledge and skills do we need to solve the identified problems?
- Learner-centered
  - In what way(s) can I use my personal or professional interests and background knowledge and skills?
  - How can I connect my prior knowledge and well-established skills to the new information presented to me or explored collaboratively?
- Assessment-centered
  - How can I get ongoing feedback on my understanding and implementation of new content and skills?
  - Who will be available to guide me and support my learning?
- Community-centered
  - How are my peers involved in collaborative explorations of new content and skills?
  - How can we build upon each other's knowledge and skills to create new understandings and practices?

10. WHAT DO RESEARCH AND BEST PRACTICE REVEAL ABOUT PROFESSIONAL-DEVELOPMENT AND LEARNING COMMUNITIES?

Sergiovanni (2000) offers a leadership framework for school administrators to create a unique *culture, community,* and *personal meaning* in our schools. He notes that

> community is at the heart of a school's lifeworld. It provides the substance for finding and making meaning and the framework for culture building. Think of community as a powerful antioxidant that can protect the school's lifeworld, ensuring that means will serve ends rather than determine them. Communities are collections of people who come together because they share common commitments, ideas, and values. (p. 59)

Sergiovanni discusses five key dimensions of a professional-learning community, which we have adapted to the ESL context here:

1. Learning communities
   a. All members of the school community are deeply engaged in lifelong learning.
   b. Learning is differentiated to match the learners' abilities and needs.
   c. Learning is valued both as an activity and as a way of life.

2. Collegial communities
   a. All members of the school community are meaningfully connected to each other.
   b. A common vision and mission is articulated and implemented.
   c. Shared goals are pursued by all members.
   d. A sense of camaraderie, interdependence, and mutual obligation pervades the community.

3. Caring communities
   a. All members of the school community are committed to the well-being of others.
   b. Concern, thoughtfulness, and respect are not just displayed but are morally embedded in actions.

4. Inclusive communities
   a. All members of the school community are respected.
   b. Linguistic, cultural, ethnic, and all other differences are accepted and valued.
   c. A sense of belonging permeates the community.

5. Inquiring communities
   a. All members of the school community are engaged in collective inquiry.
   b. All members participate in collaborative problem solving.

Most recently, Darling-Hammond and Richardson (2009) have reviewed 20 years of research on effective teacher learning and professional development. They examined the content, context, and design of high-quality professional development. Their conclusions are that teachers learn most effectively when

(a) their content knowledge is addressed as well as how to best convey that knowledge to their students; (b) they understand how their students acquire specific content; (c) they have the opportunities for active, hands-on learning; (d) they are empowered to acquire new knowledge, apply it to their own practice, and reflect on the results; (e) their learning is an essential part of a reform effort that connects curriculum, assessment, and standards; (f) learning is collaborative and collegial; and (g) professional development is intensive and sustained over time. (p. 49)

Darling-Hammond and Richardson note that the most successful framework for teachers' professional learning is one based on professional-learning communities.

A FINAL NOTE

This appendix is not designed to be all-inclusive; it merely highlights key areas of research and a knowledge base that general-education and ESL teachers may benefit from sharing. For further reading on current research related to effective strategies for English learners, please see the following:

Genesee, F., Lindholm-Leary, K., Saunders, W., & Christian, D. (Eds.). (2006). *Educating English language learners: A synthesis of research evidence.* Cambridge, UK: Cambridge University Press.

Goldenberg, C. (2008). Teaching English language learners: What the research does—and does not—say. *American Educator, 32*(2), 8–44.

Goldenberg, C., & Coleman, R. (2010). *Promoting academic achievement among English learners: A guide to the research.* Thousand Oaks, CA: Corwin.

Short, D. J., & Fitzsimmons, S. (2007). *Double the work: Challenges and solutions to acquiring language and academic literacy for adolescent English language learners—A report to the Carnegie Corporation of New York.* Washington, DC: Alliance for Excellent Education.

References

Agirdag, O. (2009). All languages welcomed here. *Educational Leadership, 66*(7), 20–25.

Airasian, P. W., & Gullickson, A. (1994). Examination of teacher self-assessment. *Journal of Personnel Evaluation in Education, 8*(2), 195–203.

Allen, D. W., & LeBlanc, A. C. (2005). *Collaborative peer coaching that improves instruction: The 2 + 2 performance appraisal model.* Thousand Oaks, CA: Corwin.

Allen, M. B. (2005). *Eight questions on teacher recruitment and retention: What does the research say?* Education Commission of the States. Retrieved August 31, 2009, from www.ecs.org/html/education/issues/ teachingquality/trrreport/home/TeacherRecruitmentRetention.pdf

American Association of School Administrators. (n.d.). *ABC's of school safety.* Retrieved May 27, 2009, from www.aasa.org/edissues/content .cfm?ItemNumber=7427

American Evaluation Association. (2004). *Guiding principles for evaluators.* Retrieved August 31, 2009, from www.eval.org/Publications/ GuidingPrinciplesPrintable.asp

Arkoudis, S. (2006). Negotiating the rough ground between ESL and mainstream teachers. *The International Journal of Bilingual Education, 9*(4), 415–433.

ASCD. (2007). *The learning compact redefined: A call to action.* Retrieved August 31, 2009, from www.ascd.org/ learningcompact

Association of Teacher Educators. (n.d.). *Standards for teacher educators.* Retrieved April 22, 2009, from www.ate1.org/pubs/uploads/tchredstds0308.pdf

August, D., Carol, M., Dressler, C., & Snow, C. (2005). The critical role of vocabulary development for English language learners. *Learning Disabilities Research and Practice, 20,* 50–57.

August, D., & Shanahan, T. (Eds.). (2006). *Developing literacy in second-language learners: Report of the National Literacy Panel on language-minority children and youth.* Mahwah, NJ: Erlbaum.

Ballantyne, K. G., Sanderman, A. R., & Levy, J. (2008). *Educating English language learners: Building teacher capacity.* Washington, DC: National Clearinghouse for English Language Acquisition. Retrieved April 29, 2009, from www.ncela.gwu.edu/practice/mainstream_teachers.htm

Ballot Proposition #203. (2000). Retrieved August 8, 2008, from www.azleg.gov/jlbc/ballotprop203.pdf

Berger, J. G., Boles, K. C., & Troen, V. (2005). Teacher research and school change: Paradoxes, problems, and possibilities. *Teaching and Teacher Education, 21,* 93–105.

Blase, J., & Kirby, P. C. (2009). *Bringing out the best in teachers: What effective principals do* (3rd ed.). Thousand Oaks, CA: Corwin.

Blythe, T., Allen, D., & Schieffelin Powell, B. (2008). *Looking together at student work* (2nd ed.). New York: Teachers College Press.

Boe, E. E., Cook, L. H., & Sunderland, R. J. (2008). Teacher turnover: Examining exit attrition, teaching area transfer, and school migration. *Exceptional Children, 75*(1), 7–31.

Borden, L. M., & Perkins, D. F. (1999). Assessing your collaboration: A self-evaluation tool. *Journal of Extension, 37*(2). Retrieved August 18, 2009, from www.joe.org/joe/1999april/tt1.php

Boulding, K. (1989). *The three faces of power.* Newbury Park, CA: Sage.

Boyle-Baise, M., & Sleeter, C. E. (1996). Field experiences: Planting seeds and pulling weeds. In C. A. Grant & M. L. Gomez (Eds.), *Making schooling multicultural: Campus and classroom* (pp. 371–388). Englewood Cliffs, NJ: Merrill/Prentice Hall.

Boyson, B. A., & Short, D. J. (2003). *Secondary school newcomer programs in the United States.* Washington, DC: Center for Applied Linguistics. Retrieved April 29, 2009, from www.cal.org/crede/pdfs/rr12.pdf

Brown, H. D. (2006). *Principles of language learning and teaching* (5th ed.). New York: Addison Wesley Longman.

Calderón, M. E. (2007). *Teaching reading to English language learners, grades 6–12: A framework for improving achievement in the content areas.* Thousand Oaks, CA: Corwin.

Calderón, M. E., & Minaya-Rowe, L. (2003). *Designing and implementing two-way bilingual programs: A step-by-step guide for administrators, teachers, and parents.* Thousand Oaks, CA: Corwin.

Carrasquillo, A. L., & Rodriguez, V. (1996). *Language minority students in the mainstream classroom.* Philadelphia: Multilingual Matters.

Causton-Theoharis, J., & Theoharis, G. (2008). Creating inclusive schools for all students. *The School Administrator, 65*(8), 24–31. Retrieved July 30, 2009, from www.aasa.org/SchoolAdministratorArticle.aspx?id=4936&terms=theoharis

Chamot, A. U. (1995, Summer/Fall). Implementing the cognitive academic language learning approach: CALLA in Arlington, VA. *The Bilingual Research Journal 19*(3, 4), 379–394.

Chamot, A. U., & O'Malley, J. M. (1987). The cognitive academic language learning approach: A bridge to the mainstream. *TESOL Quarterly, 21,* 227–249.

Chamot, A. U., & O'Malley, J. M. (1994). *The CALLA handbook: Implementing the cognitive academic language learning approach.* Reading, MA: Addison-Wesley.

Christensen, L. (2008). Welcoming all languages. *Educational Leadership, 66*(1), 59–62.

Clark, K. (2009). The case for structured English immersion. *Educational Leadership, 66*(7), 42–46.

Cloud, N., Genesee, F., & Hamayan, E. (2000). *Dual language instruction: A handbook for enriched education.* Boston: Heinle & Heinle.

Cochran-Smith, M., & Lytle, S. L. (1999). Relationships of knowledge and practice: Teacher learning in communities. In A. Iran-Nejad & C. D. Pearson (Eds.), *Review of Research in Education* (Vol. 24; pp. 249–305). Washington, DC: American Educational Research Association.

Cohan, A., & Honigsfeld, A. (2006). Incorporating "lesson study" in teacher preparation. *The Educational Forum, 71*(1), 84–93.

Collier, V. P., & Thomas, W. P. (1989). How quickly can immigrants become proficient in school English? *Journal of Educational Issues of Language Minority Students, 5,* 26–38.

Collier, V. P., & Thomas, W. P. (1999). Making U.S. schools effective for English language learners, part 1. *TESOL Matters, 9*(4), 1–6.

Collier, V. P., & Thomas, W. P. (2002). Reforming education policies for English learners means better schools for all. *The State Education Standard, 3*(1), 30–36.

Collier, V. P., & Thomas, W. P. (2004). The astounding effectiveness of dual language education for all. *NABE Journal of Research and Practice, 2*(1), 1–20.

Collier, V. P., & Thomas, W. P. (2007). Predicting second language academic success in English using the prism model. In C. Davison & J. Cummins (Eds.), *International handbook of English language teaching, Part I* (pp. 333–348). New York: Springer.

Conderman, G., Bresnahan, V., & Pedersen, T. (2009). *Purposeful co-teaching: Real cases and effective strategies.* Thousand Oaks, CA: Corwin.

Cook, L., & Friend, M. (1995). Co-teaching: Guidelines for creating effective practices. *Focus on Exceptional Children, 28*(3), 1–16.

Council of Chief State School Officers. (2008). *Educational Leadership Policy Standards: ISLLC 2008.* Washington, DC: Author. Retrieved April 30, 2009, from www.ccsso.org/projects/isllc2008research/documents/ISLLC%202008%20final.pdf

Crandall, J. (Ed.). (1987). ESL through content-area instruction: Mathematics, science, social studies. *Language in Education: Theory and Practice, 69.* (ERIC Document Reproduction Service No. ED283387)

Crawford, J. (2008). *Advocating for English learners: Selected essays.* Clevedon, UK: Multilingual Matters.

Creese, A. (2002). The discourse construction of power in teacher partnerships: Language and subject specialists in mainstream schools. *TESOL Quarterly, 36*(4), 597–616.

Creese, A. (2004). Bilingual teachers in mainstream secondary classes: Using Turkish to learn curriculum. In J. Brutt-Griffler & M. M. Varghese (Eds.), *Bilingualism and language pedagogy* (pp. 97–111). London: Multilingual Matters.

Creese, A. (2005). *Teacher collaboration and talk in multilingual classes.* London: Multilingual Matters.

Cummins, J. (1979). Cognitive/academic language proficiency, linguistic interdependence, the optimum age question and some other matters. *Working Papers on Bilingualism, 19,* 121–129.

Cummins, J. (1984). *Bilingualism and special education issues: Issues in assessment and pedagogy.* London: Multilingual Matters.

Cummins, J. (1987). Bilingualism, language proficiency and metalinguistic development. In P. Homel, M. Palif, & D. Aaronson (Eds.), *Childhood bilingualism: Aspects of linguistic, cognitive, and social development* (pp. 57–74). Hillsdale, NJ: Lawrence Erlbaum Associates.

Cummins, J. (1991). Interdependence of first- and second-language proficiency in bilingual children. In E. Bialystok (Ed.), *Language processing in bilingual children* (pp. 70–89). Cambridge, UK: Cambridge University Press.

Cummins, J. (2001). *Negotiating identities: Education for empowerment for a diverse society.* Los Angeles: California Association for Bilingual Education.

Cummins, J., & Man, E. Y. (2007). Academic language: What is it and how do we acquire it? In J. Cummins & C. Davison (Eds.), *International handbook of second language acquisition* (pp. 797–810). Norwell, MA: Springer.

Danielson, C. (2009). A framework for learning to teach. *Educational Leadership Online, 66.* Retrieved August 31, 2009, from www.ascd.org/publications/educational_leadership/summer09/vol66/num09/A_Framework_for_Learning_to_Teach.aspx

Darling-Hammond, L., & Richardson, N. (2009). Teacher learning: What matters? *Educational Leadership, 66*(5), 46–53.

Davison, C. (2006). Collaboration between ESL and content area teachers: How do we know when we are doing it right? *The International Journal of Bilingual Education and Bilingualism, 9*(4), 454–475.

Deal, T. E., & Peterson, K. D. (1999). *Shaping school culture: The heart of leadership.* San Francisco: Jossey-Bass.

DelliCarpini, M. (2008). Teacher collaboration for ESL/EFL academic success. *The Internet TESL Journal, 14*(8). Retrieved March 22, 2010, from http://iteslj.org/ Techniques/DelliCarpini-TeacherCollaboration.html

DelliCarpini, M. (2009, May). Dialogues across disciplines: Preparing English-as-a-second-language teachers for interdisciplinary collaboration. *Current Issues in Education* (Online), *11*(2). Retrieved July 29, 2009, from http://cie.ed.asu.edu/volume11/number2/

Dewey, J. (1933). *How we think: A restatement of the relation of reflecting teaching to the educative process.* Boston: D.C. Heath and Company.

Dieker, L. A. (2001). What are the characteristics of "effective" middle and high school co-taught teams for students with disabilities? *Preventing School Failure, 46,* 14–23.

Dieker, L. A. (2002). *Co-planner (semester).* Whitefish Bay, WI: Knowledge by Design.

Dieker, L. A., & Murawski, W. W. (2003). Co-teaching at the secondary level: Unique issues, current trends, and suggestions for success. *The High School Journal, 86*(4), 1–13.

Dong, R. (2009). Linking to prior learning. *Educational Leadership, 66*(7), 26–31.

DuFour, R. (2005). What is a professional learning community? In R. DuFour, R. Eaker, & R. DuFour (Eds.), *On common ground: The power of professional learning communities* (pp. 31–43). Bloomington, IN: Solution Tree.

DuFour, R., & Berkey, T. (1995). The principal as staff developer. *Journal of Staff Development, 16*(4), 2–6.

DuFour, R., & Eaker, R. (1998). *Professional learning communities at work: Best practices for enhancing student achievement.* Bloomington, IN: Solution Tree.

Dunn, R., & Dunn, K. (1999). *The complete guide to the learning styles inservice system.* Boston: Allyn & Bacon.

Dunn, R., & Honigsfeld, A. (2009). *Differentiating instruction for at-risk students: What to do and how to do it.* Lanham, MD: Rowman & Littlefield.

Dunne, K., & Villani, S. (2007). *Mentoring new teachers through collaborative coaching: Linking teacher and student learning.* San Francisco: WestEd.

Easton, L. B. (February/March 2009). Protocols: A facilitator's best friend. *Tools for Schools, 12*(3), 1–2, 6–7.

Echevarria, J., Vogt, M., & Short, D. J. (2008). *Making content comprehensible for English learners: The SIOP model* (3rd ed.). Boston: Pearson.

Elmasry, S. K. (2007). *Integration patterns of learning technologies.* Dissertation submitted to the faculty of Virginia Polytechnic Institute and State University. (No. AAT 3286982)

Elmore, R. F. (2000). *Building a new structure for school leadership.* Washington, DC: The Albert Shanker Institute. Retrieved October 1, 2007, from www.ashankerinst.org/Downloads/building.pdf

Epstein, J. L., Sanders, M. G., Simon, B. S., Salinas, K. C., Jansorn, N. R., & Van Voorhis, F. L. (2002). *School, family, and community partnerships: Your handbook for action* (2nd ed.). Thousand Oaks, CA: Corwin.

Evans, G. W. (2004). The environment of childhood poverty. *American Psychologist, 59*(2), 77–92.

Fattig, M. L., & Taylor, M. T. (2007). *Collaboration, lesson design, and classroom management, grades 5–12.* San Franciso: Jossey-Bass.

Fearon, K. (2008). *A team teaching approach to ESL: An evaluative case study.* Master's thesis. Union, NJ: Kean University. (No. AAT 1456437)

Ferguson, R. F. (2006). Five challenges to effective teacher professional development: School leaders can improve instruction by addressing these issues. *Journal of Staff Development, 27*(4), 48–52.

Fernandez, C., & Chokshi, S. (2002). A practical guide to translating lesson study for a U.S. setting. *Phi Delta Kappan, 84,* 128–134.

Fichtman Dana, N., & Yendol-Hoppey, D. (2008). *The reflective educator's guide to classroom research: Learning to teach and teaching to learn through practitioner inquiry* (2nd ed.). Thousand Oaks, CA: Corwin.

Fradd, S. H. (1992). *Collaboration in schools serving students with limited English proficiency and other special needs.* ERIC Clearinghouse on Languages and Linguistics. Washington, DC: Center for Applied Linguistics. (ERIC Document Reproduction Service No. ED352847). Retrieved August 26, 2009, from www.ericdigests.org/1993/english.htm

Fradd, S. H. (1998). Literacy development for language enriched pupils through English language arts instruction. In S. Fradd & O. Lee (Eds.), *Creating Florida's multilingual global work force: Educational policies and practices for students learning English as a new language* (pp 47–56). Tallahassee, FL: Florida Department of Education.

Freeman, D. E., & Freeman, Y. S. (1988). *Sheltered English instruction* (ERIC Document Reproduction Service No. ED301070). Retrieved January 18, 2005, from http://thememoryhole.org/edu/eric/ed301070.html

Freeman, D. E., & Freeman, Y. S. (2003). *Essential linguistics: What you need to know to teach reading, ESL, spelling, phonics, grammar.* Portsmouth, NH: Heinemann.

Freeman, Y. S., Freeman, D. E., & Mecuri, S. (2003). Helping middle and high school age English language learners achieve academic success. *NABE Journal of Research Practice, 1*(1), 110–122.

Friend, M. (2005). *The power of 2.* DVD. Greensboro, NC: Marilyn Friend Inc.

Friend, M. (2008). *Co-teach! A handbook for creating and sustaining classroom partnerships in inclusive schools.* Greensboro, NC: Marilyn Friend Inc.

Friend, M., & Cook, L. (1992). *Interactions: Collaboration skills for school professionals.* White Plains, NY: Longman.

Friend, M., & Cook, L. (2007). *Interactions: Collaboration skills for school professionals* (5th ed.). New York: Prentice Hall.

Fullan, M. (2007). *The new meaning of educational change* (4th ed.). New York: Teachers College Press.

Gajda, R., & Koliba, C. J. (2008). Evaluating and improving the quality of teacher collaboration: A field-tested framework for secondary school leaders. *NASSP Bulletin, 92*(2), 133–153.

Garmston, R. (2007). Balanced conversations promote shared ownership. *Journal of Staff Development, 28*(4), 57–58.

Gately, S., & Gately, F. (2001). Understanding co-teaching components. *Teaching Exceptional Children, 33*(4), 40–47.

Gay, G. (2000). *Culturally responsive teaching: Theory, research, and practice.* New York: Teachers College Press.

Gay, G. (2002). Preparing for culturally responsive teaching. *Journal of Teacher Education, 53*, 106–116.

Genesee, F. (1999). *Program alternatives for linguistically diverse students (educational practice report no. 1).* Washington, DC and Santa Cruz, CA: Center for Research on Education, Diversity & Excellence.

Genesee, F. (2001). Evaluation. In R. Carter & D. Nunan (Eds.), *The Cambridge guide to teaching English to speakers of other languages* (pp. 144–150). Cambridge, UK: Cambridge University Press.

Genesee, F., Lindholm-Leary, K., Saunders, W., & Christian, D. (Eds.). (2006). *Educating English language learners: A synthesis of research evidence.* Cambridge, UK: Cambridge University Press.

Gersten, R., Baker, S. K., Shanahan, T., Linan-Thompson, S., Collins, P., & Scarcella, R. (2007). *Effective literacy and English language instruction for English learners in the elementary grades: Report # NCEE 2007–4011.* Washington, DC: U.S. Department of Education.

Gibbons, P. (2002). *Scaffolding language, scaffolding learning.* Portsmouth, NH: Heinemann.

Glatthorn, A. A., Boschee, F., & Whitehead, B. M. (2006). *Curriculum leadership: Development and implementation.* Thousand Oaks, CA: Sage.

Glatthorn, A. A., & Jailall, J. M. (2008). *Principal as curriculum leader: Shaping what is taught and tested* (3rd ed.). Thousand Oaks, CA: Corwin.

Glickman, C. D. (1998). *Renewing America's schools: A guide for school-based action.* San Francisco: Jossey Bass.

Goddard, Y. L., Goddard, R. D., & Tschannen-Moran, M. (2007). A theoretical and empirical investigation of teacher collaboration for school improvement and student achievement in public elementary schools. *Teachers College Record, 109*(4), 877–896.

Godwin, P., & Gross, K. (2005). Education's many stakeholders. *University Business, 8*(9), 48–51.

Goldenberg, C. (2008). Teaching English language learners: What the research does—and does not—say. *American Educator, 32*(2), 8–44.

Goldenberg, C., & Coleman, R. (2010). *Promoting academic achievement among English learners: A guide to the research.* Thousand Oaks, CA: Corwin.

Good, T., & Brophy, J. (2000). *Looking in classrooms* (8th ed.). New York: Longman.

Goodlad, J. I., Mantle-Bromley, C., & Goodlad, S. J. (2004). *Education for everyone: Agenda for education in a democracy.* San Francisco: Jossey-Bass.

Hakuta, K. (2000). *How long does it take English learners to attain proficiency?* Retrieved May 27, 2009, from http://repositories.cdlib.org/cgi/viewcontent.cgi?article=1001&context=lmri

Hammerness, K., Darling-Hammond, L., & Bransford, J., with Berliner, D., Cochran-Smith, M., McDonald, M., Zeichner, K. (2005). How teachers learn and develop. In L. Darling-Hammond & J. Bransford (Eds.), *Preparing teachers for a changing world: What teachers should learn and be able to do* (pp. 358–388). San Francisco: Jossey-Bass.

Harvey, S., & Goudvis, A. (2007). *Strategies that work* (2nd ed.). Portland, ME: Stenhouse.

Haver, J. (2003). *Structured English immersion: A step-by-step guide for K–6 teachers and administrators.* Thousand Oaks, CA: Corwin.

Hill, J., & Flynn, K. (2006). *Classroom instruction that works with English language learners.* Alexandria, VA: ASCD.

Honigsfeld, A., & Cohan, A. (2007). The power of two: Lesson study and SIOP help teachers instruct ELLs. *Journal of Staff Development, 29*(1), 24–28.

Honigsfeld, A., & Dove, M. (2008). Co-teaching in the ESL classroom. *The Delta Kappa Gamma Bulletin, 74*(2), 8–14.

Howard, E. R., & Sugarman, J. (2001). *Two-way immersion programs: Features and statistics.* Retrieved November 27, 2008, from www.cal.org/resources/digest/0101twi.html

Hull, J. (2004). Filling in the gaps [Electronic version]. *Threshold,* 8–11, 15.

Hurst, D., & Davison, C. (2005). Collaboration on the curriculum: Focus on secondary ESL. In J. Crandall & D. Kaufman (Eds.), *Case studies in TESOL: Teacher education for language and content integration.* Alexandria, VA: Teachers of English to Speakers of Other Languages.

Inger, M. (1993). Teacher collaboration in secondary schools. *Centerfocus, 2.* National Center for Research in Vocational Education. Retrieved September 25, 2009, from http://vocserve.berkeley.edu/centerfocus/CF2.html

Interstate New Teacher Assessment and Support Consortium (INTASC). (1992). *Model standards for beginning teacher licensing, assessment and development: A resource for state dialogue.* Retrieved April 27, 2009, from www.ccsso.org/content/pdfs/corestrd.pdf

Irujo, S. (1998). *Teaching bilingual children: Beliefs and behaviors.* Boston: Heinle & Heinle.

Irvine, J. J., & York, D. E. (1995). Learning styles and culturally diverse students: A literature review. In J. A. Banks & C. A. Banks (Eds.), *Handbook of research on multicultural education* (pp. 484–497). New York: Macmillan.

Jacobs, H. H. (1997). *Mapping the big picture: Integrating curriculum and assessment K–12.* Alexandria, VA: ASCD.

Jacobs, H. H. (1999). *Breaking new ground in high school curriculum.* Reston, VA: NAASP.

Jacobs, H. H. (2004). *Getting results with curriculum mapping.* Alexandria, VA: ASCD.

Jalongo, M. R., Reig, S. A., & Helterbran, V. R. (2006). *Planning for learning: Collaborative approaches to lesson design and review.* New York: Teachers College Press.

Jin, S. (1996). *My first American friend.* Boston: Houghton Mifflin.

Johnson, A. P. (2008). *A short guide to action research.* Boston: Pearson.

Joyce, B., & Showers, B. (1980). Improving inservice training: The messages of research. *Educational Leadership, 37*(5), 379–385.

Joyce, B., & Showers, B. (1988) *Student achievement through staff development.* White Plains, NY: Longman.

Kaufman, D., & Crandall, J. A. (Eds.). (2005). *Content-based instruction in elementary and secondary school settings.* Alexandria, VA: TESOL.

Kaufman, R., Guerra, I., & Plat, W. A. (2006). *Practical evaluation for educators: Finding what works and what doesn't.* Thousand Oaks, CA: Corwin.

Kindler, A. (2002). *Survey of the states' limited English proficient students and available educational programs and services: 2000–2001 summary report.* Washington, DC: National Clearinghouse for English Language Acquisition.

Krashen, S. D. (1981). *Principles and practice in second language acquisition.* London: Prentice-Hall.

Krashen, S. D. (1999). *Condemned without a trial: Bogus arguments against bilingual education.* Portsmouth, NH: Heinemann.

Lachat, M. A. (2004). *Standards-based instruction and assessment for English language learners.* Thousand Oaks, CA: Corwin.

Ladson-Billings, G. (1994). *The dreamkeepers.* San Francisco: Jossey-Bass.

Ladson-Billings, G. (2000). Reading between the lines and beyond the pages: A culturally relevant approach to literacy teaching. In M. Gallego & A. Hollingsworth (Eds.), *What counts as literacy: Challenging the school standard* (pp. 139–151). New York: Teachers College Press.

Langer, G. M., Colton, A. B., & Gott, L. S. (2003). *Collaborative analysis of student work: Improving teaching and learning.* Alexandria, VA: ASCD.

Langer de Ramirez, L. (2009). *Empower English language learners with tools from the web.* Thousand Oaks, CA: Corwin.

Levi, D. (2007). *Group dynamics for teams* (2nd ed.). Thousand Oaks, CA: Sage.

Lewis, C. (2002). *Lesson study: A handbook of teacher-led instructional improvement.* Philadelphia: Research for Better Schools.

Lieberman A., & Miller, L. (1984). *Teachers, their world, and their work: Implications for school improvement.* Alexandria, VA: ASCD.

Little, J. W. (1982). Norms of collegiality and experimentation: Workplace conditions of school success. *American Educational Research Journal, 19*, 325–340.

Lortie, D. (1975). *Schoolteacher: A sociological study.* Chicago: University of Chicago Press.

Louis, K. S., Marks, H. M., & Kruse, S. D. (1996). Teachers' professional community in restructuring schools. *American Educational Research Journal, 33*(4), 757–798.

Love, N. (2009). *Using data to improve learning for all: A collaborative inquiry approach.* Thousand Oaks, CA: Corwin.

Ma, J. (2002). *What works for children: What we know and don't know about bilingual education.* Boston: Harvard University Press.

Marshall, P. (2002). *Cultural diversity in our schools.* Belmont, CA: Wadsworth/Thomas Learning.

Marzano, R. J., Pickering, D. J., & Pollock, J. E. (2001). *Classroom instruction that works: Research-based strategies for increasing student achievement.* Alexandria, VA: ASCD.

Marzano, R. J., Waters, T., & McNulty, B. A. (2005). *School leadership that works: From research to results.* Alexandria, VA: ASCD & Aurora, CO: McRel.

Maslow, A. H. (1970). *A theory of human motivation and personality* (2nd ed.). New York: Harper & Row.

McEntee, G. H., Appleby, K., Dowd, J., Grant, J., Hole, S., & Silva, P. (with Check, J.). (2003). *At the heart of teaching: A guide to reflective practice.* New York: Teachers College Press.

McLaughlin, M. W., & Talbert, J. E. (2006). *Building school-based teacher learning communities: Professional strategies to improve student achievement.* New York: Teachers College Press.

Murawski, W. W. (2009). *Collaborative teaching in secondary schools: Making the co-teaching marriage work!* Thousand Oaks, CA: Corwin.

Nair, P., & Fielding, R. (2005). *The language of school design: Design patterns for 21st century schools.* Retrieved June 18, 2009, from www.DesignShare.com

National Commission on Teaching and America's Future. (2009). *Learning teams: Creating what's next.* Retrieved May 15, 2009, from www.nctaf.org/documents/NCTAFLearningTeams408REG2–09_000.pdf

National Institute of Child Health and Human Development. (2000). *Teaching children to read: An evidence-based assessment of the scientific research literature on reading and its implications for reading instruction: Reports of the subgroups* (Report of the National Reading Panel, NIH Publication No. 00–4754). Washington, DC: U.S. Government Printing Office.

National Research Council. (2000). *How people learn: Brain, mind, experience, and school: Expanded edition* (2nd ed.). Washington, DC: National Academies Press.

National Staff Development Council. (2001). *NSDC standards for professional development.* Retrieved June 17, 2009, from www.nsdc.org/standards/index.cfm

NCES. (2001). *Teacher preparation and professional development: 2000.* Retrieved January 18, 2010, from http://nces.ed.gov/pubsearch/pubsinfo.asp?pubid=2001088

NCES. (2002). *Schools & staffing survey, 1999–2000: Overview of the data for public, private, public charter, and Bureau of Indian Affairs elementary and secondary schools.* Washington, DC: Author.

NCES. (2006). *Crime, violence, discipline, and school safety in U.S. Public schools: Findings from the school survey on crime and safety: 2003–04.* Retrieved May 29, 2009, from http://nces.ed.gov/pubs2007/2007302rev.pdf

NEA. (2009). *NEA reiterates collaboration as key to keeping teachers.* Retrieved April 29, 2009, from www.nea.org/home/31477.htm

Nieto, S. (2002). *Language, culture, and teaching: Critical perspectives for a new century.* Mahwah, NJ: Lawrence Erlbaum.

No Child Left Behind (NCLB). (2001, §3102(2)). Retrieved April 28, 2009, from www.ed.gov/nclb/landing.jhtml

NYSED. (2004). *New York State ESL performance standards.* Retrieved July 18, 2008, from www.emsc.nysed.gov/ciai/biling/resource/ESL/standards.html

NYSED. (2006). *New York State native language arts standards.* Retrieved July 18, 2008, from www.emsc.nysed.gov/biling/resource/NLA.html

NYSED. (2009). *2009–2010 Part 154 comprehensive plan and reporting requirements for the education of limited English proficient (LEP) students.* Retrieved July 18, 2009, from www.emsc.nysed.gov/biling/docs/PART15409–10Final-2.pdf

O'Day, J., & Bitter, C. (2003). *Evaluation study of the immediate intervention/underperforming schools program and the high achieving/improving schools program of the Public Schools Accountability Act of 1999: Final report.* Sacramento, CA: California Department of Education, Policy and Evaluation.

Olsen, L. (2006). Ensuring academic success for English learners. *University of California Linguistic Minority Research Institute Newsletter, 15*(4), 1–8.

Osterman, K. F., & Kottkamp, R. B. (2004). *Reflective practice for educators: Professional development to improve student learning* (2nd ed.). Thousand Oaks, CA: Corwin.

Panofsky, C., Pacheco, M., Smith, S., Santos, J., Fogelman, C., Harrington, M., et al. (2005). *Approaches to writing instruction for adolescent English language learners.* Retrieved May 29, 2009, from www.alliance.brown.edu/pubs/writ_instrct/apprchwrtng.pdf

Pardini, P. (2006). In one voice: Mainstream and ELL teachers work side-by-side in the classroom teaching language through content. *Journal of Staff Development, 27*(4), 20–25.

Partnership for 21st Century Skills. (2007). *21st century support systems.* Retrieved May 29, 2009, from www.21stcenturyskills.org/route21/index.php?option=com_content&view=article&id=58&Itemid=17

Payán, R. M., & Nettles, M. T. (2008). *Current state of English language learners in the U.S. K–12 student population.* Retrieved October 28, 2008, from www.ets.org/Media/Conferences_and_Events/pdf/ELLsympsium/ELL_factsheet.pdf

Payton, J., Weissberg, R. P., Durlak, J. A., Dymnicki, A. B., Taylor, R. D., Schellinger, K. B., et al. (2008). The positive impact of social and emotional learning for kindergarten to eighth-grade students. Retrieved October 29, 2009, from www.casel.org/downloads/PackardTR.pdf

Price, H. B. (2008). *Mobilizing the community to help students succeed.* Alexandria, VA: ASCD.

Proposition 227: Full text of the proposed law. (1998). Retrieved August 8, 2008, from http://primary98.sos.ca.gov/VoterGuide/Propositions/227text.htm

PTA. (1997). *National standards for parent/family involvement programs.* Retrieved July 12, 2008, from www.pta.org/archive_article_details_1118251710359.html

Rance-Roney, J. (2009). Best practices for adolescent ELLs. *Educational Leadership, 66*(7), 32–37.

Reeves, D. (2006). *The learning leader: How to focus school improvement for better results.* Alexandria, VA: ASCD.

Richardson, W. (2008). *World without walls: Learning well with others: How to teach when learning is everywhere.* Retrieved December 31, 2008, from www.edutopia.org/collaboration-age-technology-will-richardson

Risko, V., & Bromley, K. (Eds.). (2001). *Collaboration for diverse learners: Viewpoints and practices.* Newark, DE: International Reading Association.

Roberts, S., & Pruitt, E. (2009). *Schools as professional learning communities: Collaborative activities and strategies for professional development.* Thousand Oaks, CA: Corwin.

Ross, J. A., & Bruce, C. D. (2007). Teacher self-assessment: A mechanism for facilitating professional growth. *Teaching and Teacher Education, 23*(2), 146–159.

Rossell, C. H. (2003). *Policy matters in teaching English language learners: New York and California.* Urban Diversity Series No. 117. New York: ERIC Clearinghouse on Urban Education.

Rong, X. L., & Preissle, J. (2009). *Educating immigrant students in the 21st century: What educators need to know.* Thousand Oaks, CA: Corwin.

Rubinstein-Avila, E. (2006). Connecting with Latino learners. *Educational Leadership 63*(5), 38–43.

Sanders, J. R., & Sullins, C. D. (2006). *Evaluating school programs: An educator's guide* (3rd ed.). Thousand Oaks, CA: Corwin.

Saphier, J. (2005). Masters of motivation. In R. DuFour, R. Eaker, & R. DuFour (Eds.), *On common ground: The power of professional learning communities* (pp. 105–109). Bloomington, IN: Solution Tree.

Schmoker, M. J. (2006). *Results now.* Alexandria, VA: ASCD.

Schon, D. E. (1990). *Educating the reflective practitioner: Toward a new design for teaching and learning in the professions.* San Francisco: Jossey-Bass.

Scruggs, T., Mastropieri, M. A., & McDuffie, K. A. (2007). Co-teaching in inclusive classrooms: A metasynthesis of qualitative research. *Exceptional Children, 73*(4), 392–416.

Sergiovanni, T. J. (1994). *Building community in schools.* San Francisco: Jossey-Bass.

Sergiovanni, T. J. (2000). *The lifeworld of leadership: Creating culture, community, and personal meaning in our schools.* San Francisco: Jossey-Bass.

Short, D. J., & Fitzsimmons, S. (2007). *Double the work: Challenges and solutions to acquiring language and academic literacy for adolescent English language learners—A report to the Carnegie Corporation of New York.* Washington, DC: Alliance for Excellent Education.

Simplicio, J. S. C. (2007). *Educating the 21st century student.* Bloomington, IN: AuthorHouse.

Smith, S. C., & Scott, J. L. (1990). *The collaborative school: A work environment for effective instruction* (Report No. ISBN-0–86552–092–5). Eugene, OR: University of Oregon. (ERIC Document Reproduction Service No. ED316918)

Spillane J. P., & Diamond, J. P. (Eds.). (2007). *Distributed leadership in practice.* New York: Teachers College Press.

Spraker, J. (2003). *Teacher teaming in relation to student performance: Findings from the literature.* Portland, OR: Northwest Regional Educational Laboratory.

Stiggins, R., & DuFour, R. (2009). Maximizing the power of formative assessments. *Phi Delta Kappan, 90*(9), 640–644.

Stufflebeam, D. L., & Shinkfield, A. J. (2007). *Evaluation theory, models, and applications.* San Francisco: Jossey-Bass.

Tanner, C. K., & Lackney, J. A. (2006). The physical environment and student achievement in elementary schools. In C. K. Tanner & J. A. Lackney, *Educational facilities planning: Leadership, architecture, and management* (pp. 266–294). Boston: Pearson.

Téllez, K., & Waxman, H. C. (2005). *Quality teachers for English language learners.* Retrieved May 31, 2009, from www.temple.edu/lss/pdf/ReviewOfTheResearchTellezWaxman.pdf

Tennessee State Board of Education. (2007). *ESL program policy 3.207.* Retrieved April 29, 2009, from www.tennessee.gov/education/fedprog/doc/FPDTBO4NewESLPolicy.doc

TESOL preK–12 English language proficiency standards. (2006). Alexandria, VA: TESOL.

Thomas, W. P., & Collier, V. P. (2002). *A national study of school effectiveness for language minority students' long-term academic achievement. Final report: Project 1.1.* Washington, DC, and Santa Cruz, CA: Center for Research on Education, Diversity & Excellence.

Thompson, G. (2009, March 15). Where education and assimilation collide. *New York Times.* Retrieved April 18, 2009, from www.nytimes.com/2009/03/15/us/15immig.html?_r=1&scp=7&sq=ginger%20thompson&st=cse

Thornburg, D. (2002). *The new basics: Education and the future of work in the telematic age.* Alexandria, VA: ASCD.

Tomlinson, C. A. (1999). *The differentiated classroom: Responding to the needs of all learners.* Alexandria, VA: ASCD.

Tremmel, R. (1999). Zen and the art of reflective practice in teacher education. In E. M. Mintz & J. T. Yun (Eds.), *The complex world of teaching: Perspectives from theory and practice* (pp. 87–111). Cambridge, MA: Harvard Educational Review.

Udelhofen, S. K. (2005). *Keys to curriculum mapping: Strategies and tools to make it work.* Thousand Oaks, CA: Corwin.

Uline, C., Tschannen-Moran, M., & Wolsey, T. D. (2009). The walls still speak: The stories occupants tell. *Journal of Educational Administration, 47*(3), 400–426.

U.S. Census Bureau. *Census Brief 2000: Language use and English-speaking ability.* Retrieved July 30, 2009, from www.census.gov/population/www/cen2000/briefs/

U.S. Department of Education. (2001). *NCLB and other elementary/secondary policy documents.* Retrieved August 31, 2009, from www.ed.gov/policy/elsec/guid/states/index.html

U.S. Department of Education, Office of Elementary and Secondary Education. (2007). *Assessment and accountability for recently arrived and former limited English proficient (LEP) students.* Retrieved July 11, 2008, from www.ed.gov/policy/elsec/guid/lepguidance.doc

U.S. Department of Labor, Bureau of Labor Statistics. (2010–11). *Occupational outlook handbook.* Retrieved December 23, 2009, from www.bls.gov/oco/

U.S. Government Accountability Office. (2009). *Teacher preparation: Multiple federal education offices support teacher preparation for instructing students with disabilities and English language learners, but systematic departmentwide coordination could enhance this assistance.* Washington, DC: Author. Retrieved November 25, 2009, from www.gao.gov

Van Note Chism, N. (2006). Challenging traditional assumptions and rethinking learning spaces. In D. G. Oblinger (Ed.), *Learning spaces* (pp. 2.1–2.12). Retrieved June 12, 2009, from www.educause.edu/LearningSpaces

Vaughn, S., Schumm, J. S., & Arguelles, M. E. (1997). The ABCDEs of co-teaching. *Teaching Exceptional Children, 30*(2), 4–10.

Villa, R. A., Thousand, J. S., & Nevin, A. I. (2008). *A guide to co-teaching: Practical tips for facilitating student learning.* Thousand Oaks, CA: Corwin.

Walkin, L. (2000). *Teaching and learning in further and adult education* (2nd ed.). Cheltenham, UK: Nelson Thornes.

Waller, W. (1965). *The sociology of teaching.* New York: John Wiley & Sons.

Wertheimer, C., & Honigsfeld, A. (2000). Preparing ESL students to meet the new standards. *TESOL Journal, 9*(1), 23–28.

Williams, J. A. (2001). Classroom conversations: Opportunities to learn for ESL students in mainstream classrooms. *The Reading Teacher, 54,* 750–757.

York-Barr, J., Ghere, G. S., & Sommerness, J. (2007). Collaborative teaching to increase ELL student learning. *Journal of Education for Students Placed at Risk, 12*(3), 301–335.

York-Barr, J., Sommers, W. A., Ghere, G. S., & Montie, J. (2006). *Reflective practice to improve schools: An action guide for educators.* Thousand Oaks, CA: Corwin.

Yoshida, M. (2004). *A summary of lesson study.* Retrieved March 5, 2008, from www.rbs.org/lesson_study/conference/2003/papers/defining/a_summary_of_lesson_study.shtml

Zabolio McGrath, M., & Holden Johns, B. (2006). *The teacher's reflective calendar and planning journal: Motivation, inspiration, and affirmation.* Thousand Oaks, CA: Corwin.

Zeichner, K. M., & Liston, D. P. (1996). *Reflective teaching: An introduction.* Mahwah, NJ: Lawrence Erlbaum Associates.

Zigler, E., & Weiss, H. (1985). Family support systems: An ecological approach to child development. In R. N. Rapoport (Ed.), *Children, youth, and families: The action-research relationship* (pp. 166–205). Cambridge, UK: Cambridge University Press.

Index